sis
and the Millennium Meltdown
1995 – 2000

Where Did It All Go Wrong?

Nick Amies

Oasis and the Millennium Meltdown 1995 – 2000
WHERE DID IT ALL GO WRONG?
By **Nick Amies**

Ordering Information:
Quantity sales. Special discounts are available on quantity
purchases by corporations, associations, and others. For
details, contact the author via the website:
https://ligger.wordpress.com/

Printed in the United Kingdom.

For B

My girl in the dirty shirt

When you say something, you make me believe...

1. *morning glory*

2. *champagne supernova*

3. *be here now*

4. *all around the world*

5. *gas panic!*

6. *who feels love*

1.

morning glory

"Today's the day that all the world will see"

August 11, 1996. A crowd of 125,000 people stretches far and wide in the rainy darkness of Knebworth Park as Oasis, the biggest band in Britain, if not the world at this point in time, brings to an end the defining weekend of the Britpop era. Instead of considering the sheer magnitude of the event while staring out onto the rolling, steaming sea of fans, many of whom are so far away they are in another county, Noel Gallagher has other things on his mind. At the moment when his band undoubtedly makes good on their numerous claims of greatness, the Oasis guitarist is instead overwhelmed by what's happening beside him on stage. The next day, Gallagher will watch the footage of that moment with the awe and excitement of a star-struck fan.

"Just now, I was watching a video playback of 'Champagne Supernova' from last night," Gallagher told Select magazine with a mixture of pride and disbelief. "It's like, that's me onstage with John Squire. He's playing this mad fucking Jimmy Page stuff, all over the place on his guitar. I turn around to my manager who's stood behind me, and he goes, 'Look at the crowd with all the lighters'. I go, 'fuck the crowd, look at that cunt there! Check him out, what he's doing!' I'm thinking, that's another moment in my life." On the night when Oasis leave no-one in doubt that they are the country's premier rock act, Noel Gallagher was more excited about sharing the stage with one of his heroes and watching in wonder as the Stone Roses guitarist elevated one his own songs to new heights.

In the context of the many interviews he would do in the weeks and months which followed the all-conquering Knebworth shows, the small fact that Gallagher was happiest watching John Squire in action at close quarters would be lost in the deluge of enquiries about his future plans. This personal milestone, however, would carry greater significance than any of the grandiose claims and arrogant boasts which would come in the next two years. It would mark the point when Noel Gallagher stepped off his cloud into a swirling storm of media hype, suffocating adoration and rock mega-stardom which would test his sanity, punish his body and make him question even the most trusted of those around him. It would initially appear to be everything he ever wanted and more but even for Noel Gallagher, a man who has professed on numerous occasions throughout his career to waking up every day and giving thanks for the life he leads, there will be days when he yearns for the wide-eyed disbelief of a kid from a Manchester council estate who ended up trading guitar licks with one of his idols on the biggest stage of all.

Before Oasis started changing opinions in 1994 with debut album *Definitely Maybe*, few people outside of the band believed that they would become the biggest rock act on the planet. They were a raw, exciting, incendiary bunch of Manchester scallies with a volatility which made them both dangerously attractive and potentially self-destructive. This explosiveness did little to convince those who saw brothers Liam and Noel at each other's throats that Oasis had a long-term future. Rather than growing into a band which would sweep all before them and smash record upon record, Oasis were initially viewed as a combustible flash in the pan which would leave an indelible scorch mark on British music before burning out in a blaze of short-lived, expletive-laden and blood-splattered glory.

Noel Gallagher, however, had other ideas. "The plan was always to become the biggest band in the world," he told Uncut magazine in the wake of the two era-defining Knebworth gigs. "And as much as everybody used to say it, I was the only one who fucking believed it was going to happen. Like Alan McGee (head of Creation, the band's label), like Liam...They would say the words and all that, but, in hindsight, everyone was just going along with what I was saying. But I knew it was fucking going to happen. I knew in my bones it was going to happen."

"We weren't thinking that we'd got the biggest band of the next ten years on our hands," Alan McGee admitted in the documentary which accompanied the 20-year anniversary remastered release of *Definitely Maybe*. "We just thought we could get a record out before the next Stone Roses album, maybe sell about half a million copies and that would have been a result for everyone."

"You usually know when the next big thing is coming along; it's almost like a fucking storm, you can feel it six months before it's going to happen; it's like, 'Get out the fucking way'," Noel told Uncut in 2000. "You could hear Oasis on the fucking horizon before the first single come out. We spoke to a lot of people around at that time, people who were in bands or in the music business, and they were going, 'Everybody better just make way, man, because there's a big fucking train coming through here'."

"The funny thing is, all that fucking mouthing off about how we were going to be the biggest band in the world, we actually went and done it. And it was a piece of piss. We were talking out of our arses as well, though. We hadn't even recorded a record at that point. You could sense that the vacuum was there. It was in the air. You could sense that something big was going to happen. There wasn't a band for the kids to get passionate about, so along comes us singing about gin and tonic, shagging

birds and doing drugs, and everyone went, fucking hell, that's a bit more like it! We just took it from there."

"Doing Knebworth was above and beyond any of my expectations for that band," rhythm guitarist Paul 'Bonehead' Arthurs later admitted to the NME. "But I never ever doubted that what we had and what we were doing was going to reach out and people were going to take it. We were cocky, we were arrogant and we had a lot of self-belief which a band has to have. When you've got a guy like Liam on stage and a guy like Noel writing your music and your words, then that's going to give you confidence no end, isn't it? But never did I imagine that it would get as big as that, though. No way."

But despite his assertion that his band were destined to be the biggest and the best, and the acclaim that was being heaped on them, Noel Gallagher was still taken aback by the plans his management had for the crowning achievement of a year spent scaling ever-more impressive heights.

"There was a six month period leading up to Knebworth where we were the biggest band on the planet because we were selling the most records and playing to the most people and writing the best songs, I feel," Noel told Uncut.

In the Creation Records documentary *Upside Down*, the elder Gallagher returned to the theme of the band's unstoppable march through the early part of 1996 to the pinnacle of their career: "When [second album] *(What's the Story) Morning Glory?* came out, it got universally slated by the British press...and then it went on to do whatever it did and it was madness," he said. "We sold more singles than most bands sell albums. 'Don't look Back in Anger' sold over a million singles. It got to a point after *(What's the Story) Morning Glory?* and 'Wonderwall' had taken off that it felt that everything was leading up to something that would

define not only the size of the band but what British pop music was about at that time so it all felt like it was leading to Knebworth but we were too busy doing it to worry about that."

While a maelstrom of madness and hype blew around Oasis wherever the band went, Noel Gallagher and the band's manager Marcus Russell escaped the whirlwind for one day and drove to the lush rolling parkland and grounds of a stately home in Hertfordshire. But this was no retreat or weekend break to recharge the batteries, this – as with most things at this time – was about business. This was a reconnaissance mission for what would be the crowning glory of the band's rise.

Peering out of the window of his chauffeur-driven Rolls Royce, Noel's head flashed with imagined scenes from the great rock concerts which had graced Knebworth Park across the preceding decades. "Someone had told me that Led Zeppelin and the Stones had played there so we went there and I got out of the car and had a look round. I said to my manager, do you think we could do it?" Noel recollected in an interview with GQ magazine in 2000. "He said, 'I think we could do two nights'. I nearly choked on the cigarette I was smoking. 250,000 people, are you sure? He said, 'yeah'. Okay, you're the manager, I suppose you'd know and then we gave the go-ahead. That was it."

"The promoters were like: 'You're the biggest band in the world, you have to do it now'. They were saying we could do six nights. Three million people applied for tickets."

At the time, Noel was still convinced that playing to as many fans as possible, in the biggest arenas possible, was the best way to remain close to the people. "It's weird that we're having to move outdoors but I suppose that comes from being a fuck-off dirty great big horrible rock band," he told NME in February 1996. "You have to move outdoors unless you play to an elitist audience and we've never been about that."

The months leading up to Knebworth saw the band gain an unstoppable momentum and put away any remaining doubts about the decision to play what would be two era-defining concerts that summer. In two years, Oasis had gone from five-up in a Ford Transit, with designated tour manager Bonehead ("9 am in the lobby or else") behind the wheel, to a touring party of 45, transported around the world in four articulated lorries and two tour buses. They'd certainly come a long way from their days of playing to a dozen disinterested locals at the Manchester Boardwalk. On top of that, the band had seemingly emerged victorious in the media constructed war with fellow Britpoppers Blur. Despite losing the battle for the Number 1 slot – both bands released below par singles on the same day with Blur's 'Country House' beating out 'Roll With It' – Oasis put that sleight behind them to outsell Blur's *The Great Escape* album by roughly three to one with *(What's the Story) Morning Glory?* eventually winning more favourable critical points as well as commercial ones.

Despite the growing acclaim and the undeniable feeling that everything was going to plan, Noel Gallagher was beginning to privately worry that Oasis were losing a bit of the fire and edge which they had employed to slash and burn their way through the British pop landscape. There was a tiny burr in the songwriter's mind, like a snagged fingernail which always caught on a sleeve, that as things started to get bigger and bigger, the huge machine that had been constructed to steamroller the band to the top was now merely using it as a cog. "I listened back to *(What's the Story) Morning Glory?* and thought only an egomaniac would convince himself that some of the songs were worth putting on," he told the Guardian in 2008. "I said to my manager, 'You told me it was brilliant'. And he went, 'Well, you don't tell the goose that laid the golden egg that his arse is blocked up, do you?'" If he'd been really brave, he said, he would have called it a day after *Definitely Maybe*."

10

Instead of imitating the Sex Pistols and going out in a one-album blaze of glory, Oasis now had a multi-million selling second LP on their hands and a whole country ready for the taking. Now the fun was really going to begin. Oasis were cultivating not only a hugely loyal fan base which was getting ready to have a very large summer but also a slowly growing troupe of detractors, particularly in certain sections of the music press which had been battered by the band and in the right-leaning tabloids where Liam and Noel's behaviour stirred middle-class outrage. The coming tour would target both parties – for very different reasons.

The offensive for Britain would begin once the band returned from a brief six-date tour of North America and Canada. The putsch would start at Maine Road.

In April 1996, the band played two sold-out nights at Manchester City's Maine Road football ground, playing to a 38,000 capacity strong crowd on each occasion. Less than six months previously, Oasis had played the biggest indoor gigs in UK history with their two shows at London's Earl's Court exhibition centre. Crowds of 20,000 people on each night witnessed what Alan McGee later called "pure storming hedonism" and "one of the few moments where Oasis truly captured the pop culture zeitgeist."

By playing Maine Road, the band were not only taking their first assured steps into the upper echelons of the stadium rock league but were about to kick the whole phenomenon into overdrive by doing it in the Gallaghers' place of worship, and in the band's home town. For the local lads in the band who had been living off government hand-outs in the same city just five years previously, this was the dream becoming reality.

"There was a euphoria in the music and the way it was delivered, and, as the crowds started to get bigger, it fed off itself," said Noel, recalling the heady days leading up to the huge summer shows of 1996, in

11

an interview with the Daily Telegraph in 2007. "It became less about the band and more about being with all those people, jumping up and down, drunk to the music."

Oasis possibly delivered one of their finest live performances to date on the second night, eclipsing the euphoria of the first with a performance bulging at the seams with hunger and passion. Even by their own colossal standards, the confidence and belief were sky high as the band kicked off with 'Swamp Song' before Liam, dressed in baggy jeans, a Burberry coat and Darcy-esque billowy white dress shirt, swaggered into view, displaying more simian gait than the entire cast of *Planet of the Apes* put together. Balancing on the edge of the stage, he challenged the crowd to increase the noise. Then, casually smoking a joint that had been thrown on stage, he stood and admired the chaos his appearance had inspired. It was a flawless entrance brimming with arrogance and star quality.

Storming into 'Acquiesce', the nerveless energy was evident for all to see. The night before they had performed on adrenaline, buzzing on the incredulous high which came from playing a venue that held so much history for them. It had been the kind of show fuelled by the power of dreams; after playing it so many times in their heads, it was a desire to do those imaginings justice which drove them on – that and the unbending will of the thousands in attendance to see them triumph. This was a different proposition. This was a performance built on belief. 'Can we play Maine Road? Yes we can – and we did. Now we get to do it again, we're going to really show them how it's done'. Noel's guitar fired arrogant but assured flourishes into the dying light as he surged to new heights with every embellished solo, his voice growing with every song; Liam melded threat with delivery to produce one of his finest – and maddest – vocal performances, singing crisply and in tune throughout but with the snarling menace of a caged tiger on crack. Bonehead and Guigsy made light of

claims that they were "the luckiest men in pop" by putting in a flawless shift, anchoring the flights of fancy swirling off into the Manchester night around them while Alan White's tireless drumming took old and new songs alike to a whole new level. Oasis would go on to create sporadic nights of magic in the years to come but few would come close to this display of synergy.

By now, those songs off *(What's the Story) Morning Glory?* which had been chosen for the live set were becoming standards, anthems in the bands burgeoning cannon of come-together classics. 'Some Might Say', 'Roll With It' and 'Morning Glory' – so leaden a year previously when delivered for the first time to a perplexed Glastonbury crowd – were all sung at full volume by the Main Road faithful, each greeted with ecstatic screams. Such sing-a-longs were now becoming the norm, and the word-perfect playback from the crowd was clear evidence of the growing devotion of the band's fan base.

Never a band to hide, Oasis now had the tools at their disposal to put on full-blown stadium shows with all the whistles and bells, and they didn't hold back. Now they had the cash, the tunes and the balls to roll out the strings, the horns and the projections, they employed every single one to great effect. The brass section, debuted on 'Round Are Way', were soon joined by violins for 'Whatever' and when Noel's acoustic version of 'The Masterplan' needed beefing up, the full orchestra was on hand to take the song to new cinematic heights.

In addition to the huge scope of the live songs, the overall spectacle and the masterful musicianship on show, the most enduring memory of the Maine Road shows was Liam Gallagher's emergence as a true rock star. It would be churlish to suggest that his antics and performances up until this point had just been practice but at Maine Road, those in attendance were seeing the personification of the rock 'n' roll

persona that Liam had been cultivating in his mind since he experienced his musical epiphany as a teenager at a Stone Roses gig. Mixing self-deprecating humour with surreal banter, and passionate singing with a punkish sneer – all while delivering a performance of such magnetism that few eyes could stray from his actions, the Oasis singer could rightly look back at the Maine Road gigs – and the second night in particular – as his personal high point on the *(What's the Story) Morning Glory?* tour, if not of his entire Oasis career. There were no strops, no sloppiness, no lapses into thuggery. It's a shame that, by his own admission, he can only recollect one thing about the shows: that he watched the BBC TV programme *Antiques Roadshow* before going on stage. "To be honest, that's all I can remember," Liam told Esquire in February 1997. "I know they were top gigs, though."

Others would view the Manchester gigs with a more reverential sense of occasion. Alan McGee described the homecoming double-header as "rock as religious spectacle", while Noel Gallagher would rate Maine Road as the band's pinnacle, eclipsing even the Knebworth shows which were soon to follow. "Maine Road was the high point," Noel told Mojo in March 2000. "Knebworth was just a money-spinner. Maine Road was where it all made sense to me. After that it was all downhill. That was the beginning of the end. After that we were so big we had no control of the vehicle anymore."

Noel, while obviously enjoying the wild ride he and his band were currently on, was increasingly talking with a certain resignation about the distance which was growing between Oasis and their fans at the front of the stage. "I'd like to be nearer to the crowd," he told MTV at the time. "I'd also like to be closer to the rest of the band because we're a bit spread out these days what with the stage being about 200-foot long. I suppose the

fans would like to be nearer to us too but when you get this big and this successful, that's just the way it goes."

Liam was also beginning to notice the difference in intimacy between past and present shows. "To be honest, I don't really want to do stadiums," he told the NME in the month of the Maine Road gigs. "But people want to see you, and it's sometimes the only way to do it. Wherever you play, there's always a space between you and the fans. That's just the way it is, like the world is round." The singer's performances in Manchester didn't appear to suffer from the size of the venue. In fact, he grew to fill its space. He'd overblown this growing stadium persona at the previous summer's headlining slot at the Glastonbury festival, concentrating more on filling the massive space before him with aggression rather than his charisma to the detriment of the music and the performance, but at Maine Road one could see all the pieces starting to fall into place – even though, during 'Whatever' on the first night, he spat the dummy over a comment from Noel about his singing and refused to continue, instead choosing to sit, smoke and sulk on a monitor as his brother completed the song. But it wouldn't have been an Oasis gig without some kind of drama. That was, after all, as well as the rousing, life-affirming music, why people wanted to be part of what was happening with this band. And despite Liam's five-star display on the second night at Maine Road and his maturing into an even more commanding presence at the huge gigs the band would play over the coming months as their status rocketed, his performances, in even the biggest and most important concerts, would continue to be highly unpredictable in both delivery and attitude.

Oasis had been forced into the realm of the mega-gig by the clamour of the public. Liam had been right; it was really a case of supply and demand. As much as they may have wanted, it was now impossible for

the band to go back to the intimate venues in which they had built their reputation as a blistering live act. Even mid-range theatres would be a massive logistical headache. As Noel would say a year later in an interview with Select Magazine, "In an ideal world we'd be playing Shepherd's Bush Empire every night. That'd be fine because it's big enough, but small enough to create an atmosphere. But y'know, they'd have to fucking shut down Shepherd's Bush. They'd have to build a wall round it."

This was the reality of the situation. More and more people wanted to experience the band and the demand for bigger shows was growing. The crowd figures continued to rise for the last big warm up gigs for Knebworth at Loch Lomond on the 3rd and 4th of August.

Balloch, on the shores of Loch Lomond, was to play host to 80,000 Oasis fans over that weekend, showcasing the huge stage and video screens which would soon dominate a part of the Hertfordshire countryside and two new songs which would eventually appear on the band's hugely-anticipated third album.

However, amid the excitement, the first Loch Lomond show was overshadowed by the tragic and accidental death of a worker at the concert site who was crushed between a forklift truck and a lorry the day before Oasis were due to play. As the relationship between the band and sections of the press continued to sour in the months following Knebworth, during which the band – and Liam in particular – would become subjected to increasingly intrusive tactics and sensationalised (and at times, dubiously reported) accounts of their lives, a number of tabloids would attempt to lay the blame for James Hunter's death at the feet of the band. There was even a suggestion that Liam had been partly to blame because it was alleged he had shouted at a lorry driver from the stage during the soundcheck, a distraction that led indirectly to the fatal accident. "I was fucking fuming at that," Liam remembered in a Q interview in December 1999. "I wasn't

even there. I don't do soundchecks normally. I was gutted. What about the parents? If they think I had anything to do with it they must hate me. But honestly... I'm not carrying that cross, brother."

The concerts went ahead despite the fatality and a bus crash involving fans in the nearby hamlet of Luss. More than that, they were triumphant with the Melody Maker writing that "Loch Lomond started out like Altamont [the infamous Rolling Stones concert where a fan was stabbed to death by Hell's Angels at the front of the stage] and ended up as our Woodstock."

Both Gallaghers were in fine fettle and the concerts were at times as much stand-up comedy routines as they were rock spectacles. But despite the celebratory atmosphere, the death of James Hunter seemed to haunt the performance in places, specifically when some drunken fans climbed a lighting rig near the front of the stage. A worried-looking Noel tried to coax them down, saying there had been too many injuries already, but the drunks continued to swing perilously from the scaffolding throughout 'Supersonic' – the performance of which was marred by the band's obvious concern. Liam made a second attempt to bring the fans safely back to earth: "Get off the fucking scaffolding...It's confusing me. I'm singing 'Supersonic' but I'm thinking 'Get off the scaffolding'." His plea was enough and the fans gingerly climbed back down to terra firma.

The Loch Lomond gigs followed the same set list and orchestration as the Maine Road concerts with two exceptions. Both 'It's Gettin' Better (Man!!)' and 'My Big Mouth' were given their debuts; the songs destined to be on the much-anticipated third album were so new at the time that Liam was forced to read the lyrics to 'My Big Mouth' off a sheet of paper and introduced the other song as 'It's Better Gettin' Mad' on the first night.

The media coverage the band had been subjected to over the previous few weeks had mostly centred on unsubstantiated stories and rumours about Liam and girlfriend Patsy Kensit. One such rumour, that Patsy was pregnant, had been broadcast to the nation by BBC Radio 1 DJ Chris Evans. Evans had, perhaps unwisely, decided to attend the first Loch Lomond show and was spotted in the crowd by an irate Liam Gallagher. According to The Sun tabloid, Liam "unleashed an astonishing foul-mouthed attack" on Evans from the stage, shouting: "Oi, twatty face. She's not fucking pregnant, so shut it, you ginger bastard. You're fucking getting it. Come back stage and meet me, you fucking ginger bastard." The Sun reported that Evans left before the end of the show. Liam used the gig to clarify other rumours, confirming that he and Patsy had become engaged. He didn't, however, address press rumours that he was suffering from the skin condition psoriasis – which just went to show how anything could be made into Oasis news.

The music press were generally effusive in their praise for the shows but there were a few rumblings of discontent. The NME questioned what Noel was trying to say with the songs off *(What's the Story) Morning Glory?* – described by the music paper as an album of "extraordinary clichés" – and that if these were supposed to be the anthems of a generational mouthpiece then they were disappointing. "Maybe being the biggest means being the best but with so many people at his command, it would be heartening to think he could offer us something more," wrote Steve Sutherland in the gig review featured in the August 10, 1996 issue. "Something useful and lasting beyond the kick and the thrill and the power." Sutherland added that there was "a tinge of regret" that the songs and the performances already seemed tired and that overexposure and overfamiliarity had robbed the material and the band itself of any real

danger and surprise, something the writer claimed that Noel Gallagher was all too aware of.

The Melody Maker's review on August 10, 1996, however, was gushing in its praise to the extent that it appeared to have been written in the immediate aftermath of the first night while the effects of the love drug were still at their most potent. (Whether it was written while the journalist was high on ecstasy or any other mind-altering substance is pure conjecture, of course.)

Filled with cosmically-tinged platitudes and spittle-drenched acclaim, this was a piece of journalism which in time could be held up as an example of the utter devotion some sections of the British music press would lavish on Oasis while they were soaring towards the stratosphere. Not content with comparing Oasis to the Beatles as many papers had over the previous two years, the Melody Maker's Dave Simpson went as far to say that the Beatles were "shit" and that, on the evidence of the Loch Lomond shows, "Oasis are miles and miles better than the Beatles ever were, partly because their best songs match anything Lennon and McCartney ever tossed off but mainly because you just get the pure unadulterated rock fix without all the extraneous nonsense."

Such was the state of euphoria surrounding the band's live shows at the time, most of the 80,000 fans in attendance at Balloch would have whole-heartedly agreed.

If the success of the Loch Lomond shows and the massive display of adoration on show in the Scottish highlands wasn't evidence enough that their time to ascend to the throne had arrived, flying into Knebworth by helicopter six days later and seeing the massed ranks of fans streaming into the park below sharply brought things into focus.

"Flying in on the helicopter to Knebworth from Battersea was a bit of a journey," Noel admitted in the Uncut interview from 2000. "I don't like flying: it's fucking petrifying. Anyway, coming over Knebworth and seeing the crowd...it was like, 'Fuck me, now that's a proper rock 'n' roll gig'. Even though for those who were stood four and half miles away from the stage watching five ants blasting away to something you can't hear must have been pretty fucking boring."

"There were so many people going that we had to fly in by helicopter," Bonehead remembers in the Creation Records *Upside Down* documentary. "I remember circling the site, looking at all these thousands of people just swarming in and filling the place up. It was just something else...beyond."

Despite the awe-inspiring sight below then, when Oasis landed they were aptly and typically down-to-earth. "Once we were backstage, however, we were worried about other stuff," laughed Noel. "Have you got the beers? Have you got Stellas? Are they cold? And have you got Sky? Yeah, but is it Sky Plus? Stuff like that!"

There was still a joyous naivety within the band at this time, even when it was at its most obvious that they were now very far from the council estates of Burnage. Noel would be self-deprecating and dismissive of the gigs in the years that followed, telling this writer in a 2002 interview that the band were just "fat alcoholics having a laugh" and "basically being on the piss" in front of 125,000 people each night. But this belies the professionalism which they exhibited once they took up their instruments and positions. They had slaved for this moment and they weren't going to blow it – but in true Oasis fashion, they were going to enjoy it.

"If we had sat down and calculated that we were going to make history...well, I would have made sure I'd have worn a better outfit, let's put it that way...and maybe gone to bed a little bit earlier...and maybe have tried to keep Liam off the sauce," Noel admitted in the 2003 John Dower-directed documentary *Live Forever: The Rise and Fall of Britpop.*

"I'm very proud of it, I am," Liam would say about Knebworth in the same documentary. "What do I remember? Not a lot, really. Nothing. I remember forgetting that we were doing a second night. I thought we were doing just one, so I got really drunk after the first night. I woke up because someone was knocking on the door and saying, 'Come on, you've got to do it all again'. I thought I was back in my own bed at home. But I can't remember anything else."

It seems unbelievable that Liam would have so little recollection. Few concerts before or since had generated such scenes.

The Knebworth gigs opened with the roar of 125,000 people which rolled towards the stage like a tsunami, crashing into the barriers in front of the band with a powerful, almost tidal surge. While each night had its own idiosyncrasies, both shows followed a similar pattern and set-list. Each night Oasis would walk out to the ecstatic screams of a generation and set about fulfilling everyone's dreams – including their own.

As the extended intro to 'Columbia' thudded out into the early evening air, all eyes turned to Liam as he stood impassive behind massive shades; surveying his subjects, embracing their mass adoration as if he was accepting a long overdue birth right. "Are you mad for it?"

For an occasion such as Knebworth – the crowning of an extraordinary rise that the whole country seemed to have been invited to – the opening song carried great weight: "There we were" – in the mire, in the dark, in the past; "now here we are" – living the dream, burning bright, writing the future. This was goodbye to the doldrums, an arrogant, straight middle-finger to all the struggles and doubt. The chains were off. Oasis had set their fans free.

It was an unrelenting spectacle. In the space of a dozen songs, the full power of Oasis was unleashed with barely any respite, reminding everyone in attendance why these five young men were able to command an audience of some 250,000 people over one glorious weekend. 'Acquiesce' shot the crowd through with an initial heady rush of adrenaline, getting the hearts racing for an amphetamine sprint through 'Hello' which had acres of breathless fans bouncing. After a brief surreal interlude during which Liam bizarrely riffed on crockery items, 'Some Might Say' chugged out of the monstrous PA and the whole crowd lost the plot, only for the insanity to reach greater heights when 'Roll With It' followed. The crowd was given a chance to gasp for air with the anthemic 'Slide Away' but most decided that their breath was better served belting out the words while swaying along. There would be other opportunities to take in oxygen.

There were no doubt some who regretted sucking in a few welcome lungfuls when they had the chance when a massive 'Morning Glory' started pounding out and the entire crowd went into overdrive as the gig moved into a higher gear, sending a new energy flowing over the masses.

The serious moshing really got underway when the stomping 'Round Are Way' heralded the arrival of Party Oasis, a band which excelled as much when it embraced its pop sensibilities as it did its rock heritage. Following that up with 'Cigarettes & Alcohol', Oasis once more reduced the pit to a relentless surge of bodies as the glam celebration ignited primal instincts and pushed the crowd closer to spontaneous combustion.

Some respite was afforded the steaming mass when the mellower mid-section of the gig signalled a modicum of calm. For those fighting for breath and recovery, the sight of Noel moving his stool onto the stage and picking up his acoustic guitar for 'Whatever' was a welcome one.

Returning to the stage after the acoustic interlude, Liam dedicated 'Cast no Shadow' to Rob Collins, the keyboardist for support act the Charlatans who had tragically been killed just days before the gig in a car accident – "Live forever mate" – and a sense of sombre reflection settled over the crowd as the song drifted into the Hertfordshire air. In a bid to rally the masses, the Gallaghers then called for a "really fucking massive big fuck-off boo for Man United" – which everyone responded to with venom, regardless if they were a football fan or not.

After a stirring rendition of 'Wonderwall', Noel and Bonehead took centre stage for the '*The Masterplan*', sitting either side of the massive performance space armed with acoustic guitars, looking like two kids sent to defend their village from a rampaging army with only homemade catapults for company. Even the atmospheric harmonica injected into the song couldn't dispel the feeling of vulnerability as the song began but by the time the swirling chorus had peaked, there was only hope and resolve.

'Don't Look Back in Anger' followed and was celebrated like a victory cry, as if this alone was evidence that the battle had been won and the slog of a mundane life was over. With the party now in full swing, Oasis launched into 'My Big Mouth' – one of the new songs debuted at Loch Lomond a few days before. It may have been unknown to many but the song's punky onslaught and Liam's insane delivery was enough to get the masses ebbing and flowing across the turf. Capitalising on the fact that the crowd were reacting well to the new songs, the band continued with another, unleashing 'It's Gettin' Better (Man!!)' with similar effect.

After a rousing version of 'Live Forever', played out in front of the now regular backdrop of rock icon faces (with Liam knelt in front of John Lennon as the song closed and Noel telling the crowd to "show your respect"), special guest John Squire arrived on stage to assist on 'Champagne Supernova' in what Nicky Wire of the Manic Street Preachers would later call "the coming together of the great Mancunian mafia". Remaining on stage for the finale of 'I am the Walrus', Squire and Oasis combined to expand the Beatles cover into a monstrous finale of squalling

23

feedback and spiralling solos as a million fireworks exploded in the sky above Knebworth as a soft rain began to fall.

The euphoria was palpable and hung over the heaving, sweaty crowd as they filtered away under the cover of darkness. "I turned to Alan McGee and said 'The battle has been won'," James Brown, the former editor of Lad Culture bible Loaded recalls in the *Upside Down* documentary. "It seemed that all the time throughout the 80s when we putting on bands in little clubs or doing fanzines or putting out flexidisks or just trying to get an article on a small band in the music press...everything which had been done was finalised at Knebworth. That's what it felt like. It was the greatest band in the world, the biggest band in the world and for once, the biggest band in the world were the best band in the world."

"I'm not sure Oasis realised the gigantic nature of what they were doing," Nicky Wire added in the same documentary.

Noel admitted to struggling in the immediate aftermath to comprehend what the band had just achieved. "I can't put it into words. I can only understate it really, because you can't see the back of the gig because it's dark and it's fucking two miles away from where you're playing," he told Select Magazine. "Out there, last night you could only see the first... and it's a fucking shitty thing to say, like...but I could only see the first 50,000! Y'know, there's another 75 somewhere! But you've just got to try and put your head down and play. I've been trying to put it into words and I'd rather not fucking try to tell you the truth. Absolutely mind-blowing."

"Now I know what the word big means," he added. "We thought we were big when we played Earls Court, then Maine Road. But after last night... There's big, then there's bigger than big and then there's fucking like last night... Now that is big. Now that is big. It's big."

24

In the years that followed, with the benefit of hindsight, Noel would say that the immensity of Knebworth had an adverse effect on him for long time. "I remember sitting there, at Knebworth, in the backstage area, and someone saying, 'Well, what now?' And I was like, 'I couldn't fucking tell yer'," he told the Guardian in 2000. "And that was how I felt for a good couple of years afterwards. I really suffered. It's like, what do you do when you've done everything? I suppose it's like getting a massive, massive pay rise and buying everything you want. What do you do after that? You kind of sink into boredom, into a kind of directionless state."

"It was the only time that I've seen Noel gobsmacked actually," reminisced Alan McGee in the *Upside Down* documentary. "The second night of Knebworth. He was gobsmacked. He didn't have anything to say...which was a first."

"I remember talking to Noel at Knebworth and we couldn't quite believe that it had only been two years since they got the first copies of their debut album," Charlatans singer Tim Burgess told the Manchester Evening News in May 2014. "I'd seen Oasis quite early on supporting someone at The Boardwalk. Even from the earliest gigs you could tell they were going to be massive but that massive? That was something else."

The hugeness of the event and the achievement, while awe-inspiring, had brought a realisation with it. The possibilities were no longer endless, unless someone was seriously considering getting Oasis to play to a one-off crowd in the range of millions. And even if the massive amounts of cocaine blowing around the band had convinced that person to attempt to stage such a bloated spectacle, the hope would have been that someone of greater sense and clarity would have seen the potential damage that such a widening of the slowly spreading chasm between band and fans would have inflicted.

"I can safely say we won't be going any fucking bigger than this, because to be quite honest, we can't supply the demand for the band at the moment, right?" Noel told Select after the gigs. "We're trying, but to do things like this, it's just a fucking pain in the arse. It's brilliant to do it, but I wouldn't fancy doing it again. You then get into the territory of four nights at Wembley Stadium, but by the third night, it must become a bit of a fucking chore. You've got to keep it special for the band."

"But that's it, you see. When the last note came out of the speakers at Knebworth, that was the end of an era for us. We achieved everything that we ever set out to be: to play the biggest gigs, to sell the most records, to write the best songs, and we've done that. But it's too much pressure, these big gigs. It's too much pressure to fuck it up."

Alan White, the band's drummer, would put it succinctly: "What's the point of doing it again? You've done it once."

"This is history...Right here, right now...This is history!" Even Noel Gallagher, already a man who was well aware of the impact a well-chosen statement could have on his growing legacy, could not have foreseen how portentous this emotional exclamation would turn out to be. In literal terms, his greeting to the Knebworth crowd stated the obvious: these were the biggest free-standing gigs that Britain had ever seen. Oasis and those in attendance were writing a chapter into the annals of rock folklore. But more than that, Noel could have been making a prediction about the changing nature of the relationship and the dynamic between the band and their fans. While many future Oasis gigs would enjoy that same celebratory atmosphere, that energy crackling through the crowd with fanatical fervour, the feeling that those on stage and those in the pit were cut from the same cloth would essentially be gone forever. Knebworth brought down the curtain on the first age of Oasis and ushered in the era of rock superstardom which effectively consigned their image of the people's band to the history books.

Oasis had been the band of the people, for the people. Now, at a point when even their lofty dreams had been eclipsed by the reality of their stratospheric rise, they had become something else.

"People have talked about Knebworth being a cultural watershed which I don't think it was," Noel would tell RTE's Dave Fanning in an interview in Dublin a year after the event. "I think Spike Island was more of a cultural watershed because there were people from just one age group. At Knebworth we had families there, people coming along with their mams and dads and the kids to see Oasis...It's like punk never happened."

Members of Oasis have come out in the years since Knebworth and admitted that it should have been the grand finale of the band, that the realisation that nothing could ever top such an achievement was reason enough to finish on an incredible high. "I think if anyone had the bottle we would have come offstage at Knebworth and said, 'Do you know what, it's been a fucking top scream, let's just kick it in the head now'," Noel told Uncut magazine in March 2000. "But, of course, it was, you know; 'Let's have one last fucking trawl around America; let's bleed the life out of the album'. And that almost broke us in a way. But when you're on a roll, nobody wants to say, 'Let's just pack it in and be like The Jam and go out and be cool', Everyone's like, 'Fuck it, man, the bar's still open', you know what I mean? It's not last orders yet."

"If someone, especially Liam, had backed me up and said, 'Yeah, finishing it now is the right thing to do', then I'd have done it," Noel later admitted in an NME interview that same year. "But they didn't see the point. I suppose the alternatives for everybody else weren't up to much because they're not songwriters."

"The whole thing about Oasis was that we were supposed to be the ones poking fun at the Establishment and getting pissed and getting on everyone's nerves," Noel told Uncut in 2000. "As it panned out we became the Establishment, and I didn't particularly like that."

A year after the concert, even the usually mad-fer-it Liam was beginning to see a missed opportunity: "What it was, as far as I'm concerned, on my behalf, we'd done Knebworth, yeah? Big gig. Really big gig. After Knebworth we should've gone on holiday for a couple of months. We needed a break. We needed to sit in the garden with those polystyrene gnomes."

"I think we should have done Knebworth and on that second night we should have all taken a bow and said, 'thank you and good night, we were Oasis'," said Bonehead in an interview with Oasis fansite Stopcryingyourheartout.com in 2012. "We should have bowed out but we didn't, we carried on. It was a bit of a struggle after Knebworth, to go over to America and play for a few thousand people."

While recovering backstage after the triumphant, yet slightly more chaotic, second night, Noel was privately presented with the chance to cut and run when he was approached by a record company executive. "I distinctly remember somebody sidling up to me," he recalls, "saying, 'It's time for the solo record now'. It would've been pretty naughty of me because them lot would be like, 'What the fuck are we going to do?"

"I should have had a decade off after Knebworth and gone 'Well that's enough for me, I need to go on holiday and I'll see you in 10 years'," he added. "At Knebworth nobody really knew what we were doing. Normally when people play Knebworth it's the pinnacle of their achievement and they put on these awe-inspiring shows. We were just on the piss really.

"We'd come off the dole five years before and just played the biggest ever free-standing gig in England, 250,000 people. And that's never going to be topped by anyone. That rounded everything off and we should have ended it there. But nobody else wanted to do it because they haven't got the balls to do it. We should have split up when we came offstage because that would have been the logical conclusion of everything."

The band weren't the only ones to feel that Knebworth should have been the point when Oasis called it a day. Many of those involved have since admitted that the unique essence of the band's early incarnation had evaporated among the pyrotechnics of the finale and its ethos trampled by the notorious 7000-strong guest-list.

"It was fun but there was a horrible side to it," said Dick Green, co-founder of Creation Records in the label's documentary *Upside Down*. "Everything was overblown to every degree. VIP tents within VIP tents, within special areas where you had to have 15 different wristbands to get anywhere near. Then you'd find out...I couldn't get into that one! And I'm paying for this!"

Label boss Alan McGee had similar recollections. "I'd paid for the world class tent and I asked for a glass of water and they told me to go away," he says with a wry smile in the documentary. "The security were like, 'who are you?' I couldn't get backstage. It was my tent. I'd paid a quarter of a million quid for it and I couldn't even get a Diet Coke. They didn't have any so I couldn't even get a drink because I was on the wagon."

"They sent crazy Bentley limousines to pick up everyone who was on Creation Records and drive them to Knebworth," said Gruff Rhys of label mates Super Furry Animals. "So we went to Knebworth in a Bentley... and we weren't even playing."

"When I signed Oasis to Creation, I thought they were going to be big, but I'd be lying if I said I thought they would get that big," continues

McGee. "When the fireworks went off, it all went a bit AC/DC. It wasn't the band, it wasn't the management, it was 'the event'. I just thought, that's not us, that's not Oasis. I don't know what it is. We should get out. We probably should've ended it after Knebworth. In our heads, that's when Creation started ending. It was all a bit detached. I lost interest. I was proud of Oasis for living the dream but now, I look back and think it was all kind of ridiculous. Oasis should have split and we should have shut Creation. But it's easy to say that now."

"It was amazing to see that many people in a field watching Oasis and the whole buzz around the band and the label at that point was massive but everybody was under a lot of pressure to deliver," Andy Saunders, Creation's head of communications, remembers in Alan McGee's book *Creation Stories*. "I didn't enjoy that period much to be honest, it had all got out of control and messy. A lot of people acted like arseholes around that time. They know who they are…"

"Ego is a horrible thing, but I got one," McGee added. "I was delusional. If it had been up to me, I'd have got Oasis to do a gig from Antarctica. But maybe we needed those big egos to achieve what we wanted to."

The Scottish author Irvine Welsh, himself somewhat of a cultural icon of the time, summed up the Knebworth weekend succinctly: "It was like the Roman Empire," he lamented in *Upside Down*. "When it looks like it's at its strongest, that's when it's actually beginning to crumble."

2.

champagne supernova

"Some day you will find me, caught beneath the landslide"

At a time when craving fame and all its trappings were frowned upon, Oasis stood out among their contemporaries as a band that wanted nothing short of world domination and was not afraid of admitting it. Even from the beginning, the Gallaghers would tell anyone and everyone who would listen about their hunger for adoration, their desire for mansions and limousines and their belief that their talent was going to bring them everything they ever wanted and more. "Before we came along, success was a dirty word," Noel told the Daily Telegraph in 2007. "We kind of reinvigorated ambition."

That ambition appeared to have no bounds. Oasis didn't just want to be the biggest band in Britain but the world and if the universe was up for the taking, then they'd have a good crack at that as well. "There's no point starting a band and wanting to be big just in England, you've got to want to be the biggest band in the world and sell 50 million records all over the world and if you don't then there's no point being in a band," Noel told Sweden's ZTV channel in 1994. "What's the point of wanting to sell 3000 singles in England and couple of hundred round Europe? That's ridiculous. We won't sit here and be embarrassed about how good we are and tell people that we're really sorry that we've sold this amount of records or that we're sorry for being on this many covers or we're sorry for being this big. No chance."

"We just want to be the biggest band in the world and that is it...I want all the things that go with it, I want to be a big pop star and do loads of people's heads in," Liam told presenter Zoe Ball on the BBC's O-Zone programme in the same year, just after the release of fourth single 'Cigarettes and Alcohol'. "I want it and I'm not embarrassed about wanting it. These people who get all the success and then say 'oh, I don't want it'...of course you want it because that's what you do it for. I want to be mobbed everywhere I go with loads of birds chasing me down the street shouting LIAM! I want it all."

"It's nice to get noticed," Noel told Addicted To Noise at the start of 1995. "I could never understand pop stars who go on about fame. I wouldn't say I like it, but it gives you a good feeling when you're walking down the street and somebody stops you and says, 'Can I have your autograph?' If you can't enjoy that there's no point in being in a fucking band. Or like when people come up to me and will say, 'Can I take a photograph with you?' And I always say, 'Well, yeah'. That's what I'm in a band for. I'm not in a band to sit at home and hide under the blankets and be ashamed of what I am. I'm in it to be on the cover of every single magazine. On the telly 24 hours a day. Total Oasis, 24-7."

When Oasis emerged after the first flush of what would eventually become the all-encompassing title of Britpop, the British music scene was still taking its first tentative steps out of the shadow of US grunge. It had retreated after the waning of the Madchester movement of the late 1980s, when bands like the Stone Roses and Happy Mondays sunk under the weight of litigation and drug addiction, and the invasion of punk-orientated Stateside rock had sent the last remnants of the indigenous music scene scurrying for cover. A generation of young Britons who had spent their formative years popping Es, dodging police batons and facing tabloid demonization during the late-80s rave scene started to emerge in the early 90s in search of an alternative to the "I hate myself and I want to die" ethos of grunge. Early exponents of the new British sound such as

32

Blur and Suede suddenly found themselves confronted with ravenous, identity-starved audiences craving leadership. They wanted bands to inspire them with their message, their lifestyle and their fashion as they went looking for what it meant to be British in the last decade of the 20th Century.

"It was pretty obvious from the start that something amazing was happening with Oasis," said Clint Boon, keyboardist with Inspiral Carpets, in the *(What's the Story) Morning Glory?* album documentary. "Not solely through their music but through the lifestyle they were representing. Oasis tapped a nerve in a way that no band in the last 30 years had done, not even the Sex Pistols."

Andrew Mueller, a journalist with the Melody Maker at the time of the band's breakthrough, said in the same documentary that the arrival of Oasis was like an alarm call for British music. "Loads of bands were running around in flannel shirts with stupid little goatee beards wanting to be Soundgarden," he said. "Oasis appeared in the middle of all this with very obvious British influences – the Beatles, Slade, the Kinks – and people were reminded that, oh yeah, we can do it over here as well."

"Before we came along, the greatest hope for British music was Suede," Noel told GQ in 2000. "Bernard's a genius, as a matter of fact, and Brett seems to know what he's going on about in interviews, but I'm sorry, man, they don't write songs that mean anything to people living in council blocks in Glasgow."

"When we came along at the arse end of '93, it was Suede and all that lot, and we were, like, 'Right. They're shit. They're shit. You're fucking totally shit'," he told the Guardian that same year. "'Right, chop 'em out...get us a fuckin' beer...hello darlin'...' And the kids went berserk, because they were, like, 'that's me incarnate, how cool is that'. And the more people said it, the more we just went berserk. And we lived up to it for a while."

"We weren't into chin-stroking," he continued. "We were very naive. We were quite pure in a way. It was just all about rock 'n' roll. After that came the rock 'n' roll behaviour. We were a wake-up call to a lot of kids who maybe thought, 'Well I'm a little bit of an obnoxious twat too'."

"The reason the majority of the people in the country like my band is because we're like the majority of people in this country," Noel told the BBC in the 1997 documentary *Right Here, Right Now*. "We still go to football matches; we still go to the pub. We get nicked and busted like everybody else. We're still outspoken and we still don't give a shit. I wouldn't say we're the voice of a generation but we'd definitely be leading the march if there was anywhere to march to. We'd be at the front singing."

"Oasis had balls of steel," Johnny Hopkins, Oasis's publicist and the Head of Press at Creation, said. "They needed to. They wanted success and everything that went with it. That attitude was refreshing at the time. Because they were so open and honest about everything that they did and thought they were very newsworthy for the media and very exciting for the public. Apart from the Stone Roses, Happy Mondays, Nirvana and a few others, musicians had become manicured and boring. Oasis were the real deal."

Britain first started to wake up to Oasis when Creation released a white label, limited-edition 12" version of early live favourite 'Columbia' in late 1993. Originally sent out as a primer for the band to journalists and radio programmers, the song was unexpectedly picked up by BBC Radio 1 which played it 19 times in the first two weeks after its release, an unusual move for the station given the record had not been available in stores. It was a pleasant surprise to everyone associated with the band, none more so than the song's writer who later claimed that the version which made it onto the national airwaves was a drugged-up, psychedelic jam.

"Everyone claims to have written the words for that one," Noel said of 'Columbia' in the *Definitely Maybe* documentary. "We had an instrumental version we were playing at the Real People's studio in Liverpool when someone said, 'Eh, la', you need some words for that'. But we were all tripping on acid so if anyone wants to try and prove they wrote it, be my guest. I'm the one with the publishing deal. Anyway, that was the version which ended up getting played about 50 times on Radio 1, with all of us totally fucking cabbaged on it."

'Columbia', with its spiralling riff and trippy, disoriented lyrics, had whetted many an appetite. At a time when British guitar music was tentatively beginning to find its feet again, 'Columbia' was a very different proposition to offerings of other bands which were leading the nascent revival. It would prove to be a portent of things to come.

"I knew, as soon as we had the first single out, what was gonna happen," Liam told Melody Maker in April 1996. "Suede were the only big band in Britain at the time and although we weren't doing gigs, we were stuck in a room all day, getting better and better, and I just knew that if we did a few gigs and got a bit of interest, that'd be it. It would just go fucking mad. And as soon as 'Supersonic' come out, it did."

Unlike many of Noel Gallagher's other songs which would become ubiquitous over the next few months, 'Supersonic' hadn't been conceived in the fabled Hit Hut - the British Gas storeroom where, pre-Oasis, a teenage Noel had penned a number of songs which would eventually become future hits. The genesis of 'Supersonic' was more immediate.

"We did 'Supersonic' in one night," Noel remembered. "We were in Liverpool to record 'Bring it on Down' because McGee wanted that to be our first single but we couldn't get it right so someone said 'why don't you just write one?' So I went away and wrote it in half an hour, then we recorded it and the rest is history. That demo version is the one you hear. It was that fucking good, why mess with genius?"

Creation boss McGee had enough belief in Oasis to let them make most of their creative decisions without consulting him but with so much potentially riding on the first single, he was compelled to visit the band to see for himself why this new song had been chosen ahead of his own preference.

"So we were at Maida Vale and McGee turns up going, 'right let's hear this song then'. It's the first single and he hasn't even heard it," Bonehead added. "'Supersonic'? What's that?' So we played it and it blew his head off."

The song was performed by the band on their debut national TV performance on Channel 4's The Word on March 18. As is often the case with momentum, when something is rolling few things can stop it and obstacles just seem to evaporate in the face of unrelenting progress. So it was for Oasis who had cajoled presenter Terry Christian for months to get the band on The Word to promote their debut single. A cancellation opened up a space on the running order and suddenly Oasis were in. Playing in front of a psychedelic backdrop with Liam waving a Super-8 camera at the badly-dressed audience (Britain was not only struggling to find an identity in music), Oasis introduced themselves to the general public.

"I was languishing in drug rehab and watching Oasis on The Word playing 'Supersonic'," Alan McGee told the Guardian on February 10, 2009. "I thought 'What have I unearthed?' and then it was 'Yes, this is going to be massive'. And guess what? They were."

36

When 'Supersonic' was released on April 11, 1994, it went straight into the UK singles chart at number 31. It wasn't long before it was being regarded by many as a declaration of war, that the old order had better step aside or get trampled underfoot.

"When it opens up and Liam sings 'I need to be myself, I can't be no-one else', that's a statement of intent right there," Stone Roses bassist Mani said in the *Definitely Maybe* documentary. "Bang, this is how it's going to be."

"This was us saying, 'right, out of the way, we'll take charge here'," said Bonehead. "This is what you're getting. This is how things are going to be from now on."

The buzz around the band was now growing by the week. When 'Shakermaker', their second single, hit Number 11 in the UK singles charts in June 1994, Oasis were invited to perform on BBC music show Top of the Pops – achieving a life-long ambition for Noel Gallagher at the age of 27. The band was afforded the then rare honour of playing the song live, rather than miming to the track, and performed with drummer Tony McCarroll at the front of the stage with Bonehead and bassist Paul 'Guigsy' McGuigan either side of him and the Gallaghers elevated on a platform at the back in front of the band's swirling flag logo. Pogoing fans proudly wearing the band's t-shirts added a further twist of originality and authenticity to the usually staid and choreographed proceedings. With each release, interview and appearance, the band's message was becoming stronger: here's something different – get on it.

With the release of 'Live Forever' in August of 1994, things really changed. While the first two singles had been swaggeringly defiant, the third single knocked fans and critics sideways. Okay, so these Manc casuals could sneer and pout their way through coked-up terrace rock 'n' roll better than most but this was a hugely affecting and well-crafted anthem. This was not what an exploding phenomenon was supposed to deliver in its first flush of fame; this was a song which should have taken years for them to aspire to. In reality, it had. Noel had written 'Live Forever' in 1991 but for all intents and purposes for those who considered Oasis to have come from nowhere, this was a bolt from the blue. And it had been planned that way. By releasing 'Live Forever' as the third single, Oasis had already shown their rock credentials but 'Live Forever' had quickly slammed the brakes on anyone's perception sliding towards an idea of the band as one-trick ponies.

'Live Forever' did more than change people's ideas about the band, it gave those who were gathering in a swelling legion of fans their own banner to rally to. "Maybe you're the same as me, we see things they'll never see...you and I are gonna live forever..." Here was a song that spoke to the fans, connected with the fans, and gave the people hope. It told them that the band would stand together with them against all others and that together they would be triumphant. The embracing of this message by the fans, as well as the song's anthemic arrangement, was one of the main reasons that 'Live Forever' remained the band's hymn for the entirety of their career.

"For me, 'Live Forever' is the most important Oasis song because it announced us to the world," Noel told The Hour programme in 2006. "We were already getting pretty famous in Britain but when this came out, people all around the world went 'hang on'. I was writing a certain type of song before 'Live Forever' and after that, everything changed."

"'Live Forever' was the song that got us the record deal," he added in the *Lock the Box* documentary which accompanied the release of the *Stop the Clocks* compilation in 2006. "When McGee heard that, he was like 'fucking hell...' We didn't get any more money out of the cunt though..."

That same month, when *Definitely Maybe* went straight into the UK charts at Number 1 on its way to becoming the fastest-selling British debut album of all time, Oasis started getting a real taste of the fame that they had craved from the beginning. "The summer of '94, when our debut album came out, that was fabulous because we were either on the road or in the studio or doing interviews, and we were being courted by this person and that person and everyone wanted to meet us," Noel told Melody Maker in March 1998. "We were just living it, man."

The demand for all things Oasis was beginning to grow as the album and its singles became ubiquitous throughout that summer. "There was a point after 'Cigarettes and Alcohol' came out when Creation wanted to put out 'Slide Away' as a single," Noel explained in the *Lock the Box* documentary. "But I said, 'you can't have five singles off a debut album, man...because if you do, someone's gonna have to get me a Lear jet...' Michael Jackson is putting out five singles off an album and he's got a monkey and a jet...I don't want the monkey but I fucking want the aeroplane."

"I'd already been leant on to release the fourth single. I remember we were in Detroit and we got the phone call that not only had 'Cigarettes and Alcohol' got in the charts but it was the biggest selling single we'd ever had – the fourth single off *Definitely Maybe*! I just remember putting the phone down and thinking, 'now we're fucking talking, this is gonna get stupid...bring me the fucking chimp!'"

It wasn't just the people who needed Oasis. The media soon caught wind of the growing excitement around the band and the euphoria they were creating through their music and behaviour. Here was a band that had all the elements of a tabloid wet dream and one with such an exponentially expanding fan base that any story featuring them could almost guarantee a flood of sales. "The press have always needed a bad-boy, dirty, druggy rock 'n' roll band," Noel told the Sunday Times in February 1996. "Before us, pop stars were becoming arty-farty, limp-wristed, fey bastards like Brett from Suede. We're not that wised-up on books in Oasis, but we know what's what. And the press will always need a band who speak their mind. The people in the fucking tabloids want the two obnoxious twats from up North because it makes for good copy."

But Noel in particular, as the man responsible for the songs which were pushing the band higher and higher, was already starting to feel the frustration of making headlines for every reason other than the quality of the music when the band were enjoying the first surge on the back of *Definitely Maybe*'s release.

"Journalists in England look at a band and say, where do they come from, how many drugs do they take…they don't talk about the music, they just write about the things they find it easy to write about," Noel told ZTV in 1994. "They don't write about our records, they just write about us taking drugs and how many hotel rooms we've smashed up. It's just lazy and stupid journalism."

"When you start a band, you're given a stereotype in the first year of your existence and unfortunately for us, for the first year we were pretty fucking out of control so that's stuck with us all the way," he added in an interview with Select Magazine three years later.

"The thing is the media write something and twist it and it becomes lies," Noel told Melody Maker in its March 7th 1998 issue. "Say if I went out to a nightclub and got pretty drunk but left at six in the morning, it would be I went to a nightclub, got violently drunk, had two fights and left with four women at six the next afternoon in a police van."

"Much of the bad press added to the mythology of the band as it did with Sex Pistols, Led Zeppelin and the Stones...though some of it detracted from the music," admitted Johnny Hopkins. "However many

40

'bad' stories there were in the press, believe me…the majority of really bad stories were never printed."

Oasis had been cultivating a reputation for hell-raising pretty much from the start but now, with a hungry press pack increasingly on their tail, the band's exploits as they began to fully embrace what it meant to be rock 'n' roll stars at last were beginning to fill column inches. At this point, things were still at their most chaotic on the road. It would be a year or so before the madness would infiltrate everyday life. As such, the *Definitely Maybe* Tour presented the media with the best opportunity yet to stock up on outrageous quotes and reports of excess and abandon as the press followed Oasis across the world on their biggest tour to date. And true to form, the band didn't disappoint.

"One night, someone had given us 300 quid, put us in a bar with all the gear and said, 'You're playing at Bath Moles tonight, and it's 300 miles away'," Noel reminisced in a Select interview with the band in 1997. "Marcus was like, 'Right, I'll see you tomorrow', and we were like, 'If you're fucking lucky mate'. And we were off. It was like The Magnificent Seven riding into town. We were having it. Fucking big, large one. Every night. I saw Liam in a room with a fire extinguisher in one hand and a chainsaw in the other..."

"We were off our tits," added Bonehead.

"We were crazy," said Liam. "We should have died."

Already a band with a growing notoriety with hotel chains up and down the UK, the release of 'Supersonic' and the embryonic adoration which came with it would launch the band headlong into a period of first-flush-of-fame hedonism which would make all their previous hi-jinks look distinctly restrained.

"From 'Supersonic' to the first album, we were seriously fucking out of control," Noel told Melody Maker in the April 27th 1996 issue.

"People at Creation and managers of other bands were all saying 'These guys ain't gonna last a year. They're either gonna die or kill each other'. Me and our kid were just like fucking Punch and Judy then. The others were just as bad. We would walk into a hotel and just empty it out the window. The best one was in Sweden, in a hotel with Primal Scream and the Verve. We got deported and banned. Thirty grand damage..." It was a careening, foot-to-the-floor joyride which would continue at life-threatening speed for the rest of the year. "In the middle of the *Definitely Maybe* tour, they gave us till Christmas," Noel added.

The highs – both natural and narcotic – which the band had experienced throughout 1994 were beginning to take a toll by the time they flew out to the United States in September. The band had already played around 50 dates since the turn of the year before *Definitely Maybe* was released in August. After a short European tour that month, the band jetted off to Japan and then onto North America for 12 dates in the US and Canada.

America, though, was always going to be a tough nut to crack – as it is for many UK bands, especially those with innately British attitudes and approaches. Touring the massive land mass on the back of a debut album meant that Oasis weren't only having to spread the message to more receptive ears in those big cities with established music scenes but also having to roll into one-horse towns to try and reach as many new potential fans as possible. Road monsters they may have already been and a band who had educated themselves in the hard school of self-motivated touring in the early days, Oasis still found the US to be a chore and increasingly distracted themselves from the monotony by acting up.

"All bands go there for about two weeks, do four gigs and then come home," Noel told Select magazine in 1997. "We ended up going over there for two months, doing shitloads of gigs and that, and you just get bored, and you start getting pissed. All the rows that ever started, we've been drunk: 'Look at your shoes, you dick'..'.Who are you calling a dick?'... 'Calling you a dick'...'Who's a dick?'"

The band's behaviour was beginning to generate some uncomplimentary reports in the US media, prompting Liam to call the American press "wankers," before adding: "They want grungy fucking people, stabbing themselves in the head on stage. They get a bright bunch like us, with deodorant on, they don't get it." Liam continued to antagonise the locals – and Noel – by changing the lyrics to some songs to include references that Americans would find offensive.

The hedonism which had been spiralling out of control for most of the year continued unabated as the tour staggered across the States. Oasis managed to make it relatively unscathed through the first four gigs but when the band rolled into Los Angeles for a show at the Whiskey-a-Go-Go on September 29, the wheels were already starting to come off. Previously chucked out of a KROQ radio station interview for swearing on air and brawling with the bouncers at Johnny Depp's Viper Room club, Oasis rocked up at the legendary venue on Sunset Boulevard after spending the early hours drunkenly rolling about the streets and trading insults with the LAPD.

Struggling onto the stage, the band started the shambolic performance by blowing an amp in the middle of opener 'Rock 'n' Roll Star'. The band, dishevelled and off the pace to a man, then battled to keep the show from veering off into violence with the tension on the stage and between the band and audience almost palpable. Events took a turn for the worse during 'Shakermaker' when Liam, delivering each song with a strangled yowl, started to drop lines and lose interest until a glare from Noel sent the singer storming across the stage in search of a confrontation. Squaring up to his brother, Noel told Liam to go fuck himself before a bout of pushing and shoving came to an end with the singer swinging his tambourine into his sibling's head. The apathetic crowd then came to life, shouting for the fight to escalate. While a major ruck failed to materialize, the gig lurched towards its malevolent conclusion like a fatally wounded bear with a seething Liam making wanking motions at his brother throughout the remaining songs before totally giving up halfway through "I am the Walrus" and wandering off stage, down Sunset and into the night.

The next day, Noel quit the band.

"I was disgusted by what had happened," Noel is quoted as saying in Paul Mathur's book *Take Me There*. "It was complete shit. I said to the others, 'I don't want to do this if you're not going to put everything you've got into it. If you're going to fuck about then do it when we've finished the band. There'll be plenty of time then but right now I'm going to be in a group who want to do something'. Everyone just looked around and no one said anything so I thought, 'that's it, fuck it, we're splitting up'." Noel got his passport, took all the money from the tour float and got the first plane out of LA in the direction of Las Vegas. "I had half an ounce of coke with me and I thought, 'right I'm having this, then I'm going home. That's it'."

While Noel was holed-up in hotel rooms in Las Vegas and then San Francisco, suffering from cocaine psychosis and thinking the FBI were tapping his phone, the rest of Oasis were marooned in LA, their passports confiscated to stop anyone else doing a runner. Creation's managing director Tim Abbot was dispatched to track Noel down and after locating him and secretly – as not to upset the already fragile songwriter – relaying his progress back to the band and the management, he managed to get the guitarist to meet up with the rest of the band. "Honestly," Noel admitted in *Take Me There*, "I really didn't want to be in Oasis after that. It had been building for a bit but then it had come to a head. What was happening was the complete opposite of why we'd started the band in the first place. We were all getting caught up in the madness."

"It was all exploding, all over the world, in our faces, and we probably didn't know how to deal with it. All right, I knew how to deal with it, but I didn't know how to deal with the rest of the band, who didn't know how to deal with it."

"The situation was often volatile," remembered Johnny Hopkins. "But the only time it really felt like it was the end of the band was after the LA gig in Oct 1994 when Noel went missing for a few days. But there weren't really any fears of them splitting up. Noel had a vision. There was unfinished business. Neither Noel nor the rest of the band were going to give up on it. They could have done but they wanted to make more records and play more gigs. The fans were important to them."

Eventually, Noel was persuaded to reconcile with his brother. Four gigs had been cancelled so Oasis took the opportunity to grab some down time in Austin, Texas where the band recorded some new songs. Noel used the opportunity to showcase 'Talk Tonight', the song inspired by a meeting with a woman in San Francisco who had talked to him about the benefits of giving Oasis another chance. The tour restarted and concluded with the two remaining gigs in New Jersey and New York going off without incident. After spending November touring Europe and then the UK in December, in support of new single 'Whatever' – which hit Number 3 in the singles charts, Oasis ended 1994 on a high. It could have been very different.

It's hard to believe in the context of what was about to happen with the band but the drama of Noel's lost weekend barely made a ripple back home in the British media. The music press had reported the incident but at this time, Oasis were an exciting indie band but one which was only making minor waves, albeit choppy ones, on the periphery of the mainstream.

One of the first times Oasis smashed their way into the mainstream consciousness was at the 15th annual BRIT Music Awards, British music's biggest back-slapping event which honours that year's successful acts. While 1995 would prove to be Blur's year, with the band and their *Parklife* album sweeping the board, Oasis would win the British Breakthrough Act award, announcing the band's arrival on the industry awards scene. After an audacious attempt at nabbing the Christmas Number 1 with 'Whatever' two months earlier and with *Definitely Maybe* still exceeding expectations, both critically and commercially, Oasis had earned an invite to dine at pop's top table – and proceeded to litter it with cigarette butts, beer cans, spent champagne bottles and white powder.

"When we were at The Brits for the first time in 1995, we had a big table with about 10 seats around it and in between the awards being dished out, because it had a big table cloth over the top, we ended up sitting underneath most of the night, just fucking messing about," Noel told Uncut magazine. "And we had lots of Jack Daniels, and it was like, 'And the best newcomer is Oasis' and we were climbing out from under the table!"

"We were blatantly flaunting it in front of the whole establishment of the music industry. I remember the tables round us were pretty major league pop stars who were all fucking disgusted at our behaviour. But at the end of the night, right, there must have been about 500 people round our table! Everyone else was, 'That's where the party is'."

The awards ceremony came at the beginning of yet another extensive US tour. Oasis had headed back over the Atlantic at the start of January, flew home for the BRIT mayhem and the now legendary concert at Southend-on-Sea's Cliffs Pavilion before heading across the channel for a Paris show (after which drummer Tony McCarroll quit the band) and back to the UK for a gig at the Sheffield Arena (McCarroll's last show). During this time, the first single from what would be the new album was released. 'Some Might Say' came out on April 24 and went into the UK singles chart at Number 1, giving the band their first chart topper. New drummer Alan White's first appearance with the band was the Top of the Pops rendition of the hit single, a day after joining Oasis as Tony McCarroll's replacement.

"'Some Might Say' was the first song I ever wrote when I moved to London and it was inspired by listening to The Faces," Noel told the NME in 1996. "Alan McGee wanted the A-side to be 'Acquiesce' because he didn't think 'Some Might Say' sounded like a number one. He's a great man but his one fault is that he has absolutely no idea how to pick singles."

"I got a call from him, seven in the morning, and he's going, 'Och Noel, I've just heard 'Acquiesce', it's got to be a single'. And I'm going, 'Fucking not now mate, I've got a really bad head, not now'. He went into this big rant about it and sang it down the phone, really badly. And I'm thinking, 'Fucking hell – it sounds shit!' So we had this argument. I'm going, 'Well, I think 'Some Might Say' is a better song', and he's going, 'Well, I think 'Acquiesce' is'. But I suppose I was just being a stubborn cunt because he's from the record company and I'm from the band and if he wanted it then I was gonna do the opposite."

"But saying that, as soon as I'd written 'Some Might Say' I was absolutely certain it would be a number one and I was right. I never had even the slightest doubt."

With May set aside for studio time before the band headed out on another set of UK dates which would feature their headlining slot on the Pyramid Stage at the Glastonbury Festival, the band took the opportunity to head to Rockfield Studios in Wales and record the follow-up to *Definitely Maybe* with Noel and producer Owen Morris at the controls.

It was an inauspicious start, however. When recording was supposed to begin, everyone was there apart from the man with the songs. Noel had apparently had a bit of a late night in London and was running behind schedule. "At about three o'clock he bundles in, Jack Daniels in hand, note up nostril," Owen Morris told the now defunct Official Oasis Magazine in December 1996. "He shouts the odds for ten minutes and passes out. A star performance. At about five o'clock he comes round. The football's on at six so we decide to have a run through of 'Roll With It', to sort out headphone levels and the like. The band run through. It's mayhem. Nobody can hear themselves, Liam's effing and blinding, Noel's swaying, Alan – and this is his first day of recording with Oasis – is wondering what he's let himself in for."

"By the end of that night we've recorded Guigs, Bonehead, and most of Noel's guitars," he added. "Liam sang it the next afternoon, in three takes. He was on fire. Totally charged up by Alan's performance. Most singers will do loads of takes before getting enough good bits to compile a complete vocal, some go into hundreds. Liam wasn't having any of that. Apart from 'Champagne Supernova', which he tried when his voice was shot, Liam never did more than three takes on the entire album. He was singing his heart and soul out. Liam Gallagher is by fucking miles the most passionate singer I've ever known."

After the early setbacks *(What's the Story) Morning Glory?* took shape quickly with the band averaging almost one song every twenty-four hours. But, as with most things involving the Gallaghers, eventually tensions would rise and derail the now smoothly running process. The problem this time was Noel's insistence that he would sing lead vocals on either 'Wonderwall' or 'Don't Look Back in Anger'. As the singer of Oasis,

Liam reacted angrily at what he saw as his brother's efforts to snatch this distinction from him. An all-out war was averted when Liam's take of 'Wonderwall' was deemed perfect by Noel, although tempers frayed again when Liam failed to match that quality on 'Champagne Supernova', leading Noel to openly criticise him. When Noel recorded his vocal for 'Don't Look Back in Anger', Liam took the opportunity to find the nearest pub. When he returned in the middle of recording with a group of locals he'd invited back, Noel went mad and a vicious fight ensued. The session was abandoned and recording was suspended.

"We all went home," Owen Morris remembered. "Rockfield was booked for another five weeks, but there was no point in hanging around. Noel had spoken to Marcus and was going away for a while. No-one knew if he was coming back. We were all gutted. Eventually we got the call. Noel was back, everybody get their shit together. All the band turned up at the weekend, but we were still waiting for Noel; again he was late. This time though, he'd been stuck on the train for two hours. When he strolled in at dinner time Liam got up and hugged him."

The sessions resumed and recording completed after Liam and Noel had patched things up, with Noel writing the last song for the album, 'Cast No Shadow' on the delayed train back to the studio. With the recordings in the can, the band headed back out on the road while Owen Morris took the master tapes to London for the post-production work. "We finished mixing by the end of July," Owen concluded. "Noel and I worked out the running order and *(What's the Story) Morning Glory?* was done."

With a first Number 1 under their belts, Oasis decided to buck the standard industry procedure of releasing the single chosen to directly precede an album's release three weeks before the LP was due out. The decision was made to release 'Roll With It' on August 14, six weeks before *(What's the Story) Morning Glory?* hit the shops. With Blur intending to release their next single 'Country House' a week later, Food Records – Blur's label – pushed the release back a week, fearing 'Roll With It' would impact on their single's chances of hitting Number 1.

The ensuing 'Battle of Britpop', manufactured as much by the NME as by Food's decision to change the release date of the Blur single, became the biggest news story in the country, triggering unprecedented amount of exposure for both bands in national newspapers and on television news bulletins. The fascination was fuelled by a media-constructed battle between the middle class of the south and the working class of the north, the "Working Class Heroes" versus "Art School Trendies" as the Guardian called it. The chart battle even made the BBC's Six O'clock News on the night before the release of both singles and Liam was interviewed on Channel 4's main news programme. "Just about every voice in the media felt compelled to express an opinion on the freshly inaugurated age of Britpop," John Harris wrote in his book *The Last Party*.

"The thing that still pisses me off to this day is that cuntfuck [Damon Albarn, if you're wondering] said we engineered the battle with his bunch of wankers," Noel told Q magazine in May 2002. "Oasis don't need to compete with a bunch of cunts who did A-level music. They're fakers."

"The whole thing was manufactured by the NME and Blur's camp who moved their single release to coincide with ours," Noel told the BBC's Mark Lawson in 2012. "It was a media wet dream, a made-up class war. There couldn't have been more contrast: there was this lot from Manchester who robbed shit and this lot from Colchester who went to art school. But what annoyed me the most was that everyone blamed us because we had this reputation for manipulating the press."

"Blur and Food [Blur's record label] deliberately moved the release of 'Country House' to clash with 'Roll With It'," added Johnny Hopkins.

50

"That was an act of provocation and it was hard not to react. Blur's move certainly upped the rivalry. Yes the whole chart battle elevated Oasis but it elevated Blur too. Blur got their first Number 1 single. Both bands sold around 250,000 singles each in that first week. They made the news on TV. The tabloids went crazy for it. It also raised the sales of NME too."

"[Blur] were the champions, we were wanting to be the champions and Damon brought us in the ring," Alan McGee told NME 20 years after the two bands went head-to-head. "To be fair, Damon invented the fucking whole battle of Britpop. By him doing that, it became like a Beatles versus Stones thing. It wasn't before, because they were a bigger band than us. And they beat us because they had the EMI marketing machine behind them, whereas we had some little indie fucking guy giving out fucking cards."

"I think it was Ignition [Oasis management company] more than anybody that decided we were gonna get into it," he added. "I actually thought it was dumb, but it was a dumb move that worked and it put us on the football pitch. Oasis were building in their own way, but whether we would have got that kind of exposure – the national exposure, to be in the news and stuff like that – I've got my doubts. I think we would have been big in music – we would have been headlining Reading and all that kind of stuff – but without that Blur-Oasis moment, I've got my doubts."

"Did I think it was stupid? Yes. Do I think that it worked? Unbelievably. Am I glad that it happened? Completely. It was one of the events that defined the Britpop age."

"I think that both Oasis and Blur would have reached that level of success sooner or later," Johnny Hopkins continued. "The media spectacle of the chart battle just accelerated the process. It dragged Oasis into Britpop in people's minds and made Britpop a real force. Prior to that, we had avoided Britpop. I'd turned down any interviews that lumped them in with Blur, Suede, Elastica or any of the others. That wasn't out of any disrespect for those acts. It was just that we felt Oasis were different, separate. The band didn't feature in Britpop themed retail campaigns. They didn't feature in the Britpop Now TV programme that was broadcast the week of the chart battle. It was harder to avoid the association after the chart battle but neither Oasis nor Creation ever referred to them as a Britpop group."

Both songs were among the more mediocre offerings that Oasis and Blur could have released at the time but the quality of the material was generally overlooked in the media frenzy built up around the perceived rivalry. In the end 'Country House' outsold 'Roll with It' by 54,000, and topped the singles chart for a fortnight. The Oasis camp claimed that problems with their single's barcode contributed to the Blur victory but it didn't really matter (despite the result sending Noel off on a 48-hour bender with Paul Weller). Blur had won the Battle of Britpop but the war was far from over.

"Of course I was disappointed it didn't get to Number One, but 'Roll With It' is still a great song," Noel said. "If anything, it gets better the more time goes by. It's just great, mindless, senseless pop music. It's about fuck all. It's just a simple rock 'n' roll tune. And, you know, in the end...it sold alright."

"They won that one and, of course, history rolls many ways," added Alan McGee. "*(What's the Story) Morning Glory?* definitely sold, because we ended up on the fucking national news and it was the working class boys from Burnage. We went on and sold 21 million copies worldwide."

Despite numerous public statements to the contrary, the Oasis – Blur rivalry was not as fierce as the press made out, according to Bonehead. Speaking to the NME – one of the main instigators – in 2013, he claimed that relations between the bands were mostly civil and that the media was responsible for building up the idea of an on-going war between the two biggest bands in Britain at the time.

"If I ever bumped into Damon, Graham or Alex in town, we'd have a chat and everything would be alright and I think it was the same for Noel...and even Liam," Bonehead said. "We used to drink in most of the same places and there were a few nights in London where we bumped into each other and all got on. But put Liam in front of a camera next do Damon and Liam being Liam, he'd rise to the occasion, let's put it that way..."

"But it was quite healthy, you know...we'd push each other on and sweat about whether Blur were going to win more awards than us that year but there was nothing any more dangerous than that."

Alan McGee saw things a little differently. "Oasis, being Oasis, decided to hate Blur," he told the NME in 2015. "And Blur, being Blur, thought it was a game. But Oasis actually fucking hated them at the time. They really fucking hated them. I used to go see Chelsea a lot in the '90s and used to regularly meet up for a pie and Bovril with Damon at half time. I think he was unaware that Oasis were quite serious about it – how much they hated Blur."

This perceived hatred McGee speaks of most significantly reared its ugly head in September 1995 when Noel, speaking about the rivalry with Blur, singled out Damon Albarn and Alex James for a stream of invective, telling The Observer that he hoped "the pair of them would catch AIDS and die because I fucking hate them two."

Noel would retract his comment in the next breath but the words were out. He would later issue public regrets over his comments, write a letter of apology and make a considerable donation to the HIV charity The Terrence Higgins Trust but his statement had disgusted many in the British press and beyond. He later said that "my whole world came crashing down

53

in on me then." With the new album due out the following month, there were concerns as to what damage the comments may have on sales. As things transpired, there was never any reason to worry...

With 'Some Might Say' hitting Number 1 and the 'Roll With It' versus 'Country House' face-off taking media coverage of the band to a hysterical level, everything was primed for *(What's the Story) Morning Glory?* to propel Oasis into the stardom stratosphere on its October release.

"*(What's the Story) Morning Glory?* was the least anticipated album of all time," said Noel in the *Upside Down* documentary. "Nobody was waiting for that album to come out because it came out pretty soon after the first one."

Once it did come out, the rockets blasted into life on the Starship Oasis and all those on board could only strap themselves in and hold on for dear life. A day after release, record stores in London were reportedly selling copies of the album at a rate of two per minute. At the end of the first week of sales, the album had sold a record-breaking 347,000 copies, making it, at the time, the second-fastest-selling album in British history. Only Michael Jackson's *Bad* had sold more. The album entered the UK charts at Number 1 and stayed in the top three until the turn of the year before returning to the top for a six-week stint beginning in mid-January. Amazingly, *(What's the Story) Morning Glory?* then enjoyed a further three weeks at Number 1 in March. By April 1996, the album had spent an astonishing seven months in the top three.

Despite the band's inauspicious record in the United States, by early 1996, *(What's the Story) Morning Glory?* was selling 200,000 copies a week in the US, eventually peaking at number four on the Billboard charts.

"There was an equinox with *(What's the Story) Morning Glory?* becoming so big," Tim Abbot recalled in *Upside Down*. "That was a watershed moment in Oasis's life."

"If *Definitely Maybe* was the great train robbery, then *(What's the Story) Morning Glory?* was the 'I can't believe we got away with it' celebration," journalist Andrew Mueller said in the *(What's the Story) Morning Glory?* documentary.

While there could be no arguing about the commercial success of the album with the sales figures continuing to go through the roof for most of the year following its release, the critical acclaim was taking a little longer to manifest. The thrust of those who failed to warm to the album on its release was that it was inferior to *Definitely Maybe* and that it was an album full of banal lyrics and unoriginal compositions. "They scan; they fill a hole; end of story," wrote David Cavanagh of Q Magazine, referring to the lyrics. "They say nothing much about anything." The Independent's Andy Gill picked out the tracks 'She's Electric' and 'Roll With It' for specific scorn, describing them as "laddism of a tiresomely generic kind" and "drab and chummy" respectively. The Melody Maker's David Stubbs wrote that the album on the whole was "laboured and lazy" and stated that, on this evidence, "Oasis are a limited band... they sound knackered."

The band themselves defended the album's progression which some detractors were using as a stick to beat them. *"(What's the Story) Morning Glory?* had to be different from *Definitely Maybe*", wrote Liam in the booklet which accompanied the box set release of the album's singles in November 1996. "There wouldn't have been any point in just doing all the same songs over again."

"If the first album was about going out on the piss, *(What's the Story) Morning Glory?* was about staying in and having a shag," Noel explained in the same booklet. "Actually half of it is about staying at home having a shag, the other half was about walking round the streets with a Molotov Cocktail in your hand."

This was an image which was supported by Rolling Stone journalist Rob Sheffield who described the album as "a triumph, full of bluster and bravado but also moments of surprising tenderness." Other reviewers praised the band's move away from the style of their debut with the NME writing that the album showed Oasis pursuing "an altogether different direction; away from the conscience-free overloaded hedonism towards an understanding of its consequence." In time, even those who were uncharitable towards the album on its initial release would eventually fall for its charms. But on its release, *(What's the Story) Morning Glory?* was not only a watershed moment for the band musically but it also gave Oasis a first taste of the fickle nature of the press. The criticism the album got would be mild in comparison to the vitriol which would come the band's way over the next two years. There was a lot more building up to be done before Oasis could be cut down to size.

While the public was still voraciously consuming the album which had hit the shops a mere three weeks before, Creation decided to release a third single off the album in November 1995, one which would give Oasis their first worldwide hit and send everything into overdrive.

"'Wonderwall' was the turning point for everyone," Dick Green said in *Upside Down*. "A huge international hit. No-one knew how big that record could be. I think we were all stunned."

"You just had the feeling that everything was going to go crazy and that nothing was going to be the same again," added Irvine Welsh.

The journalist John Harris credits 'Wonderwall' for re-writing the rulebook and assuring Britpop's legacy. "When Oasis released 'Wonderwall', the rules of British music were decisively changed," he wrote in his book *The Last Party*. "From here on in, the lighter-than-air

56

ballad became obligatory, and the leather-trousers era of rock 'n' roll was over."

The song, one rooted in insecurity, was in sharp contrast to the public persona of Oasis and especially the songwriter. Here was the supremely confident and arrogant Noel Gallagher opening up about his fear and emotional anxieties, admitting to his 'Wonderwall' (originally said to be Meg Matthews but after their divorce in 2001 amended to "an imaginary friend who's gonna come and save you from yourself") that you can't always get what you want, that love is uncertain, and that reaching out to others is frightening. While many had pledged allegiance to Oasis because of their ability to relate to the hedonistic side of their fans, others were falling for the band because of the sentiments now on show in songs like 'Wonderwall'. People could identify with the emotions of melancholy, loneliness and confusion as much as they could the past times of drinking, drugging and fucking. 'Wonderwall' touched the introverted as well as the extroverted; a song both appropriate for collective reflection as it was an anthem for boozy bar sing-alongs. It was a call for communal bonding and one which united many sides of the band's fan base. It was no surprise then that 'Wonderwall' became a massive and ubiquitous global hit. As well as reaching Number 2 in the UK single charts, it held the Number 1 slot on the US Modern Rock Tracks chart for an unprecedented 10 weeks and reached Number 2 on the Billboard Hot 100. It was also a Number 1 hit in Australia, New Zealand and Spain.

The song may have been an emotive ballad which, as John Harris observed, brought the leather-trousers era of rock 'n' roll to a close but it did little to calm Oasis down. On the contrary, the band's most touching song to date was responsible for sending them careening towards a new level of excess. "After 'Wonderwall' hit, we partied like fucking drug monkeys until the sun went down on a regular basis," Noel admits in *Upside Down*. "It was great."

However, such behaviour was beginning to take its toll even before *(What's the Story) Morning Glory?* was released and 'Wonderwall' took Oasis to a completely different level. After flying back home from a series of Japanese dates in August of 1995 on the wave of celebration which had continued rolling since 'Some Might Say' hit the UK chart summit four months previously, Guigsy collapsed and temporarily left the band.

"It's difficult to say what was wrong with me, really," Guigs told Select in 1997. "It's pretty weird. I went to see about 15 different doctors and the all gave me a different explanation. At first, I couldn't even get out of fucking bed; couldn't stand up or nothing, I was fucked. My body was fucked and my head was gone. Nervous breakdown, whatever you want to call it. The plot got lost. Then it got found."

"There was never any chance that Guigs would actually leave the band," Bonehead added in the same interview. "And besides, the guy who we got to replace Guigs had a crispy himself!"

That guy was replacement bassist Scott McLeod, on loan from UK indie band the Ya Ya's, who would go down in Oasis folklore as the man who had the chance to tour the US with the UK's biggest band but quit after a handful of dates because of homesickness. "He said he wanted to go home because he missed his bird and his mates," Noel remembered. "I told him if he stuck around he'd have about five girlfriends every night if he wanted." McLeod quit, leaving his inept display at dart throwing in the 'Wonderwall' video as his most telling contribution to the Oasis legend.

After returning to the UK as a four piece, Guigsy was quickly drafted back into the Oasis ranks for what would be the band's biggest shows to date. The announcement that Oasis would play two show's at the

58

Earl's Court exhibition centre had already taken the collective breath away as many critics began questioning if the band's ego and arrogance had taken them too far beyond their limits with such grandiose plans. The response of the fans dispelled any doubts that Oasis could fill a venue of this size. The release of *(What's the Story) Morning Glory?* was still two months away but the two concerts sold out in what was becoming the usual breakneck speed. More than that, the performances themselves were triumphant.

"It was fucking unbelievable," Noel told the NME in its February 17, 1996 issue. "After that first night at Earl's Court...I used to get really nervous about going onstage but now it's like, if we can pull that off, man, we've got no problems. I even surprised myself at how good we played. So now we do these big gigs of tens of thousands of people and we might as well play in our own front room because we're just totally at ease with it."

With the biggest indoor gigs the UK had ever seen under their belts – 20,000 fans each night at Earl's Court – Oasis were primed and ready on the launch pad for the interstellar voyage into mega-stardom. After the Battle of Britpop had elevated their status even further and 'Wonderwall' had put the name Oasis on even the most disinterested lips, the band were ready to throw on the thrusters as Oasis bade farewell to1995 to a chorus of popping corks and enthusiastic snorting.

The next year started just as well as the previous one had finished. At the NME Brat Awards in January 1996, Oasis won Best Band, Best Album, Best Single and Best Live Band – awards all voted for by the readers of the NME. Noel dispensed with any niceties in his acceptance speech by declaring: "It's hard to be humble at a time like this, so I won't try. You're all shit."

When 'Don't Look Back in Anger', the band's fourth UK single off *(What's the Story) Morning Glory?*, gave them their second Number 1 single a month later, all bets were off. On the day of the single's release, during a break on the *(What's the Story) Morning Glory?* tour, Oasis attended the 1996 BRIT Awards and the celebrations continued with the band winning the awards for Best Album for *(What's the Story) Morning Glory?*, Best British Video for 'Wonderwall' and Best British Group. During the evening, fuelled by champagne and MDMA, Oasis cemented their reputation as the country's most maverick rock band. No-one was safe. Arch enemies Blur were serenaded with a rendition of their single 'Parklife' or 'Shitelife' as it was renamed by the reeling Mancs on stage to collect the Best Band gong; Radio 1 DJ Chris Evans was christened "ginger bollocks" when he tried to move them off the stage; INXS singer Michael Hutchence was abused while presenting them with an award – "Has-beens shouldn't be giving awards to gonna-be's" – and Liam, fully bearded and sweating profusely in a leather parka, tried to stick a BRIT up his rectum. It was an anti-establishment coup d'état.

"We didn't know Michael Hutchence was going to present us with an award," Noel later said in an Uncut article from 2000. "It was the first award of the night and there'd been words said before the ceremony in the papers. So when he came out to present the award, we went, 'Right, these cunts have stitched us up here, because they know what's going on'. So we decided that, every time we hit that stage, we were just going to give it to everyone, and we fucking duly did. And, you know, I still haven't seen that night, but Alan McGee says it's the best. He said it was 'Ecstasy abuse gone mad.'"

"We probably wouldn't have done anything if Hutchence hadn't come out and said his little bit: 'I heard Liam wants to fight me'. We were like, 'Don't fucking try and pick a fight with us, man, because we're the best at giving verbal abuse', and off we went. If people pick a fight verbally in the press, they know that sooner or later you're going to bump into them, and if there's a scene there's going to be a lot of publicity about it. And while it doesn't do me any favours and it doesn't do Liam any favours, it does do the other person a lot of favours."

"Rock 'n' roll is about doing what you want, when you want to do it, and fuck the consequences," he added. "I mean, we've done some stupid things, but at least we were always true to ourselves. None of it was that contrived. It was like, 'Next time we go up there let's insult a few people, because we might not get invited back again', because you never know, do you?"

The level of fame that the band had been craving was now their reality with the tabloids following them everywhere they went and going to great lengths to get any kind of exclusive story on Oasis, and, in particular, the Gallagher brothers. "We have the tabloids outside my gaff, going through the dustbins," Noel told the NME in February 1996. "There's a geezer with a radio scanner outside as well. We have a cordless phone and I called Meg the other day about going shopping and I said I'd pick her up and we'd go wherever and when we got there, there's like 50 photographers waiting so someone is definitely scanning the calls."

"But you have to deal with it, man," he added. "Deny nothing because I have nothing to be ashamed of. I don't think you could do an exposé of anything we've ever done because everybody knows fucking who we are and what we are and what we do, so, if they can't deal with it, well, fuck 'em."

The fame also brought more acceptable levels of surrealism with established megastars now queuing up to rub shoulders with Oasis, eager to bask in the reflective glory.

"Two years ago, I wouldn't have been asked to the Cannes Film Festival," Noel told the New Zealand Herald in 1998. "Fine, arsed. Now of course, after 'Wonderwall' and 'Don't Look Back In Anger', they draw up

61

their celebrity wish list and I'm on it. Of course, I've never been invited to these places before so of course I'm gonna turn up, because it's a trip. 'Look, there's Elton John. Hey, Reg!' And of course, it's free. Somebody will fly me over there on a Lear jet. I'll fucking have some of that, thank you very much!

"Now all these people want to meet me. Al Pacino, Mick Jagger... Their PR will go, 'see that geezer over there, that's the bloke from Oasis, it'd be really cool if you all were over there stood beside him and you had your picture taken'. So they come over and it's like, 'hey man, I really fucking love the record... I'd like to get one thing straight, you guys kick ass!' Suddenly all the photographers are snapping."

"I've come across John McEnroe," Liam told Select magazine in 1996. "He came to New York, backstage, had a spliff. Mad bastard. Fucking proper mad-head. He had his guitar with him because he's got a band. He was playing us these songs. 'Was it in or was it out? Dum-dum-dum-dum-ding-ding-ding'. Off his head. 'You cannot be serious, dum-dum'. Double faults hurt me head. Proper mad. Simon Le Bon came back, too. Freaky. Pretty strange, him and John McEnroe in the same room."

"Adam Clayton from U2 sent us a cactus," he added. "I suppose it has something to do with us being in Oasis."

It wasn't just 'mad-head' celebrities wanting to see Oasis, the (What's the Story) Morning Glory? tour saw the band playing to the biggest crowds of their career in the UK, first with the Earls Court gigs and then Maine Road, Loch Lomond and – of course – Knebworth in the summer of '96. The clamour for the band in Europe was also reaching fever pitch. "I nearly got ripped to pieces in Italy by about 2,000 people, so I guess it's bye-bye freedom," Noel told Rolling Stone in May 1996. "This will all pass in about five or six years. We have the rest of our lives to sit around our houses and be inconspicuous. Now is our time. We're in the eye of the hurricane now, and one day it's going to blow out. We'll look back in our late 30s, no worries, and we'll still be able to get together and say, 'We were good, man. In fact, we were the best. And this is what we built'. As for now, it's a small price to pay."

Despite the huge success of the UK and European dates on the tour, it had not all gone smoothly. For once, Oasis had negotiated a number of US dates – the third Stateside leg of the world tour – without much incident but when they got back to Europe in the spring of 1996, the madness inspired by life on the road was bubbling up once again.

A News of the World sponsored stunt saw the Gallaghers' estranged father Thomas turn up in the bar of the hotel the band were staying at in March before a gig at The Point in Dublin. The man who had beaten Noel as a child and terrorised the family in drunken rages for years now stood waiting nervously to see the sons he had not had contact with for nearly a decade. "I remember Noel came up to me with one of the security people and said, see that guy over there? That's my father," said tour manager Maggie Mouzakitis in the VH-1 documentary *Oasis: Behind the Music*. "I don't know what the angle of the story was supposed to be but – there he was."

Noel ignored his father and went to his room. "As far as I'm concerned, I don't have a father," he stated in the documentary. "He's not a father figure to me. I don't respect him in any way whatsoever."

The tabloid that had paid for Thomas to be there was after either a sensational, emotional reunion or a massive ruck. They got neither despite Liam's efforts to confront his father and unleash years of anger and resentment.

"So I bowled over and said, 'come on then you cunt, if you want it, let's have it'," Liam remembered. "And his arse dropped. And that was that."

"We just got him out of the hotel as fast as we could really," added Maggie. "It was a bit sick...it just wasn't right." The News of the World still ran with a double-page spread under the headline "I thought Liam was going to kill me." The sub-headline read: "Oasis dad reveals night of torment."

Things got worse a month later as Liam appeared to be unravelling. In April, The Daily Mirror reported that "wild man Liam Gallagher rowed with managers, swore at onlookers and even slagged off his own band in a drunken foul-mouthed outburst" during the band's stay in Grenoble, France. The paper catalogued Liam's "trial of havoc" in his £200-a-night suite at the Park Hotel: "A glass lamp lay shattered on the floor, a TV was upside down, a table was smashed." Strangely though, contradicting the tabloid's attempt to describe a rampage, the hotel's head porter told the paper that "we have had no more trouble with Oasis than we did With Demis Roussos." Either the Greek crooner had a dark side which few knew about or things at the Park Hotel, an establishment with a long history of housing rock bands, were not as bad as the paper suggested.

As spring turned to summer and the band's gargantuan gigs in Manchester, Scotland and Hertfordshire grabbed the attention of the nation, Oasis were starting to feel the strain. Liam's anger at having his private life increasingly sifted through by the media exploded again during one of the band's Loch Lomond concerts. Reacting to a joke by Radio 1 DJ Chris Evans who told his millions of listeners that Liam's fiancée Pasty Kensit was pregnant, the Oasis singer let rip at the presenter who was apparently in the crowd at the time.

Noel was also starting to feel the pressure, not only from the press coverage but also from the spiralling demands his band were expecting to meet. "You couldn't say you were going away for six weeks to write some music," he told GQ in 2000. "It was, 'You're going back to America because the album's just gone Top 5. '"

"The people around you convince you you're doing it for your own benefit," he added. "You've got a pint of Guinness in one hand and a cigarette in the other and you're going, 'fucking brilliant, show me the aeroplane, I'm there!' You don't think, whether your writing is going to suffer. You think, 'no I'm the bollocks, man! I'm Noel Gallagher, I'll write it in a week! Piece of piss!' And everyone's going 'yeah, you're Noel Gallagher you can write it in a week!' But the reality is different."

"There was a point just after *(What's the Story) Morning Glory?* when I didn't have anything," he admitted. "I'd lost the will to write. There was too much else to think about, like the touring and all that shit. I didn't write one song for six to eight months. I was thinking, 'Maybe that's it'. But it didn't really bother me that much. I'd written 'Champagne Supernova', 'Wonderwall', 'Don't Look Back in Anger' and 'Live Forever', so if I never write another song, then that'll do."

The band were nearing their limit and as many of those in Oasis and around them later admitted, they should have either spilt up after Knebworth or, at best, taken a long holiday before reconvening to write and record the third album. Instead, after Knebworth, Oasis played two nights at the Páirc Uí Chaoimh stadium in Cork, Ireland to 300,000 people over two nights and then moved on to London for a special MTV Unplugged show at the Royal Festival Hall on August 23. The omens for the final leg of the tour in the United States, which was due to begin four days later, were all bad. Just minutes before the MTV show, Liam backed out citing a sore throat. Noel took on the singing duties while Liam watched the band perform from the balcony, smoking and drinking throughout, and heckled loudly between songs.

"He turns up with a beard looking like fucking Grizzly Adams after being in the pub for two days," Noel remembered in *Oasis: Behind the Music*. "He can't walk, let alone sing. This is dropped on my lap 15 minutes before we were due to walk out on stage. It was like, 'oh hang on a minute – now you're the singer'. Fucking thank you very much."

"We subsequently found out that he doesn't like to sing with the band acoustically. I wish he would have told me that before two and half thousand people turned up, expecting to see him. And then he sits in the stands heckling because he gets a bit of giggle from the crowd when he does it the first time and then thinks it's cool to keep doing it. He's not arsed about his big brother dying on stage."

"I had a sore throat," Liam claimed again in the documentary. "I'd been on the piss and I had a sore throat. Simple as that."

After the MTV Unplugged show, Liam's erratic behaviour again made the front page on a day which could hardly be described as being devoid of serious news. Prince Charles and Princess Diana's divorce was finalised; seven Iraqis had hijacked a Sudanese airliner and had flown it to London in an attempt to gain political asylum, and several hundred criminals had been released by mistake due to a huge cock-up by Her Majesty's Prison Service. But the main story of the day was that the singer of Oasis had walked out on the band at Heathrow Airport minutes before they were due to leave for Chicago for the US leg of the tour, claiming that he needed to buy a house. Liam told The Sun tabloid that he had not quit the band but that he couldn't go on tour until he had found somewhere to live. "I am Oasis, I started the fucking band, I'm mad for it but I have to move house," he was quoted as saying. "I can't go looking for a house while I'm in America trying to perform to silly fucking yanks."

A year later, when asked about the incident by the NME, Liam said: "We'd just sold our house that day, right, and we had to get out in the next ten days. I thought, 'Fuck it, I'm not going to America if I've got nowhere to live, spending two weeks in a hotel in America and then coming back and going to a hotel in England'. It's not on. No chance. Loads of people staring at you onstage all the time and you've got nowhere to live? You need a fucking home. Everybody does. It's the most important thing in life."

"All the papers saying I don't give a shit about America! I do! But we should've sacked that tour anyway. We should have stayed at home and had some time off. We should have stayed at home."

Noel gave his account of the incident in the same interview. "I'll tell you the exact story, right. He looked me in the eyes in the British Airways departure lounge and says, 'I've got nowhere to live, I've got to get somewhere to live'. And I was that gobsmacked that I said, 'Do one then'. I didn't actually think he would! He went, 'Right, see you in a bit', I said, 'Right, see you in a bit', fully expecting him to come back in five minutes time. And he didn't. The cunt. He fucked off! When we got to America everyone was asking me where Liam was and I said, 'You're not going to believe this, he didn't come. Right, we've just had three months off for the sole purpose of buying somewhere to live and he's just decided right now, NOW, that he needs to find somewhere to live'. We all laughed about it in the end because only he could do something like that, but it was out of order for the kids and that."

"Any other band would not have bothered coming in the first place," Noel added. "But we have two singers in the band, two front men. I'm more than capable of fronting this band if he doesn't want to do it."

"We wouldn't pull the gig because that would be giving in," Noel said in *Oasis: Behind the Music*. "That would make him think that he was more important than the band, which he's not. I didn't want it to seem that by the wave of his hand he picks and chooses what he wants to do."

"Personally I don't give a shit," added Alan White. "If he's there, he's there. We had a job to do. We weren't going to cancel."

"I thought they shouldn't have done it if I wasn't there," Liam argued. "Not because I think I'm the man but because we're a fucking band."

After Noel had let his brother know – via a subtle message to manager Marcus Russell – that that band would be fine without their singer, Liam was on the first flight to the States. He was back in the fold three days after walking out on Oasis, just in time for their gig at the Auburn Hills Palace in Detroit. But despite his assertion that the band had laughed Liam's antics off as just another of the unpredictable singer's many bizarre decisions, Noel was still harbouring a grudge when his errant sibling re-joined the ranks. "The first gig (at the Rosemont Horizon in Illinois) was a 16,000-seat arena, and the singer's not turned up," Noel said in an interview with NME in 2011. "This is rock 'n' roll. Would Johnny Rotten have gotten a house on the eve of an American tour? Keith Richards? John Lennon? You either want it or you don't." That resentment festered throughout the remaining shows – including the infamous MTV Video Music Awards appearance at the hallowed Radio City Music Hall in New York. During their performance of 'Champagne Supernova' Liam made gestures at Noel during his guitar solo, then spat beer all over the stage before storming off. The papers, on both sides of the Atlantic, took a dim view of the singer's behaviour with The Sun's headline 'America sickened by obscene Liam's spitting rampage' proving significant in the media's slowly turning tide of opinion against the band. "Oasis wildman Liam Gallagher was branded a disgrace last night", the paper wrote, adding that 'pop pundits' were united in their assessment that Liam had ruined the band's chances of success in the US by "swearing and insulting the audience with lewd lyrics, spitting a huge lump of saliva on to the stage, and hurling an open can of beer into the crowd."

Liam's response? "I thought the show was shit, but our performance was outstanding."

The headlines continued to turn sour and a sea change was beginning to be felt. As the most combustible and unpredictable band member, the focus shifted almost entirely to Liam with the tabloids digging up anything they could to justify putting the Oasis singer on their front page. As the severely compromised US tour limped on, Britain woke up on September 8 to details about a young woman's alleged 'Drug and Sex Hell with Liam'. British weekend tabloid the News of the World had hunted down Cerice Blakeley, an ex-girlfriend who the paper claimed had been engaged to Liam, and paid her for her story on how "Oasis wildman Liam Gallagher dragged her on to a roller coaster of sex and drugs then dumped her in tears." According to the report, Cerice met Liam in 1992 and it was love at first sight. The pair moved in together and "their sex was often fuelled by deadly cocaine." The story stated that Liam had dumped her in 1993.

"The stories were coming thick and fast," the band's press officer Johnny Hopkins recalled. "I was getting calls from tabloids 24 hours a day, seven days a week. Leaks were coming from people in the band's circle – some of it true, some of it not. A lot of my time was spent negotiating negative stories off the front pages of newspapers. Most of the anarchy that happened never made it into the press. But sometimes the anarchy was positive. That was part of the band's appeal for many fans in the public and the press."

At the time of Oasis's emergence in the early 1990s, there was a desperate readership battle being waged between media companies in the UK, one that escalated once Britpop was in full swing. Due to this bitter struggle for sales figures, some writers were under considerable pressure from their features editors to get an Oasis interview. In turn, the features editors were under considerable pressure from their superiors who themselves were under considerable pressure from people higher up in their publishing companies. As a result, any Oasis news was good news for those publications wanting to get the edge on their competitors. Many of these magazines would have been happy to have had the band on their cover every issue, such was the demand for all things Oasis. It was the same for radio and TV outlets. "When a band gets that big everyone wants a piece – all the time – and for Oasis it wasn't just the demands of the media in the UK but the media in more or less every country in the world," added Johnny Hopkins.

Less than a week after Liam's alleged "coke and sex" expose hit the newsstands, Oasis were again on the front page of every newspaper in the UK. "BLOWASIS" screamed the front over The Sun. Citing unnamed sources, the tabloid was making wild claims that the band had split up after a row between Noel and Liam had erupted into a furious fist fight before the band were due to play a concert in Fort Mill, South Carolina. According to the report, "tearful Liam Gallagher rang mum Peggy from the US before the split and told her: 'I've had enough. I can't go on. It's just not working. We all want to come home to Manchester. I can't go on and it's a nightmare. We've been fighting a lot'." The Sun had door-stepped Peggy Gallagher in an attempt to get a reaction but she told reporters: "I have got nothing to say."

Immediately Marcus Russell issued a statement. "Oasis have hit internal differences on their 9th tour of the US which has resulted in the tour being pulled two-thirds of the way through," the statement read, while the spokeswoman for Epic Records in New York, the band's US recording label, denied the story. "There is no breakup," said Lisa Markowitz, the company's publicity director.

The twister of rumours and counter rumours which had been spinning wildly ever since news of the latest bust-up had filtered back to the UK went into overdrive when an ashen-faced Noel Gallagher arrived back at Heathrow Airport alone. The media scrum was insane, with the lost and lonely-looking Oasis guitarist mobbed and jostled as security staff struggled to hold back the horde, many of whom were shouting the question everyone apparently needed the answer to: "Is it the end of Oasis?" Barely three weeks before, Oasis had played to record-breaking crowds. Now they were returning in bits with people questioning the future of the band.

The rest of Oasis returned a few days later and then the band, as a whole, dropped out of sight leaving the media scratching around for updates and sound bites as the five men at the centre of the storm desperately went in search of some breathing space.

"It was all down to little bits of arguments, you know what I mean?" Liam revealed in an interview with Select Magazine in 1997. "Little niggly bits and bobs. Like you do, every day. We didn't want to be on the road anymore. We had to come home. We left all that chaos in England, Knebworth and all that, then we were back over there again...We were just tired."

"I can't remember what we argued about," he added. "ABBA or something. I think it was about ABBA. Anyway, Noel went home, we stayed there and got pissed. I was arsed. Noel was moaning, 'Oh, that's it, it's over'. I was all like, 'Shut up, you cunt - we've got a new album to make' He's banging on, 'No, that's it - I'm sick of it'. It was having all these people around you all the time - minders and that. You can't do whatever you want...We were getting side-tracked about what we're about. Then we get home and it was like someone had stolen the crown jewels. It's only a band. It's only us. It was mad."

"It was a lot of things," Noel admitted in the same interview. "We'd just been touring for too long. We'd been touring for three years. We were sick of playing that set, we were due to come straight off that tour, go straight into the studio, record a new album and go straight back out again. It's alright working to a point where you know you're going to have two or three weeks off, but there didn't seem to be any light at the end of the tunnel. And because we're always on the verge of imploding anyway, we toured *(What's the Story) Morning Glory?* in just over 12 months all around the world, while bands like U2 take two years to do the same thing. But everything was squashed into a year so people could get their money's worth before we split up. It was ludicrous. Everybody was complaining, and not just the band but the crew as well, and I just said, 'Why don't we go home?'"

"They were like, 'We can't go home because of this and because of that', and I said, 'There's nothing stopping anyone from getting on a plane and going home'. Our Kid suddenly gets an attack of the morals and says 'we can't go home, it ain't right'. I said, 'You can shut up! You never came in the first place, you cunt'. Then they said they couldn't go home because of the press, and I said, 'I'll show you how easy it is to go home'. I went to my room, phoned for a taxi and went to the airport and came home. That was it. There was no argument - well, there might have been a bit of one, but not as bad as all that."

However, Noel revealed more details about the aborted tour in an interview with Muse magazine in 2000 which hinted at a bit more discontent than he was willing to admit three years previously. "What happened was, we went to Knebworth, did the fucking gig, blah blah blah, biggest band in the world. *(What's the Story) Morning Glory?* was still in

72

the American Top Ten and we were advised that we should go back and milk it for all it was worth," he said. "In hindsight we should have said no. I should have said, 'I want at least a year off'. We should have left on a fucking big high note.

"So we went back to America, the fucking tour fell apart, there was all amounts of shit going on: drugs and fighting and arguing and people getting nicked, hotel rooms getting trashed and all that shit. It was just becoming a fucking circus, I didn't like it so I fucked off home."

In another interview with GQ that same year, Noel went as far as naming names. "When I walked off that American tour, I was just sick of it all," he said. "On that American tour, Bonehead and Liam were just fucking out of control, man. I thought, I just don't want to be around for this anymore because it's just getting on my tits. People had just stopped talking about music, it was all about the behaviour of the band, and if it's not about music, then I'm leaving. Because I'm not busting my arse for 18 hours a day in the studio so that when we go on the road, every time we get to an airport, you two fucking act like knobheads. So I said, 'Right, I'm leaving. I quit'. If I hadn't gone home at that time and had that break, I don't think we'd have made another record."

There were rumours at the time that the disrespect that Oasis had allegedly shown in America had stemmed from a feeling of loftiness; that after playing to a quarter of a million people at the Knebworth double-header, the size of crowds and venues in the United States were beneath them. Noel was quick to dismiss these claims. "Well, I don't know where those stories came from that said it was an insult to play to 9,000 people in the middle of Texas or somewhere," he told GQ. "Most bands don't play to 9,000 in London, let alone Texas.

"No one ever said that. If anyone had said that, they'd have got the sack. Whoever wrote that, that we pulled a gig because it was only 12,000 or something is going to get a crack on the head if I ever fucking see them. Because it wasn't that. I'll play to 12 people, let alone 12,000."

"It was only three gigs at the end of the day. We came back to England and it was like the Pope had been shot. Looking back on it, we should have stuck it out for the three gigs. But we couldn't be arsed."

Guigsy admitted to being a bit perplexed by the reaction of the British press when the band returned from the ill-fated US leg of what had already been an 18-month-long tour. The stories in the papers, according to the Oasis bassist, bore very little relation to the reality of the situation on the road in America. However, his own recollection of what went on was at odds with Noel's account of the bad behaviour and excessive substance abuse which led to the songwriter walking out on the band.

"We did the US gigs with signs up saying Liam wasn't doing it and if anyone wanted their money back, fine, but us four are going to do it," Guigsy explained in an interview with Access in November 1997. "So we just did it, and it was alright, we had a good laugh. I don't know what people thought of it, but very few asked for their money back. Liam came out, but at the end Noel was like, 'Look, we need to make some new music. It's all getting a bit stale isn't it?' We all had a chat and agreed; so we said we might as well go home right then. Suddenly, we've split up!"

"We couldn't see where it was going to end, and it came to a head where it was, like, let's just go home," he added. "Nothing to do with America; we were just fed up with touring, the endlessness of it for four or five years, then an album and straight back out again."

On arrival back in London it was clear that something had to be done to patch things up. Marcus Russell spirited the brothers away to a country retreat, away from the media glare, to thrash out what would happen next. "Me and Noel went to a country house," Liam recalled in a 1997 Select magazine interview. "The pair of us stayed there and got pissed. Me and him weren't arguing. We got slaughtered. And Marcus was saying, 'Let's put a press release out'. Me and Noel were taking the piss, going 'Fuck it - if anyone asks where we are, tell 'em we're chasing sheep round the fucking country'. But it would have started to get silly. So we put one together."

Noel agreed to re-join Oasis and pledged to finish the next album but made it clear that he then intended to retire. Of course, things didn't quite work out that way. "There was some recreational activity and before I knew it, the manager's booked a tour and we were half way round the world," he said in the *Oasis: Behind the Music* documentary. "I was like, 'wait a minute, how did this happen? I was supposed to be leaving!'"

While the media had been denied the big story of an Oasis spilt, there was still plenty of copy being generated to keep the public and press interested. In October, a month after the band had returned from the US, Liam was front page news again. This time, the News of the World was reporting the latest domestic disturbance in the court of the First Couple of Britpop. "Patsy Gives Boozy Liam the Boot" the headline read. After a period of excessive drinking and disappearances, Patsy Kensit had apparently tried for hours to contact her errant partner. Failing to do so, she had left Liam a message which the paper gleefully reproduced verbatim: "Thanks a lot for your concern. You can shove MTV up your arse. I hope you have a great week shagging birds with your mates and you won't be seeing me again."

The tabloids must have thrown a week-long party when Liam and the actress got together in December 1995. Despite her size, Patsy was as much of a handful as her other half and the volatile but photogenic couple gave very good press. Portrayed as the 90s version of John and Yoko only with less bagism and added fighting, Liam and Patsy's rows – and sex life – could always be relied upon to spice up a slow news day.

"I can understand the media obsession with Liam and Patsy," Noel once said. "Rock star. Headcase. Actress. Headcase. Little blonde chick, lunatic with a beard. I can see why people wonder what's going on behind closed doors."

"The press intrusion was intense at times and didn't let up when they were outside the UK touring or on holiday, especially in regards to Liam's activities," recalled Johnny Hopkins. "He was out and about a lot having it large and was in a relationship with Patsy Kensit. Two stars together are more valuable in media terms than those two stars on their own. For the media Liam and Patsy were the rock 'n' roll version of Posh & Becks - the Anti-Beckhams. They were certainly more interesting and perhaps more valuable."

The following month was a particularly fertile period with Liam dominating the headlines on a regular basis. First were the reports of violent outbursts; The Sun reported on November 7 that Liam had bitten the nose of a female fan at an Ocean Colour Scene gig at the Hammersmith Palais. "He lunged at me with this huge open mouth, screamed 'Aaaarghhh' and bit me on the nose and lip," claimed Gaynor Simonelli. "It made my eyes water. He must have been drinking - or something." Despite the lurid details and insinuation of drug use, the police decided not to investigate.

Liam was at it again a few days later when the News of the World reported that "Oasis wildman Liam Gallagher's face was contorted with fury as he rained vicious blows on reporter Sean O'Brien" in an attack on the tabloid journalist after he confronted the singer with a photo of him with "a raven-haired beauty." Liam apparently screamed, "I didn't snog no bird, man!"

"I'm not a hooligan," Liam said in reference to the media's portrayal of him as a violent thug in the 1997 BBC documentary *Right Here, Right Now*. "I don't go around picking fights with people. I just like to get on with my own business. But the way they write about me and the way I'm portrayed is like I'm up for a fight 24/7 and I'm not. I don't want to fight."

"They're always going to be gunning for me but I'm always like, 'bring it on' because I'll always be gunning for them," Liam told this writer in an interview some years later. "That will always be there because we need the love-hate thing but deep down they've probably all got posters of us on their walls. They're just idiots who just want to take a pop at me because I slagged off Blur in 1992 or whatever. There's a lot of that what goes on and always will."

"I think rock 'n' roll is about a lifestyle," he added in the BBC documentary *Right Here, Right Now*. "It has to be. No one wants a goodie-goodie do they? You've got to have it. You've got to have a good time. I just live my life the way I want to live it. I want to have fun. How the fuck can I not have fun? I'm in the most important rock 'n' roll band in the world. What I'm going to do? Sit at home clipping me toe nails and picking me nose all day? You've got to have it."

"The reason they all pick on Liam is because he goes around punching photographers in the face," contradicted Noel in the same documentary. "I look at this logically...I don't like getting photographed when I'm out and about but if you smack a photographer in the face who works for the News of the World, he's gonna go back and tell his editor who'll say, 'Did he really? Right, we'll have that bastard'. But he courts it. He courts it more than anyone."

"But he's got the hardest life to deal with, being the singer and being with Patsy," Noel said in a July 1997 interview with NME. "To be honest, I thought he would have gone under by now. It doesn't look good, does it? He's still young and it's not very healthy but he's hung in there. He loves moaning about the press but he does fucking love the attention as well."

"If I get drunk, they have a go," Liam complained about the press. "If I'm sober, they have ago. They ain't going to be happy until I'm six feet under."

"We're fortunate – me, Guigs and Alan – we don't get it on the scale that Liam and Noel get it," added a somewhat relieved Bonehead.

"Liam gets a lot of pressure," said Alan. "He has people camping outside his door. You have to be pretty strong to deal with that, don't you?"

"It's the foul-mouthed cunt side of me they write about," Liam told Q magazine in 1999. "I keep the good side of me in the family. They're not going to get... the more sensitive side of me. But I don't read the papers. Don't have them in the house. The odd time I pick one up I always seem to be in there and it does my head in. I can't be starting my day off like that."

"People want to know why I'm always miserable, why I'm always shouting at people or punching photographers and it's because I'm not like one of these celebrity dicks," Liam told the Observer in 2002, an interview in which he seemed to forget that eight years previously he'd openly craved intrusive fame. "I don't need my gob in the gossip pages. I make music and you either like it or don't. That's it. Don't follow me down the shop. People say it's all part of fame and I should have known it before…well, no. I wanted to make records and be in a great rock 'n 'roll band. The rest is you being nosey bastards and making up for not having a life by trying to ruin mine. Go and follow someone who really wants to be photographed shopping for toilet roll, like all of those idiots in Heat magazine…because I don't want to be followed."

Liam didn't need to be followed by the paparazzi to claim the biggest story of November 1996. He just needed to wander about the streets of London, looking dishevelled with a bag of cocaine in his pocket. The Metropolitan Police would do the rest.

After accepting the Best Act in the World accolade at the annual Q Awards in London and partying in the usual fashion, Liam left the rest of the band and headed back to his hotel with his bodyguard. "We both went back to the hotel, and he goes to bed," Liam told Select magazine in 1997. "He goes in his room and I'm sitting up, and I thought, 'Fuck it - I'm going home'. I just bailed out. I should've got a taxi, I didn't get one. I was fucking walking down the street and that was it."

According to the News of the World, who were now taking even greater pleasure in reporting the younger Gallagher's wayward behaviour after the fight with Sean O'Brien, when officers approached Liam he had difficulty focusing on them but said, "It's nothing to do with you. I'm fine. I'm OK." But they weren't satisfied. "They thought he might have been a vagrant," the paper wrote. The way the story hit the newsstands first thing the next morning before most of the band's management had even heard about the incident had many in the Oasis camp suspecting a sting operation. It would not be the last time that the band's persecution complex would raise its head.

"Stuff like that ends up sending you paranoid," Liam added. "But I shouldn't have been out at that time in the morning, on me jacks, with cocaine in my pocket."

"But it was top, actually," he continued. "All the police were singing 'Roll with It'. I was thinking, 'they're either going to well do me in or they're going to let me off'. As soon as I heard them whistling 'Roll With It' I thought, 'I'm well away'. It was all, 'Can you sign this for my daughter?' While I was doing my fingerprints. It was top. The main sergeant shakes my hand and says 'I daren't wash my hands now, my daughter will kill me'. I was well away."

There was a growing feeling by now that the period of grace that had been bestowed on Oasis by the press during their imperial phase that summer was beginning to expire by the time 1996 came to an end. More often the not, the headlines in the tabloids were unflattering and the music papers were already looking past Oasis in the direction of bands such as The Verve and Radiohead. It was also dawning on members of the band that the media in general had begun to see more worth in undermining Oasis than supporting them. By side-lining the country's biggest band, there would be more opportunity for exciting potential usurpers to grab the column inches and in turn, freshen up the musical environment. The underhand tactics employed to achieve this had not gone unnoticed by Noel Gallagher.

"We're pretty up front about everything that we've done and everything we do so there's no such thing as an Oasis rumour because we live our lives in the public eye anyway," Noel told Melody Maker in 1998. "But the thing is they write something and twist it and it becomes lies. These stories are usually 50 per cent true, 50 per cent the imagination of some editor. But I wouldn't mind if half the time they were telling the truth and the other half of the time it was positive. But it's usually all negative lies. People in England don't like people in England being successful. We are a nation of shopkeepers and one shopkeeper doesn't like another doing well."

"There was this thing in the Daily Star a few months ago where I was supposed to have been with a stripper in New York," Noel told the NME in July 1997. "There's this big fat fucking stripper on the cover of the Star saying she's been with me and I was rubbing strawberries and cream all over her! I was doing an interview when I was supposed to have been in New York. I showed my passport to my solicitor and it hadn't been stamped so we had the evil bastards bang to rights but Meg was all like, 'were you really in an interview?' Look, love...I was only gone two hours, it takes three hours for Concorde to even get there..."

The old adage says that there is no such thing as bad publicity but those close to the band, especially those charged with trying to manage Oasis's unruly public persona, were already harbouring fears that the media circus surrounding the band was beginning to have an adverse effect.

"I was concerned about the press intrusion at times and instigated conversations on how to minimise it where possible," revealed Johnny Hopkins, the man handed the seemingly impossible task of keeping the flow of news under the control of the band and Creation. "Press intrusion, though, goes with the territory of being famous. That level of fame is obviously going to have an impact - at times it did take its toll. But it not just press intrusion, it's the money, the success, the lifestyle, the sycophants, the vampires...if you've got the press and everyone around you telling you that you are the greatest or some demon it's also going to have an impact."

Many would argue that the band had done themselves few favours, even when the tide of public opinion seemed to be flowing strongly with them. Incidents such as Noel wishing AIDS and death on Blur's Damon Albarn and Alex James in 1995 may not have undermined the band with the fans but sections of the British press had started to seize on Noel's more unsavoury observations and began to demonise him along with his brother. Noel's acerbic quotes and Liam's increasingly out-of-control antics continued to sell papers but for many in the media, the Gallaghers were beginning to become tiresome, bitter and less palatable as the fame train Oasis had hitched its wagons to careened at full speed towards a potential pile-up.

By his own admission, Noel couldn't resist giving his views on anything and everything but as the climate began to turn chilly between the band and the press, teams of reporters actively sought responses which could be used to hang him with.

"We were the token oiks for about four or five years," Noel lamented in an interview with Uncut magazine in 2000. "Let's invite the scruffy Northerners down and have a laugh at them." In reality, it was a two-way street. Noel exploited the press image of him as a simple lout in much the same way as Liam laid it on thick in interviews because he knew what made a good story. Both brothers were more than willing to play up to the stereotypes during their imperial phase because publicity was something they craved and enjoyed at first. It became a competition between them as the brothers fought for column inches. While Liam looked for scrapes to get into to boost his image and exposure, Noel applied his gift of the gab.

"'When certain things would happen, whenever stories would break in the press, whether it be connected to Oasis or not, they would always send somebody round to my house...a film crew, or somebody with a fucking tape recorder and microphone...knowing I would have to say something, because I'm fucking Noel Gallagher. It'd be, 'Do you want my opinion on it? You wait there a minute while I get dressed and I'll be out in a minute'. And they'd be rubbing their hands together going, 'Brilliant', and I'll be thinking, 'Fucking brilliant'. They'd be going, 'What about such and such a person?' and I'd be like, 'He's a fucking cunt and his fucking wife is, and if I ever get my way...'"

"It could be about anything," he continued. "'The fucking French? What about the French? Stealing our fish?' Then I'd go off on one and they'd be down the phone to their editor, going, 'Brilliant'. And I'd phone Marcus and say, 'Call the lawyer because it could get heavy. And he'd be like, 'Fair enough, OK'. And Marcus would get the lawyer on the phone: 'John? Yes, it's Marcus. Can you get round the house straight away?'"

An intelligent man, Noel knew that he was initially engaged in a mutually beneficial game with the media, and as someone with a burning competitive spirit and a wicked sense of fun, he was more than happy to rise to the challenge. "I'd sit down and think, 'What would be the most outrageously controversial comment I could give about that right now?' And then I would just come up with the most banal fucking stupid thing, then times it by ten, add a couple of swear words, mention somebody's name in particular, accuse them of something and then throw in the word 'allegedly' on the end. Then go back in and ring my manager. Immediately."

"There was a thing in the paper about chart-rigging, and I knew there'd been a film crew sniffing about my house in London...you can always tell they're there because they're in cars with blacked-out windows," Noel continued. "And, lo and behold, I got a call off someone to say they think they're going to pull me in the street. I was going, 'What? Chart-rigging? Yeah, that's a good one'. And they were saying, 'What do you think about people who buy records in? Do you think your record company's doing that?' And I'm going, 'I fucking hope so, I'd be glad if they bought all my records in'."

"I know sometimes my mouth can get the better of me," he admitted. "And I can't help taking the piss. But when it's in print it doesn't look like you're taking the piss, it looks like you actually mean it."

Leaving their biggest year behind, Oasis were unable to do the same with controversy. In fact, as 1997 began, Noel was rivalling Liam for the most scandalous newspaper headlines. The game was getting more serious and as Oasis got increasingly more famous, the stakes got higher.

The boy band East 17 had just sacked one of its members, Brian Harvey, for saying that Ecstasy was safe and true to form the media immediately wanted to know what Noel, one the country's most celebrated drug users, thought of the situation. "If Brian Harvey did do twelve Es in one night - if he did do, and he's saying that he did - if he's being honest, then fair enough," Noel told BBC Radio on January 29. "If you can't be honest in this country then we might as well go and live in China, know what I mean?"

"There's people in the Houses of Parliament, man, who are bigger heroin addicts and cocaine addicts than anyone in this room right now. And it's all about honesty at the end of the day," he added in an ambush interview by an MTV film crew at an awards ceremony a few days later. "As soon as people realise that the majority of people in this country take drugs, then the better off we'll all be. It's not like a scandalous sensation, or anything like that. Not when you've got our Government selling arms to people who go out and probably kill relatives of somebody in this room."

And then came the killer sound bite: "Drugs is like getting up and having a cup of tea in the morning." Cue nationwide outrage.

"When Noel said 'drugs are like having a cup of tea' in the toilets at some party somewhere, it took us six months to get over that one, off-the-cuff remark," Creation boss Alan McGee told Vice on May 1, 2011. "But he was right – drugs are endemic in society. People think drugs are rock 'n' roll, but everyone does drugs. Not to do drugs is probably more rock 'n' roll."

"There's this idea in Britain that drug addicts are all skinny white people with spots and needles hanging out of their arms," Noel told MTV's *Behind the Music*. "No they're not – they're doctors, lawyers, police officers...In my own way I was trying to make that point."

Reminiscing about the whole episode three years after making the statement, Noel described his reaction to the reception his comments received in the corridors of power in Uncut magazine. "They were asking questions in the Houses of Parliament and (then Home Secretary) Michael

Howard was on the Six O'clock News talking about it. I remember him saying that, you know, East 17 have kicked Brian Harvey out of the band and that he hoped Liam and the boys would do the same to me. And I was fucking rolling about on the floor, racking out lines of coke, going, 'If only'. For fucks sake. Could you imagine? Bonehead saying, 'yeah we've had a meeting and you're a fucking liability...and you've gotta fucking go'."

The incident also drew criticism from the parents of Leah Betts, the Essex teenager who died after slipping into a coma after taking ecstasy on her 18th birthday in November 1995. Leah's death had been held up by the press as an example of the dangers of illegal drugs in general, and MDMA in particular. When Leah's parents contacted Ignition, the band's management company, after Noel's comments went public, he sympathised but was clear on how he saw her death in relation to the debate. "They didn't ring me at home but there were letters being sent to the management office and all that shit," Noel told Uncut. "And it was just, 'I didn't sell your kid drugs. I take them. Your daughter did as well, while we're on the fucking subject, never forget that. And she died, and it's a fucking shame, it's a terrible thing, but it ain't my fucking problem'."

The controversy itself proved to be, quite aptly, a storm in a tea cup. The fact that Oasis took drugs was no longer shocking and if Noel wanted to make sweeping statements about substance abuse in Britain, well, that was also unsurprising. The fact was that he wasn't telling kids to do drugs. He was just talking about a reality in many people's lives – one that the ruling classes preferred not to think about. Those who related their anger to the media were reacting as much out of self-interest as they were some sense of moral duty. Anyone in any position of governmental power could in no way be seen to be sitting on the fence or, God forbid, taking this rock star's side in the debate. The default position had to be one which called for Noel and his cohorts to be tarred and feathered. This appeased the picket-fence brigade of Middle England and gave the politicians a feeling of being relevant by commenting on what the country's biggest rock star was shouting his mouth off about that week. In reality, as the furore died away, Noel's comments only contributed to his growing legendary status among the majority of young people in the UK – those who Noel himself would consider to be the most important. In the end, the rock star who the government wanted punished remained in his position of power far longer than any of those politicians who had called for his head.

Much to Noel's satisfaction – on a personal and political level – Michael Howard and the Conservative party were ousted from power in the May 1997 general election, with the Conservatives, who had been in power for 18 years, buried under the New Labour landslide. A lifelong Tory hater and Labour supporter, Noel took great pleasure in seeing the heinous right-wing party soundly beaten (and must have allowed himself a self-satisfying smile given Howard's comments five months earlier). The political wind had been blowing in New Labour's direction ever since Tony Blair took over as the party leader in 1994. While leading New Labour in opposition, Blair had already been publicly acknowledged by Noel Gallagher at the 1996 Brit Awards when accepting the award for Best British Group: "There are seven people in this room giving a little bit of hope to the young people in this country and that's me, our kid, Bonehead, Guigs, Alan White, Alan McGee and Tony Blair. If you've all got something about you, you'll go up there and shake Tony Blair's hand. He's the man! Power to the people!" Despite being in the throes of what Alan McGee would later call "ecstasy abuse gone mad" Noel's endorsement kick-started the campaign among the new generation of British rock stars who had grown up under the Tory yoke to support New Labour's push for power. When Blair took up residence in Number 10 Downing Street after the May 2nd landslide victory, he repaid the favour. Unfortunately, in most

86

people's eyes, the new Prime Minister's apparent endorsement of Noel Gallagher would have a less galvanising effect. It was seen by many as the moment when Noel went from man of the people to society hob-nobbing photo opportunist.

"I got fucking slaughtered for that," Noel explained in Uncut magazine in 2000. "But I dare anyone not to have gone if they'd been in my shoes. Anybody who has an official fucking thing drop in their letterbox while you're dressed like an Afghan clown at fucking five o'clock in the morning when you're off your fucking head on acid, and it's from the prime minister, asking you round to his house for a drink...of course you're gonna fucking go!"

"It all started with McGee who'd got involved with the Labour party and he said, 'they want to meet you', and I was like, 'well of course they do. Who wouldn't?' I was still on that euphoric night out that started in 94," Noel told the Guardian in 2008.

When Oasis signed to Creation Records, Gallagher told McGee that if he made enough money to buy a chocolate-brown Rolls-Royce, he'd never want another thing. After the success of *(What's the Story) Morning Glory?*, McGee bought him the chocolate-brown Roller even though Noel couldn't drive. "I'm always seen as having made a grand, selfless gesture giving Noel that chocolate brown Rolls-Royce as a gift," said McGee in the *Upside Down* documentary. "What people don't know is that five minutes before I gave him the car I was sat in it, thinking how nice it was and going, 'Why the fuck am I giving this away?' I nearly kept it for myself." McGee's gift was duly dusted down for the visit to Downing Street and Noel, Meg, the Creation boss and his partner Kate aptly rolled up for drinks with the prime minister in it.

"It was all symbolic," Noel told the Guardian. "McGee used to work on the railways in Glasgow; I used to work on the building sites in

Manchester. So we all piled in this Rolls-Royce and went down there. It was only four or five years since we'd signed off."

"People seemed to have this very sinister image of [the Downing Street event] but I went there because my wife said, 'come on, let's go for a laugh'," he said in a 1998 Q magazine article. "I thought, 'Fuck it, why not'. I've never considered myself to be a rock 'n' roll rebel. I wasn't there representing guitar music, I wasn't there representing the indie community or some twat in a bedsit. I wasn't even representing the band. I was there because the Prime Minster invited me to his house for a beer. You've got to go, haven't you?"

"But of course I went there for the infamy more than anything, and it was, like, 'You're top'. 'No, you're top'. 'No, you're fuckin' top'. 'Well, thanks a lot, here's a gold disc'."

"The fact that Noel was invited to Downing Street – and went – got up some peoples' noses for sure," Johnny Hopkins told this writer. "Again this was about the power they had achieved. At the time I sensed that the reason behind some people's problems with Oasis, was that because the band were northern working class kids done very good. Sometimes this negativity was veiled, other times it was blatant – but it was certainly there. There was resentment towards McGee for similar reasons."

"I don't have a crystal ball," Noel said about the event in an interview with SPIN in October 2008. "I didn't see he [Blair] was going to turn into a cunt. I was 30, off my head on drugs, and everyone telling me we were the greatest band since who knows. Then the prime minister invites you round for a glass of wine. It all becomes part of the high. Why not? I thought it would give me mum a laugh. I didn't go thinking, 'I endorse this government's policies in every respect'. I went to have a look at the curtains."

Noel told The Drum music programme on Australia's Channel 5 in 1997 that he didn't know why he had been invited to Downing Street but the cynic in him - "the one with the inherent distrust of politicians" – believed it was just a PR stunt. "But the dreamer in me," he said, "hopes that I might get a job in the cabinet one day...Minister for Chemicals would be nice."

Liam was among those who were dismissive of the event and the opportunity it offered. "I didn't get an invite and I wouldn't have gone anyway," he admitted in the *Live Forever: The Rise and Fall of Britpop* documentary. "Why would I? I don't have anything in common with any of them. I don't know anything about politics, I don't want to and it looks like a shit house anyway so why would I go there? Noel went 'cause he's mad for it and he wanted to have a nosey about and part of me says, yeah I'd go like Noel to have a look around but part of me says it's not my cup of tea and besides, fuck that I don't want to go out tonight. I want to stay in."

Even though the press would use the visit to question Noel's credibility and to accuse Oasis of becoming part of the establishment, the man himself had his own agenda behind enjoying the surreal experience of going to the Prime Minister's house for a drink. "All the press expected me to turn up in jeans and trainers with a can of fucking Stella and a fag and stick my fingers up on the steps of No 10," he told Q. "But I thought, for once I'll try to make me mam proud of me. The press didn't get what they wanted from me that night. I wasn't going to be the working-class kid from Manchester who was all 'fuck off, I'm just here for the beer'. It was more important than that to me. I didn't get an education. I didn't go to university. I didn't get any qualifications. I've been in trouble with the police. I've been through the drugs thing. But I'm not just some thug."

"I think they were quite concerned though," he admitted. "There were a few phone calls going in to McGee: 'He's not going to misbehave, is he?' And he was going, 'No, no, he's not going to misbehave'. And in the car, on the way there, he was going, 'You're not going to misbehave, are ya?' I was going, 'Well, no, I'm not going to go in and fucking trash the joint; I'm not going to start spraying 'The Sex Pistols' and 'God Save The Queen' everywhere'. I didn't want to go in there and act like a yobbo and give the press what they wanted. I wanted to go there and carry myself as an intelligent young man." In the years that followed, that intelligent young man eventually admitted to having a crafty line of coke in the Queen's Bathroom at Number 10, despite the best efforts of the Downing Street staff to keep an eye on his toilet visits. You can take the boy out of Burnage...

Noel was well aware that Blair's spin doctors were using him to heighten New Labour's credibility and even though he later admitted that he became disillusioned when Blair started "taking money off single mothers and students" he didn't regret going to Downing Street. "Once. I wouldn't do it again. But I'd been so vocal about voting Labour anyway that it would have been hypocritical of me to send back the invitation and go, 'No, I'm not into it now, because it's not cool'. Fuck that. In my lifetime there'd always been a Conservative government. Margaret Thatcher pinched my milk at school, you know what I mean? She was fucking owed one by me."

"And I suppose, yeah, it was a symbolic thing on my behalf, from Burnage to 10 Downing Street," he added. "I don't sit back and go, 'What a marvellous evening, Meg and me went to see the PM'. It was just one of those things. It heightened my infamy. It was a buzz just to go there and think, 'This is going to get so many people's backs up. it's gonna be great, a bit of self-publicity. Shame we haven't got a fucking record out, but never mind."

The evening ended...well...early the next morning, much like many evenings did at Supernova Heights. Sometimes the evening would end several days later. Ever since Noel and Meg moved into the Primrose Hill address in 1995, the house had been a byword for wild behaviour and bacchanalian excess. In many ways, Supernova Heights was the culmination of at least one dream Noel Gallagher had been harbouring since those days on the dole, writing future international hits in a bedsit on an acoustic guitar, fantasising about mega-stardom. It was the affirmation of making it, the bricks-and-mortar statement which said "the filthy rich and successful live here." It was the launching pad for crazy flights of narcotic fancy, of bullshit conversations which lasted days with complete strangers, and painful mornings of amnesia and sickness. This was the quintessential rock star's city headquarters; open for business, but mainly for pleasure, 24/7. Supernova Heights became a magnet for every celebrity and personality looking for the hippest party in town, for every fan waiting for the genial host to pop out in his slippers to sign autographs and listen to a nervously strummed ballad on a battered acoustic, for every tabloid journo hiding behind the bins, wanting the dirt on the devotees who passed through and then passed out in the court of King Noel. It is often said that cocaine is God's way of telling you you have too much money. When you have too much money and too much cocaine, you end up with a house like Supernova Heights.

"When I lived in Primrose Hill, I operated an open-door policy," Noel told the Guardian in 2008. "I'd spent so long on the dole, and I'd moved to London and lived in this huge house, it was like, 'this is it, I'm living the dream, man'. I invited a full awards ceremony back to mine once, George Best included. I won summat for summat or other, and it was the last award of the day and I gave out my address and said, 'Everybody back to mine'. And loads came. It was a great day."

"One night, Meg threw a 30th birthday party for us at the house in London and everybody turned up - even Gwyneth Paltrow was there. it was like, 'Who's in town, fucking come round'. So I get home and it's like, 'Since when did my house become a fucking night club?' Anyway, it got to about 11, 12 o'clock and I was thinking, 'Fuck, man, if we were going to get raided, this would be the night'. I was pretty open about what we used to get up to, and I was thinking, when I had a moment of clarity, 'Fuck'. And then, of course, the mischievous side of me's going, 'Brilliant, puts another 900 grand on the house'. You know, where the entire fucking rock establishment got nicked. And then I was thinking, 'Fuck, no, man, this is getting really serious'. As it happens, the doorbell went and it *was* the police - someone had double-parked their car outside. I just shouted, 'It's the police!' to what can only be described as a symphony of toilet flushes. Of course, the Old Bill just said, 'Do you know who owns the red Mercedes?' 'Yeah, I'll be out in a minute'. And someone moved it and that was it. And everyone's like, 'Bugger'. Good old times, though."

Noel would look back and accept that much of the camaraderie which filled Supernova Heights was artificial and that many of the friendships the house played host to were false and chemical. "I tell you what, you put a load of rock stars in a room with a big bag of cocaine and they'll love each other for the rest of their fucking lives," he told Uncut. "I've had conversations with people who I fucking hate and I know they hate me and they know I hate them. I just sit there going, 'Your record's good, man; I'm not buying them, but I like them, you know, I do, I do, I love them', and they'll be going, 'Yeah, man'. 'And that thing I said about you didn't really mean anything'."

"I'd stay up for days there doing loads of coke and fucking drinking…because that's what you do. It's your divine right as a rock star to be like that. You don't want people coming round and you're there drinking mineral water. What would they think? You've got to be lying in the corner, halfway to a coma with a bottle of Jack Daniels."

As well as making it easier to accept and welcome people into his home who he would normally avoid like the plague, the cocaine was beginning to blow Noel's ego and judgement out of whack in other areas of his life. "We were going to have a flag on top of the house," he told GQ in 2000. "We were going to have it at half-mast when we weren't here, shit like that. Our manager would go, 'Just calm down, you don't know what you're letting yourself in for'. Naming your house is basically just out of being into drugs. I was actually going to get a blue plaque put up as well: Noel Gallagher Lives Here Now! Instead of having one when I'm dead. Actually they'll probably have one outside the off-licence round the corner."

By this time, the excess – especially the alcohol and drug abuse – was reaching new levels of abandon, even for Oasis. The band who Alan McGee famously described as having a gig policy of "no snow, no show" was caught up in a cycle of partying and then coping with the aftermath; enjoying the high life and then struggling to withdraw from the attention it was bringing them. Guigsy had given up cocaine after his brief exit from the band in 1995 but maintained his prodigious weed intake while Bonehead preferred to drown himself in wine when the occasion arose. Alan stayed away from narcotics, instead indulging in a few beers when the mood took him. The Gallaghers, however, were committed enthusiasts of the marching powder. "I have no idea how much we were doing but I reckon it would have been a few grand a month," Noel admitted to Uncut. "It would have been quite a lot; you could have run a small record label off it, I would imagine."

"I was doing as much cocaine as anyone you've ever heard of," Liam admitted to Q magazine in 1999.

In an interview with GQ in 2000, Noel addressed the topic of how the levels of fame and infamy the band were reaching were pushing the brothers further into a cocaine supernova. "Most people at some point have a breakdown and go and see a psychiatrist," he said. "We just got stuck into more drugs."

While the tabloids revelled in recounting their glossy tales of these beautiful and successful millionaires indulging in lives of joyous, hedonistic abandon, the reality was that the heart of the swinging London universe that the Gallaghers had become the centre of was becoming increasingly poisonous and filled with acrimony. When egos, drugs and ambition are thrown together, there are bound to be some personalities that just don't see eye to eye. "Meg hated Liam and I was always trying to please her but I didn't get on with him myself, anyway," Noel told the Telegraph on June 21, 2001. "Meg and Patsy didn't get on. It was a vicious nightmare."

The result was that the brothers started to see less and less of each other and would socialise in completely different social circles. Their wives hated each other. They hated each other's wives. They drifted further and further apart at a time when they should have been together, enjoying the fact that Oasis were becoming what they always dreamed of – the biggest band on the planet.

Success, adoration, fame, money... Oasis appeared to have achieved everything they had ever wanted when they set out on their mission for world domination a mere six years before. But by now, the drawbacks of ubiquity were starting to become increasingly obvious.

The Gallaghers were slowly becoming the people they had complained about in their early years – those rock stars who wanted it all and then complained when they got it. It would still be a few years before the pressure became intolerable but by the time the band began working on the follow up to *(What's the Story) Morning Glory?*, life had already changed irrevocably from those youthfully naive days before *Definitely Maybe* made history.

"Keith Richards once said everybody wants to be famous until they are. I agree with that," Noel told Heat magazine in 2000. "Fame is great for about a year. Then it just becomes too much. And you can't back out, you're stuck with it. So you've got to learn how to adapt and to live with it as best you can."

"Has success changed me? You'd have to be a fool to sit here and say no," Noel told the Guardian in 2008. "Is it possible to become idolised without becoming a bit of a twat? Well, I didn't become a twat, but I started to dress like a twat. I wore sunglasses a lot and I might have had a fur coat and I thought that was the correct procedure for being in the biggest band in the world, but no, I didn't become a twat."

Noel did admit that the trappings of fame had gone a long way to drive a wedge between the band and their fans over time and that an even bigger divide which was growing between his sense of normality and his perception of how he should behave as a rock star had begun to concern him. "I don't particularly like looking around and seeing three bodyguards there and everyone's clearing a path for you before you get there. Because if I was a kid there looking at me walking past with all this entourage, I'd think, 'what a wanker!' I'm not. I'm just a normal fucking geezer, but these things are thrust upon you. I don't particularly like all that, but it's a necessary evil."

"We now have about 50 million people tagging along when we go anywhere," he added. "I do miss the days of the Boardwalk when we had that little room and we all used to go deaf. But I suppose in ten years we'll be reminiscing about now. Either that or we'll be visiting Liam in rehab…with his colostomy bag…pissing in his trousers."

"I suppose I miss the anonymity of it all," Noel added in an October 31 1998 NME interview. "Just being able to really do what you want. You could come out of a pub drunk, have a piss in a car park and nobody would be arsed. Whereas if you come out of a pub drunk now, and have a piss in a car park, the bricklayer who laid the bricks will sue you."

To this point, the problems and the changing attitudes the members of Oasis had towards their fame were based on the challenges presented by the adoration which was thrust on them. Newspapers intruded into their lives, looking for any kind of stories, because people wanted to know everything about them. The levels of protection and isolation that they had to endure were because millions of fans wanted to be near them. The reason why they could no longer play the Manchester Boardwalk and had to hire entire counties to play in was because the demand for their music was unprecedented in its colossal nature. These were all 'good' problems. These were the challenges that only the massively successful would ever face.

Very soon, however, Oasis would have to face a new set of challenges related to their fame. Soon, the problems that they had to endure would not be solely derived from their popularity. Soon, Oasis would be presented with a different reality, one in which the press would be less concerned with building them up and more preoccupied with cutting them down to size.

3.

be here now

"Open up your eyes, get a grip of yourself inside"

It could have been described as the deep breath before the plunge. Oasis had conquered Maine Road and had just over three months free before the summer gigs which would make the band, in Noel Gallagher's words, "bigger than, dare I say it, fucking God." Loch Lomond, Knebworth and true musical dominance awaited them in August 1996 but as April turned to May of that year, the band were rewarded with some much needed down time. And what does a rock star who is part of the self-proclaimed biggest band in the world do with his time off? He goes on holiday to a private island in the Caribbean and stays in Mick Jagger's house with his girlfriend, a movie star and a supermodel.

Noel had been suffering from writer's block since the winter of 1995 and admitted that he had written only a single guitar riff in the six months following the release of *(What's the Story) Morning Glory?* The intensive touring and the whole circus which had gone with it had frazzled his mind. Flying out to Mustique for a well-deserved holiday with Meg, Noel hoped that the block would ease and that he could start work on the songs for the follow-up to the band's second album. He also hoped that he would rediscover, not only his rich vein of song writing, but part of himself which had been discarded on the long road from Burnage to the West Indies.

However, the level of fame that Oasis had achieved to that point was such that even Noel's choice of sanctuary wouldn't save him from the intrusion and unwanted attention that plagued him at home. "I went out to Mustique which is out near Venezuela, right? Like, fucking no-one's gonna have heard of us out there," he told Select in 1997. "Geezer in customs in the airport pulls out a fucking copy of *(What's the Story) Morning Glory?* I'm like, 'so how do you know the band?' He's like, 'um... MTV man.'."

Noel's escape had not gone unnoticed in the UK and it wasn't long before a pasty-looking press pack from Britain was spotted scurrying across the island in search of sightings of Noel Gallagher. The leader of Oasis taking a well-deserved break was one thing – some beach shots with his lover might fill a gossip column or two – but one of the biggest rock stars on the planet hanging out with a Hollywood heart-throb and one of the world's most desirable women was a completely different story. Soon pictures of Noel, Meg, Johnny Depp and Kate Moss strolling in the shade of palms trees were being carried by the majority of mainstream international newspapers, as well as in the music press. If anyone was wondering how far Oasis had come by the spring of 1996, this was their answer. It also leant more credence to the dark mutterings which were beginning to surface about where Noel Gallagher's head was at.

"I went away to Mustique to write the album," he recalled in an interview with Uncut in 2000. "Johnny Depp and Kate Moss turned up because Meg's known Kate for years. Now, they were staying in Mick Jagger's house. This is really fucking surreal, right? Meg and Kate are out the back getting fucking pissed as arseholes, Johnny's in this little adjoining room writing a script for this film, I'm sat in Mick Jagger's fucking front room with an acoustic guitar writing a song for the new album, looking around at all these original Andy Warhol paintings, going, fucking hell..."

"You write your first album when you're young and you're broke and you're hungry and you write your third album when you're a big fat drunken rock star," he added in an interview with the Independent in the same year. "You just fall onto that treadmill."

98

For those who had witnessed the burning desire and unrelenting focus of a lean and mean Noel Gallagher circa 1993, a year before he effectively dragged Oasis from obscurity into the big leagues, the sight of the increasingly doughy, bleary-eyed 1996 version partying with actors and models in a millionaires playground while trying to relocate his songwriting mojo was an ominous one. This was a dangerous flirtation with cliché. Would Noel – and Oasis – turn out to be just another bunch of energetic chancers who over-achieved and who became neutered by the trappings of fame? There was no doubt that his world had changed irrevocably over the previous 18 months but despite the temptations and the extra-curricular responsibilities that came with his new status as an international rock star, Noel still had three things which were driving him on: fear of failure, pride in his craft and his working class attitude to getting the job done. These, he hoped, would be enough to get him over the line this time as he struggled with the pressure of writing a follow-up to *(What's the Story) Morning Glory?*, an album which was still selling around 200,000 copies a week at this time.

To start with, Noel spent his days recharging under the Caribbean sun but within a week, the cogs started turning and he started work on the songs which would feature on the next Oasis album. Some of them he already had in some form, written as they were many years before when lying beside Mick Jagger's pool would have been a young man's stoned fantasy. Others had yet to form at all. But once the ideas started to flow, Noel got to work and was spending ten hours a day working on the demos with Owen Morris who had flown out with a portable 8-track studio desk.

"I've got 15 songs on a cassette," Noel told Select magazine in August 1996. "Like I say, I went to Mustique with Owen with a digital 8-track and a keyboard to do the strings on. I played them on acoustic and Owen programmed the drums in. It's the first time I've ever done any demos, bar 'Live Forever' and 'Up in the Sky'. But it sounds good. Most of the songs were written before I even got a record deal. I went away and wrote the lyrics in about two weeks."

When he got the call, Owen Morris thought he and Noel might be able to put down a couple of songs. "But then the first night he reeled off fifteen songs on the acoustic," recalled Morris in the September 1997 issue of Q magazine. "Then we piled through them in a week, midday to seven in this chalet by the airport. It's easy with Noel because you make decisions on the hoof; chop that, stick that in, bung it down. Guitar overdubs and backing vocals as well. The Mustique tape's amazing, really cool, although it sounds shit because of the drum box. And that was the album, apart from a couple of songs got dropped and 'Magic Pie' was added later. The words, most of the arrangements and the running order were sorted on Mustique too. He's got big balls that man. He did that week's work and that was it."

Back in the UK with the demos in the bag, Noel was cagey about the direction the new album would take but the few hints he gave not only suggested a heavier approach but they also gave a glimpse of his developing state of mind. On a positive note, it appeared that he was still relatively grounded despite the insanity which was permeating his life and that he was still aware of the ridiculousness of it all. However, there were also signs that the sweet taste of fame was beginning to sour in his mouth.

"The vibe of the music is a reaction to the boredom of having to drag around in convoys with police escorts," he told Select in August 1996, shortly before Oasis hit the road again for the second half of the *Morning Glory* tour. "*Definitely Maybe* was me sat at home dreaming of being a young, free rock star living it large. *(What's the Story) Morning Glory?* was actually doing it. This one is wishing I was still fucking back at home doing what I was doing before it all kicked off."

Oasis resumed touring in August with the Loch Lomond double-header, a one-off show in Sweden and then back to make history with the Knebworth weekend. Shortly after the mammoth shows in Hertfordshire and the two stadium shows in Cork which immediately followed, the band would jet off for another ill-fated tour of the United States – one which nearly brought everything crashing down around their ears.

After returning of separate flights after Noel's decision to walk out on the band, a move which sent rumours of the band's demise in the British press into overdrive, Oasis came back together through the calming mediation of their manager Marcus Russell. The rift created by the US tour had Ignition and the band's handlers in a panic. Oasis had never been so big and yet they had never appeared so fragile and unstable. After reconciling at a country retreat, Liam and Noel decided that, to keep themselves at the very top and for them to survive, work should begin on the new album, which Noel wanted to call *Be Here Now*, in reference to a quote he had read in Mustique attributed to John Lennon in which the former Beatle had described the meaning of rock 'n' roll as "to be here now." Seeing an opportunity to meld the band back together over the collective activity of recording, Marcus Russell urged the brothers to start work as soon as they could. The songs that Noel had written a few months earlier in Mustique were considered to be good enough and so the wheels were set in motion. "In retrospect, we went in the studio too quickly," Marcus Russell admitted in a Q magazine interview in 2007. "The smart move would have been to take the rest of the year off. But at the time it seemed like the right thing to do. If you're a band and you've got a dozen songs you think are great, why not go and do it."

"After the US tour fiasco, there was endless speculation that the band was going to break up, to end that speculation I said, 'Fuck it, let's go into the studio and record an album'," Noel said in an interview with Muse magazine in 2000. "Where are the songs? I was all like, don't worry about that, we'll do that when we get there...which was the biggest mistake we ever made."

"I had all the music but not the words. We were starting in two weeks. I was heavily into drugs and I just didn't give a damn."

The arrogance with which Oasis returned to the studio when they were so clearly under-prepared had been justified on so many occasions previously that no-one was keeping an eye out for any potential pitfalls up ahead. Noel had crowed that everything Oasis laid a finger on turned to gold but he also admitted in the next breath that he was aware it could all turn to "dog shite" one day. Little did he know that the Midas touch was about to desert him and his band.

The decision was made to record *Be Here Now* at Abbey Road in London, the iconic studios made famous by the band's idols The Beatles. The sessions began on October 7 and it soon became clear that despite the reconciliation and the joint decision to record a new album as a show of strength and unity, Oasis were still at war with themselves. "So many things had been written about us and most of it was nonsense but we'd become five Robbie Williamses rather than the band Oasis," Noel told RTE later in 1997. "So we went off to make the album and it started off quite badly. No-one was really interested in doing it. We weren't getting on with one another."

"The only reason anyone was there was the money," Owen Morris recalled in Q magazine in 2007. "It was fucking awful. Noel had decided Liam was a shit singer. Liam had decided he hated Noel's songs. Massive amounts of drugs. Big fights. Bad vibes. Shit recordings." Morris admitted that he tried to get the sessions abandoned but Noel managed to convince him that these were just teething troubles and that they could work through them to complete the album as planned.

The atmosphere continued to be strained and the relationship between all the members of the band – not just the brothers – seemed to be at breaking point. The photographer Jill Furmanovsky who had documented the band's career from the early days revealed in her book *Was There Then* that there were very few occasions when all of Oasis were in the studio at the same time. Abbey Road had also become a general hangout for all manner of people with interests in the band. The constant comings and goings of sycophants, drug dealers, family and friends all added to the pressurized atmosphere surrounding the recordings. There was also a constant media presence outside the studios which should have been expected given the high profile nature of the band, what was at stake with the album and the location of Abbey Road in the heart of the capital. When Liam got busted for cocaine possession a month into the sessions, paranoia entered the equation with rumours spreading of a mole within the organization, leaking information to the press. There were so many people wandering in and out of Abbey Road as part of the Oasis entourage that it could have been anyone – if there was even an informer at large at all.

The Sun's showbiz editor Dominic Mohan recalled of the period: "We had quite a few Oasis contacts on the payroll," he told Q magazine in 2007. "I don't know whether any were drug dealers, but there were always a few dodgy characters about."

Jill Furmanovsky wrote in her book *Was There Then* that even she came under pressure from the press with the tabloid journalists living in her building hassling her for information. "They thought I had the band hiding in my flat," she wrote.

The changing dynamic around the band was also creating suspicion and distrust, with friends from before the band made it big being regarded as liabilities due to the amount of information they had on the band. There was a concerted effort to clamp down on stories being leaked to the press and so the band closed ranks. "People were being edged out of the circle around Oasis," Johnny Hopkins told Q magazine. "These were people who knew them before they were famous rather than because they were famous. Once you're in that situation you lose sight of reality."

"From the start we built strong relationships with certain journalists – great writers, great fans of music and very trustworthy people," Hopkins continued in an interview with this writer. "These became friends of the band and they would often hang out socially, come to a lot of the shows and have backstage access. They would get the full Oasis experience which made for great features in the press. However, the bigger the band got the more doors started to close. Sadly, as the doors started to close on these writers and some of the band's older friends, the door opened up to all the London liggers and starfuckers – many of whom sold stories to the tabloid press."

Liam's arrest brought even more reporters to the door of Abbey Road so the decision was soon made to relocate the sessions to Ridge Farm studios in Surrey. The music had again become hostage to the madness surrounding the band.

"I had this idea that we'd do it around the corner from our house in Abbey Road and everybody would turn up when they turned up, do their bits and fuck off, but it didn't turn out that way," Noel told the NME in 1997. "In the end we did three songs at Abbey Road. But it was good to get out of there and get to a farmhouse to record and act like a band again as opposed to a media circus. We had to deal with the tabloid press and people stealing things from the studio...leaking the contents of private conversations to the gossip press and such. There was too many tabloid journalists knocking about in corridors and shit like that. It became intolerable."

While the more rural setting and the distance from London's media maelstrom seemed to invigorate band, the band still seemed unfocused and tense with Noel vacating the studio whenever Liam was laying down his vocal track.

The amount of cocaine being snorted was also reaching unparalleled levels, even for Oasis. "In the first week at Ridge Farm, someone tried to score an ounce of weed, but instead got an ounce of cocaine," Owen Morris recalled in Q. "Which kind of summed it up."

Six months before recording began, Noel had explained his love of drugs to Rolling Stone, saying: "I just like getting out of it. I like the feeling of lying on the fucking floor, being out of my head. I guess in the long run you think about your body, but until it happens, well....As long as it doesn't affect the work." Such was the level of intake going on at Ridge Farm that no-one knew – or even cared – how much damage the avalanche of cocaine was doing to the band and the embryonic *Be Here Now*.

"At the time, I was taking a lot of fucking drugs, so I didn't give a fuck," Noel told Chuck Klosterman in an article for Grantland in 2011. "We were taking all the cocaine we could possibly find. But it wasn't like a seedy situation. We were at work. We weren't passed out on the floor with a bottle of Jack Daniel's. We were partying while we were working."

"When you're on the old cocaine, you think everything you do is incredible," Noel later recalled to Details magazine. "I was pretty much whacked out all the time. Because I didn't like the band I was in, it had become too big for me."

"I'd get to a certain point and go, 'Fuck it, that'll do' because we made the record to justify the drug habit. My personal opinion was that I was making records to justify spending fucking thousands on drugs."

"We were just pushing it to the point that it could not get any bigger, it couldn't get any more mad, you couldn't get any more fur in this coat if you tried, the shades couldn't be any more mirrored, they're mirrored on the insides," he recalled of the *Be Here Now* days in an interview with the Daily Telegraph in 2007. "When you look at yourself in the mirror at 7 a.m., wearing big fucking round sunglasses and a black fur coat with a fucking £50 note up your nose, and you say, 'Yeah, man, this is what it's all about', you might be a bit fucked."

"We were having so much fun in the studio that quality control went out the door a bit," Noel said in the 2011 Grantland interview. "We weren't analysing anything, we were just like 'that's fucking brilliant, let's have it', and of course all the people around us were saying the same thing: 'No, it IS brilliant."

"We had more money and drugs and all that kind of shit that you could deal with, and for some people, that kind of level of fame can hit you really fucking hard," Noel told Time Out in Oct 15, 2008. "But we couldn't fucking get enough of it. It was like 'come on, man!' The days weren't long enough. Every time we had to go to bed it was like, 'I don't wanna go to bed!' And in the middle of it all, you're trying to make music."

In this environment, few people were in any state of mind to put the brakes on and even fewer were prepared to take Noel to one side and admit that the new songs weren't up to scratch and that the whole album was going off the rails. When Owen Morris did manage to raise some concerns he was, in his own words, "cut down" by Noel. The producer admitted that, instead of pressing his case, he returned to "shovelling drugs up my nose."

In an interview with Uncut in 2000, Noel put his own slant on things. "If you've just sold 20 million albums and you go and write a bunch of songs, people aren't going to go, 'I don't like that, it isn't good enough'," he said. "When we invited people down to the studio everyone was going, 'It's brilliant'. But I would imagine in the taxi home, they were going,

106

'fucking hell, there was fucking two months of fucking feedback before the song started'... which is great when you're off your tits in the studio, but when you're listening to it in the back of the car on the way to work it must be fucking excruciating."

Wondering what Oasis were getting up to in the countryside with the blank cheque he had given them, Creation boss Alan McGee once turned up and was shocked at what was going on – and for a man with his own record of prodigious drug use, this was some reaction. "I used to go down to the studio, and there was so much cocaine getting done at that point," McGee told Q. "Owen was out of control, and he was the one in charge of it. The music was just fucking loud."

Noel would tell Rolling Stone in July 1997, two months after the album's completion, that *Be Here Now*'s incredible volume had been influenced by his work with the Chemical Brothers on their Number 1 hit 'Setting Sun'. "It's definitely influenced the sonic side of things," he told the magazine. "When we were laying down this mix, we listened to our drum tracks and then to 'Setting Sun'. When their drums came in, they were twice as loud as ours. So I said, 'We've got to get ours fucking louder than that'. It's all about compressors and equalizers, stuff I don't really understand. I just sit in the back drinking, pointing and shouting, 'It's not loud enough, turn it up!'"

Such was the volume of the recording sessions at Abbey Road that Oasis were actually asked to leave on one occasion after a producer in an adjoining studio had complained about the noise. "He knocked on the door and asked us if we would turn it down," Noel told the San Francisco Chronicle on January 25th, 1998. "By the time we stopped laughing, he'd left the room. It was the first time I've been in a recording studio and someone's told us to turn it down!"

"Someone told me the other day that [*Be Here Now*] wasn't as loud as the other albums," Guigsy said in an interview with Access in 1997. "Yes, I think it sounds outrageous. But in another way it's almost like the band feels more confident to express their playing, and their attitude to making a record. Now we all know how the studio works; it's a lot more relaxed and everyone is a lot more confident. Confidence makes you more relaxed."

What the band themselves failed to notice at the time was that they had become too relaxed to the point of not caring as much about the end product and that the chemical confidence which was driving Oasis at the time had instilled a belief that anything they produced would be sprinkled with genius. The fact that the whole album was sprinkled with something else soon became apparent to anybody who got involved with the whole project.

Every aspect of *Be Here Now*'s creation seemed to pursue the goal of setting new levels of excess. Even the cover shoot was described by its artistic director as "Alice in Wonderland meets Apocalypse Now." Shot at Stocks House in Hertfordshire, the cover depicted the members of Oasis in various activities around the former stately home's outside swimming pool with various visual devices Noel Gallagher had acquired from the BBC props store scattered throughout the scene. Pride of place was a white Rolls Royce sticking out of the water; homage to the great rock 'n' roll excesses of the past which Oasis seemed hell-bent on eclipsing with their own behaviour. It seemed to say that Oasis were in such a position that there was not only a Roller in every driveway but they now had spare ones which they could throw in the pool. As well as keeping the increasingly inebriated band under control, the photographer Michael Spencer Johns had actual children to deal with too. Describing how the shoot "degenerated into chaos," Johns said he struggled to get the shots he

108

needed with Oasis taking up residence in the bar and school kids running amok all over the set.

Back in the studio, events were also spiralling into unchecked chaos. The album was becoming incredibly dense with Noel filling the songs with multiple guitar tracks in an attempt to make the colossal record he heard in his snow-blown head. On some songs, he dubbed ten channels with identical guitar parts, in an effort to create a sonic onslaught. 'My Big Mouth' alone has an estimated 30 guitar parts layered over it.

As the music expanded exponentially, so did Noel's ego. "Nothing but the best album of 1997 will be good enough for us," he said in the BBC's *Right Here, Right Now* documentary. "We want to blow every band into oblivion; we want to eclipse every musician in this country because we can and we will because we're the best."

With much of the main work done on the album at Ridge Farm, the sessions moved back to London. Firstly at Beatles producer Sir George Martin's Air Studios in Hampstead, where more of the drum, bass, guitar and vocal tracks were laid down and the string sections were recorded, and then on to Master Rock studios in Kilburn where the multiple guitar and vocal overdubs were completed. Noel and Owen then took the tapes to Orinoco Studios in Southwark for the final mixing. The album was finally finished in early May 1997.

Even before any note of music was heard from the album, the anticipation and expectation was reaching fever pitch. It had been over a year since 'Don't Look Back in Anger' had gone to Number 1 in the UK and while 'Champagne Supernova' had been released as a single in Australia, New Zealand and France, there had been no new Oasis music since before Knebworth. Everyone was eager to hear what Britain's biggest band had come up with in the time in between.

With the new release on the horizon, the press began flooding its pages with anything Oasis related stories that reporters could get their hands on: Noel and Liam with new haircuts, some of the band out shopping somewhere – anything to keep the band in the headlines and provide the insatiable public with any tiny morsels before the feast to come. Liam did his best to oblige by getting cautioned by the police in July after he leaned out of his Mercedes' window, grabbed the shirt of a passing cyclist and pulled him along with the car. Witness Angela Deane told the Daily Mail: "The cyclist seemed very mild-mannered, and he didn't want the fight or the confrontation. He looked as if he had been picked on. He didn't go back and retaliate."

With the hype machine crunching through its gears, Ignition attempted to put the brakes on and slow it down before it spun out of control. The management team's efforts, however, only succeeded in hitting the turbo button on an already speeding vehicle. By acting secretively about the new record and refusing any prior information about the album to be released, Ignition aptly ignited a firestorm of interest in *Be Here Now*.

When asked by the NME what the new material was like, Noel struggled to toe the party line: "It sounds brilliant. It's quite varied, really. The single sounds sort of like…it's a lot heavier than *(What's the Story) Morning Glory?* The single's... No, I can't tell you, I'm not going to tell you." This did little to calm the situation.

With the album slated for release in August, almost a year to the day that Oasis played their biggest ever gigs, the press and public began focusing on the July 7 release date of the first single. When 'D'You Know What I Mean' finally dropped, so did the nation's collective jaw.

"The song was eight and a half minutes long and I refused to edit it, because I was so full of self-importance," Noel admitted in the 2010 documentary which accompanied the release of the *Time Flies* singles compilation. "Why edit something down to four minutes when you can listen to it for eight minutes? I remember being adamant about it at the time. We were in the studio and someone said 'it's a bit long'...and I said 'it's not long enough!' I guess if you've just sold twelve million albums and you're on Creation...Their ethos was: the artist is always right. But you know, it's too fucking long."

"At the time, the spotlight of the world was on the band...We were fucking massive in America, we were beyond big in England... This was going to be the first single. I remember I was sat in a meeting in our office and playing it to the relevant people...radio pluggers were there, people from America...people from fucking Japan, like 'what the fuck are you doing here?' It was like the fucking United Nations. And I remember this one radio plugger clicked his stopwatch when it started..."

"Now...there's one minute of feedback before there's a single musical note," he continues. "And there's a plane taking off and a seagull fucking tweeting in the background. It only dawned on me then that this was fucking out of order! It was so wrong. And all these people are nodding their heads and checking their watches...'fucking hell, it's still not started'... All these suits sitting there thinking 'These fucking jokers are riding on the biggest expectations of any band this decade, and they've recorded a plane landing'. And so a month later it ends and they're all like 'so...is there going to be an edit?' and I'm all like 'NO...IT'S NOT LONG ENOUGH...'"

With no radio edit, stations were obliged to play the dark, heavy pounding epic in its entirety. This was the new Oasis single after all. This is what the world had been waiting for and radio stations were going to give the masses what they wanted, regardless of the fact it took up the air space of three regular length songs.

"I do regret going to Mustique with Mick Jagger, Jerry Hall, Johnny Depp, and Kate Moss and trying to write *Be Here Now*," Noel admitted in SPIN in October 2008. "I was doing it for the wrong reasons. And that's how you get into a situation where you think 'D'You Know What I Mean?' is the most amazing thing you've ever recorded."

Oasis were huge and a phenomenon that was impossible to ignore. They were the first post-grunge band to be massive in every context; popular with the critics, the press and the public. They were releasing *Be Here Now* from an unassailable position. Oasis were so massive that even their B-sides made it on to mainstream radio playlists. Radio 1 was even playing 'Stay Young' on rotation, which – as the song was more upbeat, radio-friendly and much shorter than the A-side – was a relief to many. Mark Radcliffe and Marc Riley, two Manchester DJs who had championed the band from the early days, even played the single's third track on their Radio 1 show, although they did refer to 'Angel Child' as "a bit of a crap one."

Despite its length and its general weirdness, 'D'You Know What I Mean' went straight in at Number 1 and sold an incredible 370,000 copies in the first week, 162,000 of those in its first day of release. The egos which were so obviously wildly out of check if the new music was anything to go by, were now inflating at a phenomenal rate. If the new album didn't at least achieve world peace and align the planets then it would have been seen as a failure.

With the appetite whetted by the starter, everyone was eager to get stuck into the main course. But Ignition were still doing their best to frustrate the salivating masses. *Be Here Now* was to be released on August 21. Usually, a new album is brought out on a Monday but Ignition had insisted that the date be moved to a Thursday. The reasoning for this was a fear that import copies from the United States might find their way into the

UK before the country's official release date. Ignition also insisted that record stores stocking the album signed a contract pledging not to sell the new album earlier than 8am on the Thursday morning. This meant that the traditional midnight release which always led to fans lining up through the night to be the first to buy the album at the stroke of 12 would not be happening. Ignition allegedly insisted on this to limit the contact fans would have with the press who normally interviewed those camping overnight to be the first to own the record. The presumably bizarre reasoning behind this has been lost in the madness that followed.

Before the band's management had to deal with the craziness of release day, there was even more suffocating secrecy and paranoia to endure. First the people at Creation appeared to have mislaid the memo informing them to keep expectation to a minimum.

"I heard the album in the studio and I remember saying 'We'll only sell seven million copies'... I thought it was too confrontational," Alan McGee admitted to Q magazine in 2007. He, Johnny Hopkins and marketing executive Emma Greengrass had heard the finished songs at Noel's house and all had their doubts about the new material but kept their thoughts to themselves. However, when interviewed about the album a few days later, McGee couldn't help himself and indulged in some of his famous hyperbole, predicting *Be Here Now* would sell twenty million copies. Ignition and Oasis went crazy and immediately excluded McGee from any further involvement in the release campaign.

"The record company started hyping it in England against our wishes," Noel told Details. "When you've got the head of your record company saying two weeks before it comes out it's going to shift 20 million copies you think, 'what's going on here?'"

"I really wonder what would have happened if *Be Here Now* had sold like *(What's the Story) Morning Glory?* The lack of effort I was putting into songwriting would have been vindicated by the record sales," Noel mused in an interview with Grantland in 2011. "I would have gone, 'fuck it, if it ain't broke I ain't gonna fix it'. It would have been insane. Just imagine if that album had sold 30 million copies. I probably would have grown a moustache and started wearing a fucking cape."

After Alan McGee's off-message statement, things got even more cloak and dagger. Ignition and the rest of Creation went into lockdown. The extent of control deepened and when cassette copies of the album to the music press were distributed ahead of the album's release, each journalist was made to sign a contract which stipulated that the journalist "could not discuss the album with anyone – including your partner at home," Select journalist Mark Perry recounted in *The Creation Records Story* by David Cavanagh. "It basically said don't talk to your girlfriend about it when you're at home in bed." Things got weirder when, convinced that the Creation and Ignition offices had been bugged, Johnny Hopkins was told by his bosses to drive journalists around London while playing the album to them on the car stereo.

"It's been well documented that the *Be Here Now* album listening contract pissed off some writers and also people at the radio stations," admitted Hopkins.

"There was a lot of bullshit around the album," Noel recalled in the *Time Flies* documentary. "People could listen to it but they weren't allowed to tell anybody they'd heard it, and it was fucking nonsense. It was very, very embarrassing. Nothing to do with anyone in the band, I might add. I think we copped a lot of flak for that. Shit like that really annoys me when I think about it now. People were getting so up their own arses about it at the time. I remember somebody on the Channel 4 News holding up the cover and saying 'We've got it, we're not allowed to say we've heard it but this is the cover'. It was embarrassing. But it was mad as fuck.... no wonder we thought we were superhuman beings."

Ten days before the release of *Be Here Now*, DJ Steve Lamacq received a tape of three songs he could play on The Evening Session, his Radio 1 indie rock show. He was told that more songs would be sent the next day if he adhered to the rule of talking over the tracks to prevent bootlegging. He played 'The Girl in the Dirty Shirt', 'Be Here Now' and 'All Around The World'. The next day, he received a call telling him that he would not be given any more tracks because he hadn't spoken enough over the songs. "I had to go on the air the next night and say, 'Sorry, but we're not getting any more tracks'. It was just absurd," he recalled in *The Last Party* by John Harris.

"The whole campaign made people despise Oasis within Creation," the label's head of marketing John Andrews told David Cavanagh. "You had this Oasis camp that was like 'I'm sorry, you're not allowed to come into the office between the following hours. You're not allowed to mention the word Oasis'. It was like a fascist state." Another Creation employee told Cavanagh about an incident "when somebody came round to check our phones because they thought The Sun had tapped them."

Emma Greengrass later admitted in the same book that "in retrospect, a lot of the things we did were ridiculous."

With sections of the public and press alike – not to mention most of the employees in their own record company – becoming alienated by the *Be Here Now* campaign, it was no surprise that the strain was beginning to show on the band. "I just need more time to think about where the band's going," Noel told a rabid press pack shortly before the album's release.

"This is probably going to be the most important album of our career," Noel said in the BBC documentary *Right Here, Right Now.* "It'll either send us up to U2 level or see us back on the dole."

Finally, *Be Here Now* was released on August 21 and in spite of Ignition's attempts to catch out news crews, the cameras showed up outside record stores anyway. The images they caught were of the shops doing slow early trade on the album. However, business was booming by midday and at the close of trading, the album had shipped over 350,000 units on its first day of release. Two days later, that figure exceeded 696,000 making *Be Here Now* the fastest-selling album in British history. The album hit Number 1 on the UK album charts and in a dozen others around the globe. It debuted at Number 2 on the Billboard charts in the United States, despite selling 152,000 units, a disappointing return in the context of the 400,000 it had been expected to sell. By the end of 1997, *Be Here Now* had sold eight million units worldwide, largely gained in the first two weeks of release.

The album release was one of the main stories on the BBC's Breakfast News programme on August 21 while The Sun honoured the event in its own inimitable way by plastering its front cover with a picture of Liam and a topless Patsy in a speedboat while on holiday. Essentially the story was hung on the fact that Liam's new album was out and so were his wife's breasts. Again, the music had come in second (and third) to more sensationalist tittle-tattle.

"I bet there's some kid somewhere who started getting into music about six months ago who doesn't realise that we're a band, who just thinks we live in the papers for some reason" Noel told the NME in July 1997. "So we had to make a record to remind people what we're really about."

The album was initially selling well, as a much-anticipated Oasis record was expected to, but was it any good? The immediate response was encouraging with some reviews suggesting that the band had not been the

116

only ones heavily indulging in lines of ego-booster over the past 12 months. Q magazine for one seemed swept up in the moment and gave the album a 5-Star review and compared it to the Beatles' *Revolver*, describing it as "the heavy, heavy sound of the summer." Rolling Stone, whose four stars out of five suggested they weren't being sarcastic, praised the album and called 'D'You Know What I Mean' "seven minutes of simple, focused genius." British broadsheet The Guardian stated that "*Be Here Now* validates most if not all of the Gallaghers' boasts about their greatness." Select Magazine gave it five out of five describing the album as "the biggest thrill in town" and Oasis as "the finest rock synthesists the world has ever known."

In his book *The Last Party*, John Harris wrote: "To find an album that had attracted gushing notices in such profusion, one had to go back thirty years, to the release of *Sgt. Pepper's Lonely Hearts Club Band*." Such praise began to fuel rumours that those lavishing accolades on the album hadn't actually heard it at all. Others wondered if the ecstatic reaction to *Be Here Now* in some quarters was a reaction to those magazines and newspapers getting it so spectacularly wrong with *(What's the Story) Morning Glory?* Of course, such was the level of the band's popularity at the time that few editors would have considered sacrificing their circulation over a less-then-favourable review of the new Oasis record, especially when many of their competitors were praising *Be Here Now* to the heavens. Everyone stood to gain from maintaining the status quo. It was only when more and more people started saying that Oasis now actually sounded like Status Quo did the tide start to turn.

Suspicions of euphoria-inspired ill-judgment grew stronger when more considered, and then scathing reviews started to appear. The surge of early sales of the album also began to dwindle in line with the diminishing number of positive articles. Those who had stuck to their guns throughout

117

the release of *Definitely Maybe* and *(What's the Story) Morning Glory?* and maintained that Oasis had always been over-rated, felt vindicated by the growing shift to their position. Where was the worldwide hit single? Where was this album's 'Wonderwall', the song which long-term critics claimed had carried the mostly dull *(What's the Story) Morning Glory?* to such heights? More and more people were beginning to stand up, point and shout: "Look, the emperor has no clothes!" Soon, what could only be described as a full-on backlash was well underway with previously silent sections of the media finding their voices and joining with long-term Oasis detractors in the music press to roundly slate the band.

"Bloated and over-heated (much like the band themselves), the album has all that dreadful braggadocio that is so characteristic of a cocaine user," Irish Times journalist Brian Boyd wrote. Pitchfork succinctly called the album an "uninspired failure" while Stylus Magazine claimed that *Be Here Now* took "loudness, density, compression, and ugliness to a level previously and rightfully unimagined."

"In the UK, *Be Here Now* got rave reviews," recalled Johnny Hopkins. "The fans went out and bought the album in their droves: around 350,000 on the first day alone. Nearly 700,000 after three days. Incredible. However it started turning up in the second hand shops pretty soon after that once the fans had heard the album. That's where the backlash, such as it was, became evident but it was coming from some of the fans and then sections of the press picked up on it from there."

"The backlash came with the realisation that the fans didn't all share the enthusiasm of the positive reviews," he added. "People – fans and the media – invest a lot of hope in, and project their own ideas, onto bands. This creates expectations of how a band are and what they might do. This can often lead to disappointment."

118

"To an extent the backlash was also partly to do with the band's unprecedented success and productivity. *Be Here Now* was their third album in four years. Plus they'd put out all those great singles and quality B-sides. A lot of ace music. They were really prolific. Perhaps some people felt it was over-saturation."

"I don't care what anyone says," Liam said in an MTV interview in 1997. "It won't change what I feel about [*Be Here Now*] and I love it."

He was still adamant three years later when talking to Jayne Middlemiss on the BBC's O-Zone programme. "It's good, man. I think the songs are good on it, I'm good on it, everyone else is good on it and it was better than any other fucking record that was put out that year."

Hindsight provides enough safe distance from a previous embarrassment to achieve a credible *mea culpa* but it cannot make past statements look any less ridiculous when seen under its humbling spotlight. It was no surprise then that comments made by members of Oasis in the immediate aftermath of *Be Here Now*'s release were coloured by the chemicals that created it, the egos that drove it and the arrogant commitment which defended it.

When Noel was asked by Q magazine in January 1998 whether he thought *Be Here Now* as good as the first two albums, he said that he did. When asked if he'd picked up on the growing sense of disappointment surrounding the album, he said he had: "I had my manager come in earlier with a big long face because the album's been out two months and it's only sold two million. Fucking hell, what a bitch. We might as well pack it in. I just said, 'Go and tell that to Echobelly'. I don't know what everyone's moaning about."

The interviewer then asked him if he was personally happy with the album. He was uncharacteristically evasive. "I'm always happy finishing an album with the band intact, to tell the truth," he said, directly avoiding the heart of the question. "I've listened to this album more than the other two but I listened to *Definitely Maybe* the other day and I'd forgotten how good that was. There aren't many great albums knocking about. I don't actually think anyone's made a great album since *Definitely Maybe*. That was the sound of a garage band having it large and that was great, but you can't go on doing that. Every album has reflected the mental state of the band at the time."

Perhaps the last statement was the most telling. While at the time, Noel and Liam continued to promote *Be Here Now*, they could not have escaped the sound of sharpening knives coming from larger and larger sections of the public and press. Under such a sustained attack, it could only have been expected for the band to come out and defend their record but as time crept on, the will and strength to do so was beginning to wane under the constant pressure and questioning.

"I wish I hadn't written it," Noel told XFM Radio in 2000, starting the autopsy at the very beginning. "Once I'd written it, I was obliged to go and record the songs then. But I shouldn't have started writing it in the first place. I went away on holiday to the Caribbean, and I was like: 'Well, if I write a song a day, I'll have enough for an album'. So the first three days were spent drinking. So it was like: 'Alright, so now it's gone up to two songs a day'. And it shows, you know what I mean? It was just like, 'Anybody got a word what rhymes with bus?'"

The man who once famously said that he could fart and it would go Top Ten had started to believe his own hype. It certainly seemed that the heavy cocaine use and the widespread adulation had convinced Noel he could write whatever he wanted and people would still love it. But in rare moments of clarity, shards of truth were beginning to stab him through the fog.

120

"Once it was recorded, I took it back to my house and listened to it when there wasn't a party happening and I wasn't out of my mind on cocaine," Noel continued in the 2011 Grantland interview. "And my reaction was: 'This is fucking long'. I didn't realize how long it was. It's a long fucking record. And then I looked at the artwork, and it had all the song titles with all the times for each track, and none of them seemed to be under six minutes. So then I was like, 'Fucking hell. What's going on there?' When we had recorded *(What's the Story) Morning Glory?* nobody from the label bothered us, and we hatched the golden egg. So the label was like, 'Don't bother those guys. They're geniuses. Just let them do what they want'. There was nobody around to say, 'These songs are too long'."

"I didn't like it myself," he added. "I wasn't satisfied with it, which is the most important part for me. How can I expect the audience to like it if I don't like it myself? But you can't really see it if you just recorded it. You're still too caught up in it and I was in a situation where I was tired and burned out and it sounded good to me. If I listen to it now, I see it in a different light. I see the weaknesses it has and I didn't see them back then. It just sounds how I felt – tired – like a band recorded it that had no past and has no future. I think that's what we were."

"I knew I hadn't done my best," Noel told XFM. "And I knew I'd let the fans down more than anything because expectations were so high. When I listen back to 'Stand By Me' and a few of those songs I just think, 'oh fucking hell, man, why are there so many fucking verses in it? Why does it go on so long? What's all that fucking feedback nonsense going on there?' It was an album mixed on cocaine. That's why it sounds like it does. Loads and loads of trebly guitars...I wasn't prepared to make things any better."

"I think me and Owen got a bit lazy in the studio" he added, "that's my opinion and I'm allowed to say it - nobody else is. We weren't

121

taking too many risks. In hindsight we should have called it 'Fuck it, That'll Do'...that or 'The Great Rock 'n' Roll Swindle'."

"People can bitch about for the rest of their lives...but then, you know, fucking sell it," Noel added in the *Live Forever* documentary, referring to the fact that *Be Here Now* quickly earned the unwanted distinction of becoming the album most sold to second-hand record stores in the UK after its release. "You'll probably get four or five quid for it, I'd imagine. Come round to my house and I'll sign it for you. You'll probably get a tenner for it then."

Noel's honest self-assessment in the sober light of day was in contrast to that of his fellow band members. Those who made comment on *Be Here Now* in the years that followed continued to stand up for it, as if denying their previously held opinions on its greatness would further undermine the album and the Oasis legend as a whole. Most criticised or contradicted Noel, something that many people failed to do while the record was being made.

"At the time we thought it was fucking great, and I still think it's great," Liam said in the *Live Forever* documentary. "It just wasn't *(What's the Story) Morning Glory?* It's a top record, man, and I'm proud of it...it's just a little bit long."

"If Noel didn't like the record that much, he shouldn't have put the fucking thing out in the first place...I don't know what's up with him. He pisses me off when he says that. It was a great album and he knows it was great because I saw him when he was writing it. He was loving it.

"I reckon he thinks it's shit because a lot of other people think it's shit. He's saying it just to agree with the fucking people who slag him off. But fuck that. Six or seven million people didn't think it was shit and I'm with them."

"It gets on my tits because every side is negative," added Alan White, sticking up for *Be Here Now* in a July 2000 interview with Rhythm magazine. "They say that the album is shit, but there were five people in this band that made that record and think it's great. If people don't like it, then fuck them, it's our album and we love it. Most of them aren't even interested in the music, though. They only want to talk about what Liam has had for breakfast and his personal life, which is wrong. When they do slag us off, though, it only brings us closer together, and makes us stronger, so we are able to turn the negative into a positive."

Bonehead has also defended the album in the years since its release. "I don't honestly think it was shit, because it wasn't," he told the NME in 2012. "It wasn't on a par with *Definitely Maybe* but I certainly wouldn't say it was shit. If *Be Here Now* was the latest debut album, it would get rave reviews. But if you're following on the back of *Definitely Maybe* then it's hard to follow isn't it? The press jumped in and slated it because it was the difficult one after *(What's the Story) Morning Glory?*" Reacting to Noel's critical assessment of the album, he added: "Maybe Noel's just saying that to cover his back but I certainly don't think it's a shit album."

"It seemed like a big production, but only because of the extra instrumentation, really," Guigsy, in one of his rare interviews, told Q magazine in 1998. "The drums were still just straight drums, I just played the same old bass line I always play - top string! Sometimes there were 12 guitar tracks, and a lot of it was to do with some keyboards and things going on, and we also had strings and trombones and stuff. It was still pretty straightforward to do, in that way. And then there was a lot of production just to bring all the levels together, really, with that many instruments going on. I don't really think that we went for too many tricks."

As time passed, some of the magazines which reviewed the album changed their opinions. Q magazine, which had awarded *Be Here Now* a full five stars, revisited the album in a ten year anniversary issue. With the benefit of a decade to mull over its splurge of praise, the magazine concluded in 2007 that "so colossally did *Be Here Now* fall short of expectations that it killed Britpop and ushered in an era of more ambitious, less overblown music."

"The third Oasis album is a loud, lumbering noise signifying nothing," it added before describing the album as "a disastrous, overblown folly – the moment when Oasis, their judgment clouded by drugs and blanket adulation, ran aground on their own sky-high self-belief." A slightly different take to the one which put the album on a par with *Revolver*.

The Guardian, which was just as effusive in its praise in 1997, also looked back on the album on its 10th anniversary. John Harris, who didn't write the original review, spent much of the commemorative article marvelling at what on earth Oasis thought they were doing back then. "Did Noel Gallagher really listen to a playback of the impossibly over-wrought, soupy, completely meaningless 'Magic Pie' and sign it off?" he wrote. "Did no-one listen to the absurdly Bon Jovi-esque intro to 'Fade In/Out' and advise even a slight re-think? As the last five minutes of 'All Around the World' found trumpets colliding with strings, the guitar overdubs piling into infinity and the whole conceit threatening to collapse in on itself, why didn't anybody pause for thought?"

Harris would go on to describe the album as "the empty sound of being off your head and convinced of your own brilliance at the start of the Blair era and the end-times of what was known at the time as - oh, please - Cool Britannia."

The NME also went back and reappraised *Be Here Now* in 2012. Back in 1997, the music paper gave the album an eight of ten rating, while calling it "one of the daftest records ever made" and "tacky and grotesquely over-the-top." While the NME inevitably jumped on the bandwagon to sporadically slag *Be Here Now* off from time to time in various uncharitable polls, Dan Stubbs mostly stuck to the original assessment 15 years after the fact. "So where does *Be Here Now* fit in? Well, yes, it's ridiculous. Yes, it's the sound of two men's egos exploding simultaneously. Yes it's got lots of empty sentiment covered up by strings and noise. But really, this was ambition and self-belief on a grand scale, with big tunes thrown in for good measure. Can an album that includes the epic, rock 'n' roll rush of 'D'You Know What I Mean', the sing-along-y 'Stand By Me', the council estate pop of 'The Girl in the Dirty Shirt' and their most accurate Beatles pastiche, 'All Around The World' really be that bad?"

"I think a lot of critics can't make up their minds what to say about us," Noel told the Irish Times on December 6, 1997. "They're afraid to give their opinion until they've read everybody else's. When *(What's the Story) Morning Glory?* came out they slagged it off, but as soon as they saw the kids were buying more copies of it than any other album, they changed their minds and started calling it a classic. *Be Here Now* got great reviews from all the critics, but when it didn't sell as well as the last one, they turned around and went, 'I'm sorry I said that, it's really a shit album'. I wish critics would fucking stand by what they say and take the consequences. I have to take the consequences of what I say every day."

Three years later, with a clearer head, Noel looked back on the press coverage of *Be Here Now* and delivered a more honest appraisal. "I thought that the praise that was heaped on it at first was a bit over the top and then I thought the criticism afterwards was a bit over the top as well," he told Uncut in 2000. "It didn't deserve eight out of ten in any of the papers and it certainly didn't deserve the slagging it got since. I don't think it was a good record but I certainly don't think it was as bad as people made out."

The truth is, *Be Here Now* is not the disaster many described it as. Yes, most of the songs are overly long – and embarrassingly so in some cases; yes, many of the lyrics are nonsensical, banal and insipid (which could be argued was nothing new), and yes, it shows little progression and a certain amount of regression in comparison to its predecessors. But looking beyond its obvious failings and excesses, *Be Here Now* has some thrilling moments and a number of rousing songs.

Be Here Now was criticized for being a plodding and uninspired record which held the band's limitations up against an unflattering light. While the album never strays from the traditional format of guitar-based rock music – verse, chorus, verse, chorus, middle-eight, chorus – there is some experimentation such as the slowed down loop from N.W.A'.s 'Straight Outta Compton' on 'D'You Know What I Mean?' and, despite being a meandering and lazy piece of work, 'Magic Pie' plays around with psychedelically arranged vocal harmonies and adds a bizarre slab of manic mellotron into the mix – even though its inclusion sounds like an example of the band not knowing when to stop and not caring either: "All I did was run my elbows across the keys and this mad jazz came out and everyone laughed," Noel admitted in Q in September 1997.

Noel claimed that the album was just "pub rock bollocks" when asked about its direction before its release and there are more than a few examples of bloke-ish bluster and trad-glam stomping but there are also some honest, sentimental and even emotive moments on the album which bely the belief that Oasis were at their most oafish and derivative at this point in their career. 'Stand by Me' and 'Don't Go Away', while suffering in parts from the bloated production and Owen Morris' inability to hit the stop

126

button, are heartfelt and vulnerable in places, reflecting the fragility behind Noel's bluster as he faced a growing distance between friends and family, and the audience he felt held accountable by.

Liam also delivers some commanding performances on the record, most notably when 'My Big Mouth' builds on the elongated, swampy promise of 'D'You Know What I Mean' to up the ante and issue a statement of intent which sadly peters out as the album begins to sag in the middle. It's Oasis at their heaviest and Liam rises to that challenge, breaking through the wall of screaming guitars and seismic drums to deliver the song with a menacing "Northern punk whine," as Q's Paul du Noyer described it in 2000, which eclipses the building malevolence of the music.

Unfortunately, after the early promise, *Be Here Now* tails off considerably as the last chords of 'My Big Mouth' die away.

The Noel-sung ' Magic Pie' begins the slide and is a song which is symptomatic of his compromised judgment at the time. When compared to the B-sides that Noel had written to accompany the *Be Here Now* singles, the inclusion of 'Magic Pie' in the album running order seems ludicrous. It has been reported that it was in competition with 'Stay Young' for a place on the record but because the album needed at least one number sung by Noel, the more upbeat and rousing Liam-voiced track became one of the songs on the reverse of the first single. "We recorded the B-sides and then it was a choice between 'Magic Pie' and 'Stay Young' on the album," Noel told Q in 1997. "I sing Magic Pie so that's why it's on there." While 'Angel Child' would not have improved the running list, 'Going Nowhere' from the 'Stand By Me' single would have satisfied the need for a Noel-sung tune and raised the quality level.

There were also questions asked as to why 'I Hope I Think I Know' was included when 'The Fame' from the 'All Around The World'

127

single was far superior and would have fitted the criteria for a fast, upbeat track. Even Noel couldn't come up with a good reason for this decision: "The only reason ['I Hope I Think I Know'] is on the album is for balance because it's quite fast."

It has been said that Oasis were mindful of their reputation as a great B-sides band, like some of their heroes such as The Smiths and The Jam, and wanted to maintain that by keeping some of their best material for the reverse of their singles. On hearing the quality of songs that backed the four singles off *Be Here Now*, and then comparing them to the weaker tracks on the album, it is clear that the band risked a great deal to uphold this reputation.

There were perhaps also commercial considerations at play. By putting out such great songs on the reverse of the singles, the fans would have to buy all the *Be Here Now* releases to get them.

Before the hugely padded-out 'I Hope I Think I Know' leads the album into an uninspired and flabby middle section, the anthemic 'Stand By Me' offers some hope of improvement. Who Noel is asking for support in the song is unclear; it could be the legions of fans he feared might leave him as he endured this rudderless period, pleading with them to stick with him until he could plot a new course for his band. Typically, he would never admit who his plea was aimed at and would resort to self-deprecation when asked about the song: "It starts, 'Made a meal and threw it up on Sunday'," he explained in his 1997 track rundown in Q. "When I first moved to London my mam kept on ringing up and asking was I eating properly. Yes, mam. So I tried to cook a Sunday roast and puked up for two days with food poisoning. It was back to Pot Noodles after that."

"It's a bit like 'Live Forever', I suppose, with a touch of 'All The Young Dudes' in the background – though I made sure I changed the chords."

128

Despite Liam's fine vocals, Noel's defiant lyrics - "They're trying hard to put me in my place and that is why I've gotta keep running"- and the Oasis attitude rocking all over the initially upbeat melody, 'I Hope I Think I Know' quickly loses focus and wanders about for four-and-a-half minutes before eventually heading to the pub, leaving the listener to sit through nearly six minutes of cod-Faces bagginess on 'The Girl In The Dirty Shirt'.

Apparently a song about Meg Mathews and an incident where she forgot to bring a change of clothes and had to make do with what she had with her, 'The Girl In The Dirty Shirt' at least introduces a bit of looseness and air to the claustrophobic proceedings. It's like wandering out of a smoky and stifling pub with a swimming head and weaving your way home in the sunshine. Breaking from the gnashed teeth intensity of the studio, it slurs and sways about on rubbery verses before Liam gains a modicum of control with a wonderfully sung bridge. But then, with the fader once more missing in action, the remainder of the songs staggers on aimlessly, perhaps in search of a bucket.

The mood-deflating mid-point triumvirate is capped off by 'Fade In-Out' which could be what Noel was referring to when he was told reporters outside Abbey Road in October 1996 that Oasis were recording "pub rock bollocks." The song only really merits comment in articles about *Be Here Now* due to the fact that it has Johnny Depp playing slide guitar on it, and not even particularly well. Noel, of course, had plenty to say about it at the time. "The first part of the song is from the Mustique demo with Johnny playing slide guitar in a little fucking shack on the beach," he told Rolling Stone in July 1997. "We were drunk one night [in the Caribbean], and I borrowed his slide guitar and tried to play this solo, and it was absolutely dreadful," Noel recalls. "So he sat down and played it and got it in one take. He's actually a really good guitar player."

"It's going to be weird how that's perceived, having a Hollywood star on the album," he added. "But I'm glad it happened. If he hadn't been around, we'd have had to get some fat old geezer who'd be telling us about how he played with Clapton in '76 and did a slide solo that lasted for fucking months."

"I like it because it's the first blues song I've done and Liam does the best singing I've ever heard from him. I pushed him to the limit on that. I said, 'Pretend you're a black man from Memphis'. He's not got very good rhythm and we made him stamp his foot all through it. He couldn't sing for a week after."

"The scream near the end was the last bit we did," he told Q later that same year. "Me and Meg went back to Mustique over Christmas and I took the rough mix with me. It needed something and it was bugging me. Meg woke up one morning and there I was in bed with the Walkman on, screaming. She thought I'd gone into my drug psychosis phase...'oh, sorry, I'm just filling in a bit of the record...'" Filling in a bit of the record seemed to be the order of the day as the final three minutes of the seven minute-long song consists mainly of Liam repeating "you fade in-out" – which is when Noel and Owen Morris should have done precisely that.

The album then starts a slow climb back to quality with 'Don't Go Away', a restrained and weary sounding lament backed up with strings and controlled guitars which provides one of the very few humble moments on the album. While the bombastic rockers clearly point to the mental state of the band when they were coked out of their minds, 'Don't Go Away' and 'Stand By Me' provide a rare glimpse behind the ego-tripping at the frail nature and privately held fears the band had over where Oasis were going and whether they would all end up there in one piece.

The title track which follows soon veers off into the stodgy territory inhabited by the likes of Status Quo. 'Be Here Now' has Liam spitting out absurdities such as "wrap up cold when it's warm outside...your shit jokes remind me of Digsy's" while denim-clad guitars chug along in a manner which conjures up images of Noel and Bonehead standing back-to-back. "In Mustique at Mick Jagger's house, there was this toy plastic piano that belonged to one of Jagger's kids," Noel told Q. "The opening's played on that, slowed down. I was pressing that one key for about two hours, with Meg going, 'Will you fucking shut up!' Anyway, I nicked it...The piano...Me from Burnage. I can't help it. Mick can have it back if he wants."

"Back home, I was talking about drum loops with Owen Morris and he said one of the greatest was the opening to 'Honky Tonk Woman'," he added. "We played it and it was in the same time signature as that piano. So I wrote the song from there. I liked the Stones involvement at the start and the finish of writing it."

After 'Be Here Now' – finally, after years in the making – Noel delivers 'All Around The World'.

"All Around The World was written before we had a manager," Noel recalled on the *Time Flies* documentary. "It was written in a rehearsal room in 1993. I remember Bonehead saying one day, 'why don't we record that song?' and I said, 'no, that's for the third album'. And this is before we had a deal. And Bonehead's like 'third album? We haven't even done four gigs'. Nah, this is third album gear, man, this is Ivor Novello shit..."

Held back until the band could afford to lavish the right amount of orchestration on it, the song would have certainly raised eyebrows if it had made it out into the world in 1993. The album version is over nine-and-a-half minutes long with a two-minute reprise at the end of the album. There were rumours of a 13-minute version which have been rejected by Mike Marsh, who helped with the mastering of the album: "We never had a 13 minute version of 'All Around The World' – not sure where that rumour has come from? The full length version direct from the ½ inch master tape was 9 minutes 45 seconds and the final running time on the album was 9 minutes 20 seconds but this was only because we chased the end fade a little earlier to run into the next track," he told the Oasis Recording Info website. "If there was a longer version I never saw it and I'm not aware one existed unless it got scrapped and never actually made it to a finished mix."

Noel alluded to a longer version in his 1997 track rundown with Q: "I wrote this one ages ago, before 'Whatever'. It was twelve minutes long then. It was a matter of being able to afford to record it. But now we can get away with the 36-piece orchestra. And the longer the better as far as I'm concerned. If it's good. I can see what people are going to say, but fuck 'em, basically."

"It seemed, particularly once you heard the album, that this was cocaine grandeur of just the most ludicrous degree," Select magazine journalist Mark Perry said in David Cavanagh's *The Creation Records Story*. "I remember listening to 'All Around The World' and laughing – actually quite pleasurably – because it seemed so ridiculous. You just thought: Christ, there is so much coke being done here."

There is a great song amongst the needless repetition, multiple guitar overdubs and inane "na-na-na-na"s which seem to go on for an eternity. Remarkably, the song was released as the third single off *Be Here Now* and was longer than the album version. Even more incredibly, it went in at Number 1 – the longest song ever to do so – and eventually went gold.

"The lyrics are teeny-poppy," Noel told Q. "But there are three key changes towards the end. Imagine how much better 'Hey Jude' would have been with three key changes towards the end. I like the ambition of it, all that time ago. What was all that about when we didn't even have our first single out? That's gin and tonics for you."

132

Bringing the album proper to a close before yet more "na-na-na-na"s drag it out to a slammed door conclusion, is another fine example of the Oasis attitude writ large. First aired at the Loch Lomond gigs in August 1996, 'It's Gettin' Better (Man!!)' is the essence of the wild, hedonistic days it was recorded in and you can imagine the massive party which was happening at the same time the song was recorded. It's a chore to make through the entire seven minutes and more quality control and editing would have delivered a better song at around five minutes but 'It's Gettin' Better (Man!!)' is still ludicrously thrilling music set to unbridled cocaine abuse.

The unnecessary 'All Around The World' reprise then wafts in and saunters out on the sound of sleeve designer Brian Cannon's footsteps and a the door being slammed shut behind him. Many have taken this effect to represent the last person leaving the Britpop party and closing the door on a golden era. Others suggest it is Oasis shutting the door on the first chapter of their story – although, at the time, no-one knew if there would be any others to write about. In reality, it appears to be just another example of the inability of the album's creators to recognize when enough is enough after seventy-two minutes and twelve tracks.

On top of the media and public backlash aimed at the album, *Be Here Now* was already beginning to look musically out of date mere months after its release. Compared to some of the albums released in the same year by their contemporaries, the third Oasis album seemed to have been made in a bygone age. The light that burns brightest burns only half as long and Britpop had burned brightly for the few short years it had dominated the music scene. Now the ashes of the movement were being blown away by the arrival of new sounds and attitudes leaving Oasis to blink with red-rimmed eyes at the new landscape that had taken shape while they had their faces buried in mountains of cocaine. In response to the question Oasis posed: "where were you while we were getting high?" many of their rivals could now respond with the answer: "Finding a way to remain relevant."

Blur had experienced their own nadir with *The Great Escape*, which is often overlooked as another of the most self-indulgent acts of mid-90s folly due to its proximity to perhaps the greatest example, *Be Here Now*. Damon Albarn had become blinded by his own self-importance in much the same way as Noel Gallagher had but while Noel was surrounded by people who lacked the conviction to set him straight, Damon had Graham Coxon. After leading his troupe into pastiche, Albarn had been clever enough to listen to his guitarist's concerns. The result was 1997s *Blur*, one of the band's best and bravest albums. At the time, many questioned the logic of swapping lowest common denominator music hall sing-alongs for US-influenced low-fi experimentalism but once those critics saw what sticking to an ageing blueprint had done to Oasis, *Blur* began being appreciated as a necessary and admirable reinvention.

Elsewhere, Radiohead had released the game-changing *OK Computer* and had become not only massively bankable but critically lauded. It would be the album which saw them begin a steady and individualistic rise to the top and usher in a new era of cerebral rock. Oasis' Creation label mates Primal Scream, mired in heroin addiction throughout much of the Britpop era, emerged from the wreckage of the lethargic and sloppy *Give Out But Don't Give Up* with Mani from the Stone Roses on bass and a thrillingly heavy electro concept album in *Vanishing Point*. If these had not raised the bar high enough, then there was the mind-bending experimentation and heart-breaking orchestration of Spiritualized's *Ladies and Gentlemen We are Floating in Space*.

Yet the real kicker for Oasis was the success of *Urban Hymns*. The Verve had long been trailing on the coat tails of Oasis even though the

Wigan band had been recording and releasing material for a couple of years before their Manchester comrades came on to the scene. Now with their patrons stagnating and stalling, The Verve had stolen a march on the flagging Gallaghers by reproducing their own masterplan. Appealing to the same demographic and delivering a set of songs of hope and aspiration which were finely balanced between psychedelic rockers and delicate ballads, the success of *Urban Hymns*, the band's third album, had helped to position The Verve as The Next Great People's Band. Those turned off by the bloated aggrandisement of *Be Here Now* were finding empathic anthems akin to those which had raised the spirits in the days of *(What's the Story) Morning Glory?* in the words and music of Ashcroft, McCabe & Co. Few critics expected Oasis to have the tools to adapt to the new reality and rise to the artistic challenge of their emerging rivals, but it now also looked as though they would get beaten at their own game.

Be Here Now had killed Britpop and had brought down the curtain on one of the greatest, most excitingly hedonistic and optimistic eras the UK had ever witnessed but it wasn't only the music scene which was a very different place to the one Oasis had dominated a mere 12 months ago.

"The end of Britpop was, if nothing else, the third Oasis album," the author Jon Savage said in the *Live Forever* documentary. "It was supposed to be the big – BIG – triumphal record. Labour got in, Oasis were preparing their big statement...and it comes out a few days before Princess Di gets killed."

The world had changed. The euphoric bubble of the mid-90s had burst and the atmosphere as the millennium neared its end suddenly became more oppressive, darker and introverted. The death of Princess Diana – ten days after the release of *Be Here Now* – had thrown Britain into mourning. It was not a country that wanted to celebrate any more. This was a nation turning away from wanton abandon and self-love, of brash controversy and crass arrogance. Britain had been shocked into a state of self-reflection by the death of the Princess of Wales and as the Britpop party came crashing to a close, many of those who had gotten out alive were faced with the stark reality of their own mortality and their impending insignificance. As if to accentuate the shift towards painful clarity, The Verve released 'The Drugs Don't Work' the day after Diana's death and it went straight in at Number 1. It captured the new downcast mood perfectly. In contrast, *Be Here Now*'s egotistical bombast, which had arrived six months too late to catch the tail end of a national mood that Oasis had helped to create, now sounded like someone telling crude jokes at a wake.

"Everything changed after that, from the mood of the country through to the pop charts which was all Elton John," said Johnny Hopkins. "In fact the re-release of 'Candle in the Wind' kept Oasis's 'Stand By Me' off the Number 1 position. That was significant."

"At this point the press and public weren't just starting to just switch off Oasis but the other so-called Britpop bands too," he added. "After Diana's death, the upbeat celebratory nature of the music didn't seem to connect with people as much as before. Many people wanted something more introspective. Radiohead really caught people's imagination at this point."

Once clarity had returned to the Gallaghers, it became clear where things had gone awry.

"There was a lot of cocaine going on, loads of drinking, we were right fucking up there for *Be Here Now*," Liam told Uncut in April 2000. "We were getting followed to the studio by the paparazzi, five cars from my house to the studio, waiting outside, five cars back. It was like fucking *Band on the Run*. I think all that shit came out in the music."

"To me, that's no way to go to work," he continued. "If you're stressed out when you go to work, it's going to show in your work. So I was stressed out, and that was happening to everyone. That's the only problem I've got with *Be Here Now*. It was better than any other fucker's album around. There was a lot of cocaine going on, there was a lot of fucking hangers on in the studios, and it shows."

"But let's see someone else do all the gear we were doing and go in and record that album and see if it comes out any better," he added. "I bet it fucking doesn't."

To close the chapter on the third Oasis album, it's best to leave it to the man who masterminded it to sum everything up...

"It's the sound of a bunch of guys, on coke, in the studio, not giving a fuck," Noel would admit in the 2004 *Live Forever* documentary. "There's no bass to it at all...I don't know what happened to that ... And all the songs are really long and all the lyrics are shit and for every millisecond Liam is not saying a word, there's a fucking guitar riff in there in a *Wayne's World* stylie".

"To be honest," he told Q in May 2002, "I find *Be Here Now* grossly offensive. I listened to it about six months ago and I had a pillow over my ears. I won't bullshit you, we'd fucked everything up by then and we blew it."

"We lost it down the drug dealer's," he told the same magazine in 1999. "If you're given a blank cheque to record an album and as much studio time as you want you're hardly gonna be focused. There's a pub round the corner and Kentucky Fried Chicken - you just get lazy. We weren't pushing ourselves in the studio."

"Some of the songs were good, some of the songs were pretty uninspired," he continued. "You know in your heart of hearts that you don't get two massive albums back to back, nobody fucking does. I don't even think *(What's the Story) Morning Glory?* is that good to be honest with you. I think that's got a handful of good songs. It was a semi-decent album with a big fucking hit, 'Wonderwall'. *Be Here Now* was aimless. I was glad that album eventually got panned because then it was like, 'Right, the bar's fucking closed, I'm moving out of London and I'm stopping doing drugs'. I didn't have any songs left and it was like this is the fucking start again."

But before the shutters could be brought down on the band's boozy, drug-fuelled era of dominance, there was one last pub crawl to go on...

4.

all around the world

"These are crazy days but they make me shine"

A wild animal is perhaps at its most dangerous when it is wounded. It is powered by fear, pain and the all-encompassing will to live. It will fight with all its remaining strength and with every tooth and claw to survive, even when the unavoidable conclusion to its last battle is death.

The predators were circling Oasis in the wake of *Be Here Now*'s release, baying for the band's blood while under the illusion that this once proud and commanding beast was so mortally injured that its imminent demise was at hand. The media hyenas in particular were willing the staggering creature to succumb so they could strip the carcass clean and move on to the next quarry. Wounded the band may have been but it still had its most potent weapon in reserve. They may have flopped on record for the first time in their career but it would take more than a few critical reviews to undermine the band's reputation as a live act which few could rival.

Despite the battering his charges had taken over *Be Here Now*, and with his knowledge of how persuasive their concerts could be, Marcus Russell was initially wary of approaching Oasis about touring the album. The band had come close to imploding on numerous occasions while on the road promoting the two previous records but the momentum had been in their favour back then. There had always been the sense that there was still so much to achieve and that quitting would have ended the story too soon. But this time was different. Oasis had achieved everything they had set out to do and more. After Knebworth, everything had been an anticlimax even when they were enjoying the unprecedented levels of fame and success that followed. The summit had been reached. All other mountains were just rolling hills in comparison.

"To be honest with you, it's losing its magic," Noel told Q in January 1998. "Every tour we used to do would be five times as big as the last one, but once you get to Knebworth, what do you do? You can't go touring places that size all the time so you've got to step down. It's a situation forced on you by becoming as big as you do. I don't know what you do about it. You fucking tell me."

The climate around the band was also very different. The fighting spirit that Oasis had used to beat their critics into submission was in a depleted state after the mauling they had suffered at the hands of the press. The relentless reporting and intrusion which had begun around the time of *(What's the Story) Morning Glory?* continued unabated but it was now geared towards undermining the band, rather than elevating them. There were fewer triumphant editorials and light-hearted puff pieces on the band's lifestyle and antics. What passed as playful exuberance in the past was now being sold as boorish and coarse. The perception of the band in the media was one of in-fighting and that the special something that had made Oasis such a phenomenon had been lost. Where was the danger? Where was the unpredictability? Where were the rebels of old who had seemingly been replaced by these fame-bloated egotists that showed such distain for the record-buying public by releasing such a lazy and indulgent mess?

The suspicion and resentment towards the media that had been slowly growing within the band was now beginning to wear its members down. Noel in particular had started to sound weary and bitter in interviews after giving typically robust statements in defence of *Be Here Now* immediately after its release. He was increasingly surly and dismissive, retreating from his previously affable and outspoken persona into a more introverted and unapproachable one. Those around him started to notice that he only seemed happy on stage, writing on his own or hanging out with his few trusted friends. The enjoyment seemed to have deserted him, as if the responsibility of being a huge rock star, with the commitment to all those who relied on him for their living, had soured the dream. He had also started to turn on his own album by June 1997, calling it bland and referring to some of the songs as "fucking shit." There was a resignation to his growing assessment that, in reference to an earlier quote, the arse of the goose that had laid the golden egg was now blocked.

Meanwhile, Liam and Bonehead – both of whom continued to praise the record – reacted to the changing mood by playing up as usual but with their behaviour taking on a darker, more destructive edge. Guigsy and Whitey, as ever, kept their own counsel.

With the band in this thorny mood, the concern amongst the management was that a world tour in this frame of mind might be the final nail in the Oasis coffin.

"When the album was finished, I deliberately didn't mention the touring word because of all the strain that it had put on the band in the past", Marcus Russell told Paolo Hewitt in his book *Forever the People: Six Months on the Road with Oasis*. "I thought I'd let them come to me and sure enough, about a month later, they started saying things like 'well, what's happening with the gigs?'"

This response was unsurprising. Oasis might have been under fire and on the edge but they would not be swayed from doing what they had done since exploding onto the scene way back in 1993: blowing misconceptions away and changing opinions through their live shows. The band were well aware what additional pressures and strains they would be subjected to while touring the world and the effect these may have on them as individuals and as a collective but the urge to force the dissenters to eat their words overrode the nagging doubts. It was unthinkable, after all, for Oasis not to tour. While they were contractually obliged to undertake promotion of the album, it was more than that. Oasis had always been a road band and much of their success had come from their tireless circumnavigations of the globe. Their greatest achievements were measured just as much in the live spectacles they had put on as in the dizzying record sales they had chalked up. They also had a commitment to fulfil with the fans – of which there were still many millions around the planet. *Be Here Now* may have begun to be slated but it did not disguise the fact that as the summer of 1997 started to slide into autumn, sales of the third Oasis album were heading towards the eight million mark.

To quit playing live would have also been an admission of defeat, one that would have never been countenanced. Despite the darkening mood in the band and the reluctance to heap any more praise on *Be Here Now*, no-one was going to make such a public statement of failure. They may have been privately concerned for the future but Oasis were never going to give the bastards who were conspiring against them the satisfaction of seeing them in anything less than full-on belligerent denial as they raged across the continents.

For a band that had achieved so much, Oasis – and Noel in particular – still had a lot to prove. Creation were concerned over the sales of *Be Here Now* in relation to *(What's the Story) Morning Glory?* and were beginning to harbour private fears over the direction and future of the band, possibly with the label's own survival in mind. To be doubted by such ardent supporters must have set alarm bells ringing in the Oasis camp. More than anything else, the doubts in the mind of the band's songwriter were the most concerning. Noel's talent had been called into question after the release of *Be Here Now* and while he professed to not caring about

142

press opinions, even a man of such apparent self-confidence could not have been unmoved by the disappointment of the fans. It was clear that many felt let down by the new material. 'D'You Know What I Mean' had topped the charts for just one week and most of the album sales had been recorded in the first two weeks of release, with sales tapering off after *Be Here Now* was released to UK radio stations. Casual listeners didn't like what they were hearing. "I've still got a bit to prove to everybody, because I don't think I get the respect I deserve," Noel told NME in August 1997. "People think I just sit there and listen to a load of Mott the Hoople B-sides and then write a song. It's not like that. I'd like to do something mind blowing."

Suddenly Oasis looked and felt like they had lost their invincibility. To get back that feeling, to get back that confidence, they needed the validation of the crowd and the adoration of those who had stuck with them through everything.

Just as the album itself had been billed as potentially the most important of the band's career, the upcoming *Be Here Now* world tour took on even greater significance given the underwhelming performance of the record.

By way of a warm-up, Oasis supported U2 on three American dates on the Irish band's PopMart tour in June 1997. Rehearsals for the tour proper began in South London's Music Bank two months later before Oasis moved to the London Arena in Docklands ahead of the first dates in Scandinavia which would begin on September 8 with a sold out show at Oslo's 9600 capacity Spektrum venue with Ocean Colour Scene in support.

The opening three shows in Oslo, Stockholm and Copenhagen, were the first to showcase what would soon become the infamous *Be Here Now* stage set-up with its props recreated from the album cover, such as the Rolls Royce – on which Alan White's drums were arranged, a large clock face, a faux pub bar which hid the keyboards and, most ludicrously of all, a huge red telephone box through which the band would arrive on stage every night. The set-up itself would eventually become synonymous with the excesses of the album and the tour which followed.

Oasis live shows had always succeeded or failed on two things: the quality of the performance and which version of Liam had turned up (if he had turned up at all). It was as simple as that. The band were either mind-blowing or mediocre. Liam was either mesmerizing or a mess. They didn't dance around and they didn't go in for flashy stage settings. They basically stood in their familiar places, playing their tunes under a variety of bog standard lights with minimal added effects, just letting the music create the magic and atmosphere. That is until the wealth, the egos and the cocaine started to influence decisions.

"We tried it with the big telephone box and all that kind of shit," Noel told Time Out in 2008. "And that's only because I felt like that's what one does. That's what I thought the biggest band in the world did. My template for it all was U2 with their big fucking super-gigs, and we had to be as big as them, or even bigger. But instead of getting a fucking professional stage set designer in, I did it, round a table, with a load of fucking guys, doing loads of charlie."

"We were just going, 'Right, let's have a big red telephone box!' and nobody was going, 'Hang on a minute', everyone was going, 'Yeah man! Fucking hell!'" he added. "Everything I did at that point turned to gold. I could casually knock off a tune with the Chemical Brothers in less than an hour, and it would go to Number One, selling fucking 150,000 copies. So nobody was in the position to tell me what not to do. And really, looking back on it, I could have done with somebody saying, 'You might want to go and have a lie down for half an hour'."

"But I was like, 'We'll have this and this, and you go away and design it', and they'd come back with this thing and you'd go, 'It's fucking brilliant!' Until you get to the first gig and you just go, 'It just looks fucking stupid, but we've paid for it now so we might as well go for it'. Now really, we should have just got a few more lights and a few more effects pedals and been a bit mysterious, but we kind of embraced the lunacy of it all."

Liam was less keen from the start. Two months after the tour began, he spoke to SPIN Magazine about the stage show: "There's nothing better than five lads on stage, or four lads...or 25 lesbians, just doing their bit, 'cause you get side-tracked and you end up not watching the show with that million-pound fucking lemon in the air."

"The *Be Here Now* tour was kind of like Spinal Tap, complete with the elaborate stage set based on the album cover and the band coming on stage through a telephone box so there was an element of Dr Who thrown in too," added Johnny Hopkins. "It was maybe not very Oasis, but you have to do something visually in those big bland spaces. They'd seen that sort of show in operation when they supported U2 on the PopMart tour."

It wasn't just the props which smacked of the excesses of a rich cokehead's indulgence. Whereas in the past Oasis would just saunter on from the wings to take their places, they were now introduced by a pantomime performance featuring a man dressed as a concierge with a top hat who would appear onstage to excite the crowd, beckoning them to scream and clap, while the opening piano loop from *Be Here Now* began playing over the concert PA. The telephone box would then open and Oasis would appear, more often than not – as the tour progressed – with slightly sheepish expressions. If they were trying to play down the perception that Oasis had lost the plot, they weren't doing a very good job of it.

Noel had settled on a set-list peppered with hits from the first two albums with a few selected from *Be Here Now* – such as 'Stand By Me', 'All Around the World' and 'Fade In-Out' – to keep the interest in the album up as they toured. This, as much as anything else, was the main reason for hitting the road. People wanted to see Oasis so they were addressing the demand but the band, their management and their label wanted these people to buy the album if they didn't already have it. Unfortunately, by the time the tour got underway, the band were already playing catch-up. "The downside of this tour is that we're late in the context of how long the album has been out," Marcus Russell said in Paolo Hewitt's *Forever the People*. "It's sold out in the UK but elsewhere we'll have to work at it which is good...it keeps us in the real world."

The gigs at the Spektrum in Olso, the Globen in Stockholm and the Forum in Copenhagen were uneventful as the band got back up to speed but they were soon reminded of the weirdness their status created when it came to the post-gig arrangements. The band either found themselves roped off from the everyday people at parties, stuck in VIP sections with record company executives and their fawning wives, or barricaded in hotel bars as hordes of fans pressed their faces to the windows. The chasm between reality and life in the tour bubble would get wider as soon as they arrived back in the Britain for the first UK leg of the tour.

The first dates were to be played at the Westpoint Arena in Exeter on the 13th and 14th of September. As the clamour for Oasis was still overwhelming at this point, the band were effectively held prisoner at remote hotels, hidden away from rabid fans, a salivating press corps and the many temptations (and potential threats) a city centre location would offer. This state of affairs did little to improve the band's mood which had darkened on their arrival back in the UK where unflattering reviews of the Scandinavian gigs had leaked into the British papers. Despite this, the band's first photo shoot outside the cavernous Westpoint made the front page of every major paper the next day. Little was said about the low-key performance Oasis put on and there was no leak regarding Noel's attempted robbery on the hotel bar in the wake of the show with the details of his champagne grab staying within the band's entourage.

The second Exeter show was a marked improvement with the songs from *Be Here Now* growing in stature when allowed to flex their considerable muscle in a live environment. Oasis seemed more at ease and this went a long way to improving the atmosphere which had been more than a little subdued the previous night. However, despite this minor triumph, the reviews for all of the early shows were bad with the press complaining about the soupy mix, the ear-splitting volume and the widening divide between the fans and the band. With just five gigs of an 83-date world tour under their belts, the old demons started to appear. Liam in particular was beginning to sink faster than the others. After the second Exeter gig, journalist Paolo Hewitt recorded an exchange between the singer and bassist which hinted at a rapid disillusionment with proceedings: "We're just silhouettes... Shadows," Liam was heard telling Guigsy. "I know this is big what we're doing but fuck it. We're just shadows, man."

After two mediocre gigs at the Newcastle Arena, Oasis headed north of the border for their first Scottish show of the tour in Aberdeen where Alan McGee would see his charges rediscover some of the old magic. "I'll admit the *Be Here Now* tour was when Oasis lost their rock 'n' roll mojo," McGee told the Guardian on February 10, 2009. "Not every date on this tour was a highlight, but Oasis were on fire in Aberdeen. It was completely mental, unrestrained, rebellious rock 'n' roll. Oasis became a gargantuan juggernaut of electric feedback and primal beats."

Loved with a fervent passion by the Scots and inspired by the crazed adulation, the band had delivered the second best performance on the tour to date. Perversely, they followed this up with the worst – a shocking mess of a gig at the Sheffield Arena.

Sheffield Arena had been the venue of the band's first stadium show in 1995 and had been one of the many triumphs Oasis would enjoy as they scaled those early heights. On that famous night, Liam had urged the fans to jump the barriers and ignore the security in a bid to get closer to the band. Noel had described the scene as something reminiscent of a revolution. But this show, two years later, lacked everything that made that early brush with enormity so thrilling. Instead of wanting to be close to the band as they had done back in 1995, the Sheffield crowd seemed too in awe of their idols. Rather than engaging, they were frozen to the spot. Oasis had become something very different to them and all they could do was stare. "Well, that was shit," Noel was heard to say afterwards before the gulf between band and fans was reinforced by the chauffeur-driven journey back to their country hotel.

The policy of keeping the band out of the way of temptation and danger was perhaps necessary given their status but few would argue that the plan to house them in remote hotels was not a flawed one from the start. Unable to cut loose when the pressure got too much, the band became caged animals in the confines of their accommodation. After the awful Sheffield show which created a nasty atmosphere, tensions started to bubble over and while the rest of the band set about drinking the hotel dry, Noel packed his bags and headed off with Meg to a hotel in the city centre looking for some life and some escape from the rising bile.

Even as the band attempted to avoid the levels of intrusion which had caused so much havoc and chaos in the past, invasions into their private lives were still happening. It was reported that while Noel was in the north of England on tour with Oasis, someone was helping themselves to his and Meg's possessions at Supernova Heights. The police believed that the thieves had been back and forth for a number of days although they weren't entirely sure how they had managed to get in past the Gallaghers' security system. Meg had offered her own explanation which had Noel at a loss. "Meg reckons they've been coming in through the dog flap," he sighed to Paolo Hewitt while on tour. "Birds...what goes on in their heads?"

The British music press, still reporting less than favourable reviews of the first few shows, were still hunting for any story which would make Oasis front page news. With third single 'All Around the World' being prepared for release, Garry Blackburn, the band's plugger, the man responsible for getting Oasis tunes their airplay, was concerned that this event would be just what the papers were looking for. Noel was refusing to edit the song down from nine minutes, a length that would have made it a very hard sell. Garry was convinced that if the song remained in its current form, no radio station would play it and it would be a flop. (In the end, the single version – which was 18 seconds longer than the album version – went in at number one in the UK singles chart on its release in January 1998. It became the longest song ever to top the charts and eventually earned Oasis a gold disc).

With Oasis heading south for a three-night stint at Earl's Court in London, with old friends The Verve in support, the New Musical Express decided to replicate their Battle of Britpop cover, pitting the two northern bands against each other as they had Oasis and Blur back in 1995. The article, which compared the bands under a title which suggested this was the new musical battle for the heart and soul of the country, disgusted Liam. "They're our mates," he said. "It's music. What the fuck are they on about?"

The Verve, playing songs from the yet-to-be-released *Urban Hymns* album, made a massive impression on the 22,000 fans who were well and truly warmed up by the time Oasis arrived on stage. As if responding to the challenge laid down by their support band, Oasis played the best shows of the tour to date at Earl's Court, despite being targeted by some fans armed with laser pointers. Unnerved and annoyed, Liam let rip in his own fashion: "You fucking cockney Darth Vader!" he yelled from the stage. "I'll come down there and stab you in the throat with my credit card."

Noel was also targeted and his response was equally choice: "Oi cunty bollocks, I hope your house gets burnt down to the ground, you lose your job and someone shags your bird, you fucking wanker!"

Each night was the same despite announcements being made before the shows that Oasis would leave the stage if targeted by laser pens. Security personnel were instructed to wade into the crowd and eject the perpetrators but with crowds in excess of 22, 000 ever night, this was a futile order. However, the incidents were not enough to ruin what were hugely celebratory gigs. Oasis were on great form and the songs, especially the increasingly monstrous versions of the *Be Here Now* material, filled the cavernous exhibition centre and lifted the crowd to euphoric heights. The concerts were so good that even those sections of the music press looking for a negatively spun story couldn't help but be impressed, even if some chose to ridicule Liam for his decision to dedicate 'Live Forever' to the deceased Princess of Wales.

Of course, it couldn't all be positive. A number of daily papers the next day decided that complaints from Earls Court residents about Oasis fans – "scumbags that urinate in your garden, dump rubbish on your door step and openly buy drugs from dealers in the street" – made better headlines than the triumphant shows. There was even a petition started to get Oasis banned from ever playing Earl's Court again.

It appeared that a corner had been turned and there was a better atmosphere in the Oasis camp as the tour headed to the Midlands for two dates in Birmingham as September came to a close. Everything would have been perfect apart from the small fact that the band's singer had gone missing en route between Earl's Court and the NEC. When Liam finally arrived in the second city, he regaled his band mates with stories of the previous evening. Apparently, after dropping some ecstasy and being left alone by his companions who had crumbled under the effect of the drug, Liam had spent the night "howling at the moon". That night's performance was unsurprisingly below par, with Liam blaming his sub-standard vocals on "not being pissed enough."

After the NEC double-header, the band had a week off before they were due to fly to New York for two shows at the Hammerstein Ballroom. The break afforded Noel some time to assess the state of play from the comfort of his own home. The view from Supernova Heights, however, was not a pleasant one. "I'm on the road for the next year and after that I'm shutting Oasis down," he told NME. "I've got 35 songs at the moment and I don't need to do this. I'm going to wait until the people are gagging for another record. I'm going to take two years off and do fuck all."

If Oasis thought they'd had a rough deal in their home country, they were in for a shock when they flew out to the States in the first week of October for what was essentially a short promo tour of radio stations before two gigs at the Hammerstein Ballroom. They would return for a full US tour in January. The band's reputation after the aborted tours and the terrible and disrespectful behaviour while on American soil had soured their relationship with the US media who saw the Gallaghers as two childish brats with attitude problems. The press were hardly going to welcome them with open arms even if the legions of fans they had in the

States were salivating at the thought of Oasis crossing the Atlantic once again.

As expected, things didn't start well. After fielding questions on Mr Bean and whether he thought Meg would scream while giving birth to a child during a radio interview, Noel stormed out after telling the show's host to fuck off. Liam had tried to get his brother to stay but to no avail. "You spend seven months making an album, putting everything into it, and then you come out here and they ask you about Mr Bean and your missus," Noel complained.

Liam was not impressed. Back at the Hammerstein Ballroom, the Oasis singer was seething at his brother's behaviour – a role reversal not lost on those listening to Liam shouting about how a "proper fucking ruck" was on the way and how Noel was "going to fucking get it."

"All you people, telling him how great he fucking is, you just don't know," Liam shouted at those members of the Oasis entourage in attendance. "He's a right cunt. But everyone's too busy telling him how top he is. If only you knew."

When Noel arrived at the venue he issued a warning that his younger brother should stay "as far away from here as possible because if I see him I'm going to punch him right out." Until this point, Noel had been employing a new tactic when dealing with the volatile version of his younger sibling. Whenever Liam was in the mood for a fight, Noel would just get up silently and walk away. With his own sanity now being tested by the unique tensions which develop on tour, Noel had decided that the best course of action was avoidance. This time, however, both Gallaghers had cracked at the same time and that, as everyone around them knew, was bad news.

If things weren't already explosive enough, Alec McKinley from Ignition, the band's management company, arrived with news of a media storm brewing back home in Britain. Noel had been angered by Liam's regular dedication of 'Live Forever' to Princess Diana which had led to Oasis being roped into a tribute concert in Paris for the deceased royal the following month. Perhaps in response to the criticism that had come the band's way because of the tribute gig – hardly the kind of show an apparently anti-establishment, working class band from the north of England should be involved with – Noel made one of his ill-thought out, off-the-cuff comments. It seemed that most of the UK, not just the Daily Mail-reading conservatives of Middle England, took umbrage to his demand for everyone to stop whining about Diana's death: "Half the people wouldn't visit their grandmother's grave...then they go and throw flowers at the coffin of some bird they've never met."

Despite the seething animosity between the brothers and bad vibes in the camp, both the Ballroom gigs were excellent, mainly because the Gallaghers ignored each other and just got on with it. The songs were delivered with short, clipped introductions and there was no banter. It was all very business-like which, for all those who had to live with the band afterwards, was a relief. Liam and Noel left in separate cars directly after each show with no-one sticking around for the post-gig meet-and-greets which had been arranged.

No-one knew what had happened to resolve the crisis but by the time Oasis were required to record 'Don't Go Away', the US single, for the David Letterman show, the storm had passed with no reports of damage.

The peace didn't last long. With two weeks free before heading to Europe – and that Princess Diana gig – Oasis were back at Ridge Farm recording B-sides for the January release of 'All Around the World'. The single would be backed with the pre-recorded song 'The Fame' plus 'Flashbax' and a cover version of the Rolling Stones song 'Street Fighting Man', both to be recorded in the studio during the break from touring. With

Liam pegged to do both vocals (Noel had sung 'The Fame'), the session all hinged on the singer's mood. When he eventually rolled into the studio after being in the pub for two days, Liam's voice was shot to pieces. Noel was furious. After the confrontation had subsided, Noel took on vocal duties for 'Flashbax' while Liam recovered sufficiently in the next few days to lay down his voice on the Stones cover. Needless to say, it was not one of his finest pieces of work.

Lady Luck, if not the Princess of Hearts, was smiling on Noel Gallagher a fortnight later when Oasis headed off to begin the European leg of the *Be Here Now* tour. After playing to a small but very enthusiastic crowd in Lille, Oasis found themselves stranded. A truckers strike in France had paralysed most of the French transport network meaning that the Princess Diana tribute gig had to be cancelled, somewhat of a let off for the band. They managed to get to Paris by train to make a TV show appointment but by then, the Oasis touring behemoth had started to lumber across Europe by any means available in an effort to get the band's equipment to Spain for the next show in Zaragoza. While a logistical miracle was taking place unbeknownst to them, the five members of Oasis were getting hammered in the French capital. The drinking went on all night and into the next day with the band still quaffing merrily in the departure lounge while they awaited their flight to Spain. A few raised voices aside, the flight passed without incident.

The gigs in Zaragoza and Madrid were like a breath of fresh air. Oasis found Spain to be a lot more relaxed about having them around. With very little pressure from the local media and faced with less expectant crowds, the band seemed at ease and even Liam was relaxed. The casual atmosphere was also conducive to the rabid drinking spree Oasis had been on since Paris. As such, it was only a matter of time before things – and people – started to come apart at the seams.

154

On arrival in Barcelona for the third Spanish date, Bonehead – more than a little worse for wear – could barely walk off the plane and while Noel addressed a few reporters and the others slid by, keeping their heads down, Bonehead made the grandest of entrances. After being dragged through arrivals by a luggage trolley with which he had become entangled, the rhythm guitarist decided to drop his trousers to the assembled TV cameras as he exited the airport. Events went further downhill at the hotel where the drinking continued, resulting in Liam getting into a confrontation with a security guard who tried to physically remove the singer from a desk he was sitting on while talking to a fan. After some quick and polite negotiations, the hotel manager was persuaded not to throw the band out onto the street. Others, however, could not be talked round. Noel's press duties were cancelled after the footage of Bonehead's arrival was beamed all over Spanish television. Not only was his backside beamed to the many millions of viewers sitting at home but the camera angle had also managed to capture a perfect view of his testicles too. While the Spanish press did not see the funny side of this, the members of Oasis found it hilarious with Guigsy saluting his old friend for being the first member of this band of badly behaved rock stars to have his bollocks exposed to an entire nation.

From Spain, the tour continued through Switzerland and into Italy with John Squire's new band The Seahorses as support. After a lacklustre show in Geneva, the band hoped that the concerts in Italy, where Oasis had a fanatical following, would provide the energy which was beginning to wane. The good vibes of Spain were also evaporating. Noel was beginning to snap at people; he was now issuing his regular threat of the sack to members of his entourage without the usual humour and reminding people in a malevolent tone that "you work for me." As a result, those with a little more confidence started to refer to him as The Chief.

Liam was also experiencing a downswing in mood. After the first Italian date in Bologna, he began taking himself off away from the others and could be seen brooding in corners, looking withdrawn. After a lifeless show in Milan where the crowd spent all night acting cool rather than enjoying the band, he had one drink in the hotel bar and then disappeared. In his stead, Bonehead picked up the chaos mantle – and a fire extinguisher – and set about causing thousands of pounds worth of damage which almost resulted in the band being made homeless again.

After a better gig in Munich, Oasis headed east from Germany to play Prague in the Czech Republic. For the locals, this was quite an event as the Czech capital rarely featured on many tour itineraries. As such, they responded to having Oasis in town with huge gusto. A capacity 17,000-strong crowd at the Sportonvi Hala delivered one of the finest performances for an audience outside of the UK that the band had experienced since beginning the tour. However, while enthused by the reaction of the crowd, the mood back stage turned flat soon afterwards as the lack of entertainment and the freezing temperatures outside offered little for the band in terms of post-gig distractions. In addition to this, news was filtering through that Michael Hutchence – who narrowly avoided a battering at the hands of Oasis at the 1996 Brit Awards – had been found hanged in a Sydney hotel room. The INXS singer's death, and the gloominess of the Czech capital in late November, did little to raise the spirits of those in Oasis who were already starting to feel despondent.

The band returned to Germany for a gig at Berlin's Deutschlandhalle but, after drinking on the train journey to the German capital and keeping his levels up right until show time, Liam's performance was woeful and his vocals hoarse and off-key. Adhering to his new policy of making himself scarce when Liam was on the warpath, Noel and Meg quickly vacated the premises, leaving the Oasis singer staggering around the backstage area, getting increasingly belligerent and looking for a fight.

When the tour rolled into the Netherlands, it was Noel who was the liability. The drinking had begun after the previous show in Frankfurt and had continued on the flight to Amsterdam so when Oasis touched down, Noel was barely coherent. Somehow the gig in s-Hertogenbosch passed without Noel falling off the stage but it would only be a matter of time before he was too paralytic to stand. This eventually happened around five the next morning when his security guard Rob picked the highly inebriated Chief off the floor of a bar and carried him home to bed.

Unsurprisingly, the following night's gig in Oberhausen was a disaster. Both Gallaghers were off-key and out of time, the band as a whole were sluggish and off the pace, and the whole show was a struggle from start to finish. The only positive was that the European leg of the tour was now over and the band had a few days off before returning to the UK for a batch of arena shows.

After coming undone to a certain degree towards the end of the European tour, Oasis were upbeat about their return to familiar shores. And what better way to get things back on track than three nights at The Point in Dublin, rightly regarded as the band's spiritual home. The Dublin show on the 1995 *Morning Glory* tour had gone down in history as one the truly great Oasis gigs and with their Irish ancestry, a triple-header in their heartland was seen as a dead cert success.

Business, however, had to be dealt with first. Noel was finding that his time was increasingly taken up with responsibilities beyond the music. It could be argued that he had brought much of the extra pressure on himself by insisting that he retained control over many of the aspects of running the band. Even so, as Oasis got bigger, he found himself spending more time in meetings than he did sitting and composing. Before the

157

Dublin gigs, Noel had to discuss future tour dates with Marcus. The Oasis manager explained that plans had been put in place to add a South America leg to the tour, a decision which would extend the itinerary by a week and four gigs. The prospect of extending the tour after playing Australia and New Zealand didn't impress Noel but he lacked the energy or will to fight his manager over it. Marcus also wanted the band to try and fit in a few more European dates to get to the cities that had been missed, such as Paris, Hamburg and Brussels, before ending the tour in Mexico City.

There were also discussions over the fourth single from *Be Here Now*. Noel wanted to release the title track but Marcus was pushing for 'Don't Go Away' on the grounds that it was a more radio-friendly song. (In the end, 'Don't Go Away' was only released as a single in Japan in February 1998). In addition to the argument over which song to release, Noel was also annoyed by the fact that, by releasing another single at this time, he would have to write and record the B-sides for it over the Christmas break. (The single was eventually backed by a live recording of 'Cigarettes and Alcohol' taken from the Manchester G-Mex shows of December 1997, 'Sad Song' from the *Definitely Maybe* sessions and the Warchild charity album version of 'Fade Away' from September 1995, meaning that Noel had won a minor victory by cobbling together a number of pre-recorded songs rather than slaving over any new ones).

With all that out of the way, Oasis were set to kick-off the next leg of the tour with a resounding triumph at The Point. Except, it didn't quite work out that way...

First of all, the opening night was a disaster due to the terrible sound and the fact that the band seemed at odds with each other. The crowd bestowed great love on the band as expected but the energy was lost on stage and the band were dispirited and dejected afterwards. It had been a lost opportunity to get the good-time vibe back.

158

Things got worse before the second show when Liam was diagnosed as having nodules on his throat. Banned from singing under his doctor's orders, Noel replaced Liam on vocals and delivered a blistering set. The gig was a triumph and after reintroducing his acoustic set from the good old days, a reconnection was felt between band and audience. The intimacy provided by the scaled back mid-section had re-established, albeit briefly, the bond which had been lost on the road to mega-stardom. Discarding the bludgeoning heaviness of the rock onslaught that had been ubiquitous on the tour to this point, Noel had given the songs the space to breathe and the audience had embraced them as if each were sung to them individually, just as they had in the early days when the lyrics could be interpreted as speaking directly to each and every fan.

This renewed feeling of togetherness powered the band to heights so rarely reached in the preceding months and they left the stage empowered by the experience. However, after briefly celebrating, Noel and Meg left the venue early, puncturing the euphoria and sapping the energy from the reinvigorated collective. The mood turned flat in this vacuum and the gang mentality which had briefly resurfaced slowly evaporated.

Of course, Liam reacted badly to the success of the show in his absence. Feeling alienated, the stricken singer began drinking heavily despite being of prescription steroids for his condition. The effect was dark and destructive. Unable to sing for the third night in succession, a reeling Liam insisted that he wanted to come to the final show at The Point only to be told that it would be disrespectful to the fans for him to show up after they'd been told he was too sick to perform. Out of a mixture of belligerence and paranoia, Liam turned up anyway and challenged Noel to try and remove him from the premises. Noel's decision to just walk away angered the singer further and after tearing through the backstage area in a blind rage, Liam finally cracked when he bumped into Mani, now a

159

member of Creation label mates Primal Scream, who'd come to watch the show. Reacting to Mani's greeting with violence, Liam and the former Stone Roses bassist were soon on the floor trading punches before the Oasis singer could be restrained. After being dragged away by his bouncer Terry, Liam finally calmed down and apologized to the shocked Mani in the privacy of his dressing room.

Liam's behaviour was starting to worry some and annoy others – namely his brother Noel. After the Dublin incident, Noel confessed to the Irish Times that it could soon be time for Oasis to be put on ice.

"I'm bored with Oasis and I can't wait until this tour is over so I can take a long break," he admitted on December 6. "If someone told me that tonight was the last date and we wouldn't play again for another five months, I wouldn't give a fuck. I'd go home, grab a beer, turn on the telly and watch the football."

"I think everybody's getting a bit bored with Oasis...I know they're getting bored with me and Liam, and the Beatles influences, and the drug stuff, and all that other bollocks about us," he added. "It's not as exciting anymore."

"I reckon we're losing it. I really do," Noel concluded. "I said to our kid the other day, 'you're boring. You really are. And so am I'. The trouble is, Oasis have just become too safe. Things have got to change because things are too safe."

Things were far from safe when Oasis rolled into Glasgow for the next arena show at the Scottish Exhibition and Conference Centre. After playing a handful of songs, Bonehead was struck on the leg with a vodka bottle thrown from the crowd. Many things had changed in Oasis over the years but some things – like the rule that they would walk if anything was ever thrown at them – remained. So they downed tools and left. The band were safely back at their hotel before the crowd even knew that they had

160

been spirited away from the venue in speeding cars. The road crew were not so lucky, however. Once it dawned on the audience that the gig was over, the situation began to turn violent. Those members of the Oasis entourage that had been left behind had to barricade themselves in the back stage area until the venue had been cleared by the police.

Liam, now cleared for vocal duties, had not mellowed in the days since attacking Mani backstage in Dublin. He was in a confrontational mood before the band left for a two-night stint at the Motorpoint Arena in Cardiff, getting into an argument over a Paul McCartney book that Bonehead had bought at the airport. Challenging the rhythm guitarist over why he would buy a book about "Quaka the wanker," Liam eventually ripped the book from Bonehead's hands and threw it off the balcony. He then attempted to get Noel involved in the spat but, again, Noel just walked away without saying a word, leaving his younger brother hurling insults at his back.

On arrival in Wales, things got worse. The drinking that had started in the departure lounge had continued on the plane and had been expanded on once Liam had set himself up in the hotel bar. Stalking the bar area, the Oasis singer started singling out people and asking them if they were Welsh before telling them: "I fucking hate the Welsh". He then spotted a journalist in the bar, walked up to him, threw a pint over him and spat: "I fucking hate journalists too."

The tour was hanging by a thread at this point and it was not the best time for Oasis to be hearing bad news. Johnny Hopkins, the band's press officer, was concerned that reports that Oasis were struggling to stay in the top ten albums of the year list that were starting to appear in the British press would tip the band over the edge. "I remember thinking, they won't stand a chance," he said as he remembered how The Verve and Radiohead were duelling it for the top honours. From his own experience,

Hopkins knew that the decision to demote Oasis was not just based on the quality of their last album. "An editor at NME once told me that he hated Oasis because they reminded him of the bullies in his class," he added, suggesting that other agendas were also at work.

Oasis badly needed a win. Luckily, the next three nights would be spent playing to home crowds at Manchester's G-MEX arena.

Usually the band would be annoyed at having to be housed in the middle-of-nowhere and driven miles to their own gig but playing Manchester always threw up a number of sinister problems which made the idea of retreating to a sanctuary in the country a bit more palatable. Back in the days of *(What's the Story) Morning Glory?*, Liam especially had been targeted by local gangsters who thought they could extort a few million from the mega-bucks band by kidnapping their singer and holding him to ransom. Although the alleged plans were never acted upon, the continued threats emanating from the Manchester underworld were always taken seriously by the band's security.

Of course the band had a massive following in city of their birth, a city with a proud musical heritage stretching back decades and which featured some of the best British bands of all time. But there was always a dark under-current in Manchester related to its love-hate relationship with those who achieved success, one which disturbed Noel Gallagher when he started to make his name as a rock star. It was this sinister, jealous vibe that persuaded him to quit the city for London. "As soon as I got some money, I was out of there," he told Q magazine in February 1996. "In Manchester I was sick and tired of going into pubs I'd been going into since I was 15 and everyone saying, 'Tight bastard!' if I didn't buy the drinks and 'Flash Bastard!' if I did. I was sick and tired of young crack heads coming up to me in clubs sticking a screwdriver in my back and saying, 'We're doing the merchandising on your next tour' or 'We're going to be your security team'. I hate the way the working class turns on anyone from the working class who makes money."

Bearing all this in mind, it was no surprise that Oasis didn't really mind that much that they were being accommodated at a hotel well away from the centre of Manchester in the run-up to the G-MEX shows, although Guigsy admitted to being troubled by the extent of the security. On top of the high security fences around the hotel and the 24-hour guards patrolling the perimeter with dogs, the decision was made to send the band to the venue in a bus rather than in their usual cars. "It's a bit much, a bit paranoid to send us in in a coach and not in the cars," the bassist said. "It's a bit over the top."

Despite the air of menace, the G-MEX shows were among the best Oasis had played in a long time.

The Greater Manchester Exhibition Centre, or G-MEX as it was more commonly known, had become an iconic venue in the late 1980s and early 1990s, hosting some of the landmark gigs of the Madchester era by the likes of Happy Mondays, James and Inspiral Carpets. Historically, the G-MEX could hold 8000 people but for the Oasis gigs of 1997, the seats at the sides of the auditorium were removed for the first time to allow the venue's capacity to expand to over 10,000. This expansion was necessary because everyone wanted to see Oasis on their homecoming. The larger capacity allowed couples, young kids and older people to see the band for the first time; a crowd demographic which showed that Oasis were now inescapably part of the mainstream and now appealed to a lot of different people, not just the mad-fer-it fans who had started out following the band in search of some of that early 'Cigarettes and Alcohol' hedonism.

The attendance of young children and their families at the G-MEX didn't appear to deflate the atmosphere and certainly didn't make Oasis – or more specifically Liam – tone down their performance. This was

Manchester and Oasis had some bridges to rebuild here more than anywhere else, especially after some of the derogatory comments the Gallaghers had made about the city since leaving for London.

The second night, on December 14, was perhaps the better of the two shows. After a slightly self-conscious fist bump with the crowd fluffer-stroke-concierge (a sign that he was a tad embarrassed playing out this pantomime in front of his own people), Noel walked to the microphone, grabbed his crotch and shouted "good evening, town!" as Liam – sporting a pair of huge shades and the first ominous signs of the dreaded pre-meltdown beard – paced the stage in preparation, banging his tambourine and chewing manically. "Are yer mad for it?" he shouted. "Are yer?" As 'Be Here Now' blasted out of the speakers, it soon became clear that they were.

With the band sounding tight, even at this ear-splitting volume, and Liam at his vocal best, it quickly became clear that some extra effort was being made for the home crowd. "So how's Manchester been then? Good?" Liam asked to ecstatic cheers to the affirmative before 'Stay Young'. "Lying bastards..." he grinned. After a series of duff gigs and simmering bad vibes, Oasis had hit their stride just in time to bring the good times to Manchester once again. And when 'Some Might Say' cranked out and the G-MEX shook to over 10,000 people jumping up and down as one, it looked as though the band's previous indiscretions had been forgiven. "That's a bit more fucking like it," Noel beamed at the heaving, sweating crowd. The camaraderie even led to some partisan shit-stirring with Noel leading the blue half of the crowd in a chant of "who the fuck are Man United?" despite his beloved City then playing in a division lower than their red rivals, who were reigning Premiership champions at the time. (Surprisingly, it was Liam who then issued the call for unity by dedicating 'Live Forever' to all of Manchester.) Few could dispute that

164

Oasis had relocated their mojo, even if it would prove to be a fleeting discovery.

Oasis signed off on the UK leg of the tour with three nights at Wembley Arena as Christmas and a well-earned rest appeared on the very near horizon. All three gigs were sold out but despite Wembley Arena being packed to the rafters, the atmosphere in the venue was flat in comparison to the celebratory feel of the Manchester shows. The concerts lacked soul, as if the band and the fans were going through the well-rehearsed motions. The fans clapped and they sang in the right places but on more than one occasion on each of the three nights Noel had to berate large sections of the audience for remaining sat in their seats.

By now, with the festive season approaching, the crowd-agitating concierge had been replaced by a Santa Claus who – just like his predecessor – tore around the stage to the strains of the *'Be Here Now'* intro before the band entered the fray via the ludicrous telephone box.

Just as the G-MEX shows had highlighted the changing composition of the Oasis audience, the upper levels of Wembley Arena were filled with thirty-something couples out on a Christmas treat with the kids in tow, sharing pre-packaged Marks and Spencer sandwiches while their seven-year olds screamed along to 'Roll With It'. It was further evidence that the old Oasis danger had evaporated, replaced by an end-of-the-pier Christmas Special. There was no tension, no surprise. Worn out by the previous four months and jaded by the response, Oasis looked like they were running on empty. "Even the wife won't come to see us," Noel was heard to lament after Meg's refusal to attend the London shows. Something had to change before the band headed for the US in early January or America would be the scene of another major Oasis implosion.

Despite having time off over Christmas, the return to the United States felt laboured as Oasis struggled to get back into the rhythm of touring again after their break. It didn't help that a number of the early gigs were poorly attended, a situation which really hit home when the band played to just 600 people in a half full Rogers Arena in Vancouver. Recalling their last appearance there when the band played just two songs before storming off after a shoe was thrown at them, Noel mused that maybe the Canadians had very long memories.

However, the Oasis show at Rosemont's Allstate Arena had been a return to form with Marcus Russell professing to being emotionally moved by the adoration the crowd had heaped on the band. It was hoped that the affection Oasis had been shown in Illinois would continue as they headed to California.

Noel, however, was not feeling the love. His mood was dark as the tour stopped off in Seattle before moving on to San Francisco and while the gig was okay, Noel's despondency had started to affect the band as a whole. The subdued atmosphere continued as Oasis travelled to the West Coast but once in San Francisco, Noel rediscovered his energy through anger. Recalling that the Bill Graham Civic Auditorium had lavished five-star hospitality on the band on their last tour, Noel was less than pleased that there was barely any effort made this time around. Citing the perceived poor sales of *Be Here Now* in relation to *(What's the Story) Morning Glory?*, Noel was convinced that the venue was responding to what many saw as a diminishing of the band's stature. As a result, Noel and the band as a whole put on a blistering show – the best riposte to whispered suggestions that Oasis were finished.

The indignant response to the perceived sleight in San Francisco was a brief return to the fighting spirit of old but once the anger passed, it couldn't hide the fact that Noel was swinging between apathy and rage as Oasis moved on to Los Angeles. After a pre-show outburst backstage at the Universal Amphitheatre – during which he ranted about being sick of "chords, melodies, notes, fucking solos" – and a mediocre gig in front of a subdued crowd, Noel spent the next day drowning his sorrows at Johnny Depp's house in Beverly Hills. The edginess had spread by now and Liam, tour DJ Phil Smith and Alan White had attempted to expel the negative energy by hitting the bars of LA. Unsurprisingly, the mixture of pent-up aggression and alcohol led to the trio getting into a number of scuffles.

After recording 'Don't Go Away' and 'Acquiesce' for the Ivory Keenan Waylon Show the next day, Oasis boarded a flight to Dallas for a gig at the Bronco Bowl Auditorium where – by his own admission – Noel would execute the worst ever guitar solo of his career.

The tour passed through Houston without a hitch but after enduring the unavoidable rock cliché thunderstorm that threatened to crash their plane and kill the band, Oasis arrived in Florida ready to celebrate their survival. After hitting the bars in West Palm Beach and delivering a ramshackle performance at the local auditorium, the band moved on to Orlando where events took on a darker hue. Shortly after arrival at the hotel, Liam went berserk and systematically destroyed the entire contents of his room. The reason for the destruction would only become clear two days later before the final show of the US tour in Atlanta when the singer revealed that the British press was reporting that he had been having an affair with supermodel Helena Christiansen.

As Oasis left the United States behind, mostly in one piece, Liam's disintegrating relationship with the media was about to reach its nadir.

After playing the Budokan in Tokyo and the CEC venue in Hong Kong, the *Be Here Now* tour headed down under for two weeks of shows in Australia and New Zealand. The Oceania leg of the mammoth jaunt, the band's first, would be the most testing and controversial of the tour, if not of their whole career up until this point. And it all started with a scone...

"That had nothing to do with me," Liam told Q Magazine in its December 1999 edition, initially pleading innocence. "I was asleep." He then provided a more honest recollection of the incident: "I might have had one argument with a stewardess over a scone. I asked her and she wouldn't give me one. We'd paid for about twenty people on that plane and all I asked for was a fucking scone. This woman in the same row was having one so I said, 'why can she have one and I can't?' Right, well fuck you then!"

"Maybe I shouldn't have told her to fuck off," he conceded. "But on the road, these things become important. You've been away from home for a long time and you think, 'I could fucking do with one of them scones'. It's like a matter of life and death at the time. And I'd lost the plot. I had this big beard and I was pissed up and getting arrested all the time."

Reports at the time suggested Liam's scone incident was just the tip of the iceberg. According to the BBC, the captain of the Cathay Pacific flight which was taking Oasis from Hong Kong to Perth threatened to divert the plane and force the band and their 30-member entourage to disembark after they allegedly behaved offensively. He also threatened to arrange for police to meet the group at Perth Airport. The band was accused of smoking on board, swearing and throwing objects at staff and fellow passengers who described their behaviour as "disgusting, immature and dangerous."

The controversy rumbled on when Oasis landed and Liam started giving press interviews about the incident. Threatened with an airline ban, Liam told news crews that he didn't give "a flying fuck" and that he'd rather walk. He then said the captain who had tried to shut him up "wants fucking stabbing in the head with a fucking pick axe" before telling the assembled press that he hoped "every fucking plane of theirs goes down."

Initially asking the band for a good behaviour guarantee before getting on another Cathay Pacific flight, the airline retracted the offer in view of Liam's comments and banned the singer and the band's entourage from flying with them. Cathay Pacific spokesman, Chuck Fai Kwan, told the BBC: "Cathay Pacific has taken the decision to refuse any further carriage to Liam Gallagher and people known to have been causing a nuisance on the flight in question."

"Passenger safety is most definitely a priority at Cathay Pacific. We go to great lengths to ensure our operations are safe and never hesitate to take any necessary course of action when safety is in question."

The Cathay Pacific incident set the tone for the entire Australia tour. The shows were poor, some were badly attended, the band was disinterested – Noel admitted to spending one show thinking about a pair of shoes he should have bought – and the press coverage was consistently negative. Oasis had made enemies of the Australian media as soon as they arrived and it was battle from beginning to end. Marcus Russell was starting to feel the pressure: "We've only played a few gigs and this country has been relentless, absolutely relentless."

The band themselves were suffering from the intensity too. Liam was constantly talking about killing Oasis off while he and Noel could barely stand to be anywhere near each other. The others were living with raw nerves and over-reacting to everything, taking out their tiredness and frustrations on each other. Bonehead especially was feeling fragile as the anniversary of his mother's death approached and his hotel rooms took the brunt of his emotional pain. He was also becoming concerned about his inability to stop drinking, confiding in the trusted few that he can't escape the endless cycle of abuse. Guigsy also admitted that his own prodigious substance abuse had increased in line with the pressure he was feeling while on tour; he revealed that he was smoking more and more weed to get him through the days and that without it he was suffering from panic attacks and cold sweats.

In addition to their own personal collapses, the road dynamic was also splintering. The band now travelled separately from the entourage as divisions started to appear. It really felt as though the whole tour had reached its breaking point.

Liam was then accused by a female fan of making advances to her in Sydney. Julia Kerrigan said she planned to lodge a complaint, claiming that the singer had followed her from her hotel and had stuffed a used tissue down the front of her shirt, saying: "Here, I have something for you," before running away. The complaint never materialised.

Things got even worse on March 5, a day before the last Australian show in Brisbane. In an altercation outside the band's accommodation, Liam allegedly attacked Benjamin Jones, a British fan who had been trying to take photos of the singer. Jones accused the Oasis singer of breaking his nose with a head butt. A police spokesperson told reporters that "a number of people came out of the hotel including members of the band and their bodyguards. This tourist took a photograph and a band member came across the road and allegedly put his arm around the tourist and broke his nose."

A spokesman for Creation, said in a statement: "We are aware that there has been an incident involving an over-zealous photographer outside the band's hotel in Brisbane. That's all we know at this time."

Liam was charged with assault occasioning bodily harm and after pleading not guilty to the attack, he was released on bail to appear before the Brisbane court again on June 9, some three months after the *Be Here Now* tour was scheduled to end. Liam's Brisbane solicitor, Terry O'Gorman, said the singer would be "strenuously defending the matter".

The Australian media, already enraged by the Cathay Pacific incident, went into overdrive. At the same time, the news was also prompting the British press and music commentators to have their say.

Radio 1 DJ John Peel said that Liam should grow up. "It's old-fashioned rock 'n' roll, but it's also a pain in the neck," he was reported as saying in Q magazine. "It seems to be all right for him to behave like that because he's in a successful rock band, but if he did that in the real world he would probably get a kicking. It's really stupid behaviour. He should grow up, and he'd probably find he'd enjoy life a lot more if he did."

Steve Penk, of Capital Radio, said: "The guy is a thug. It's a good job he got a lucky break in a pop band, or he would certainly be in the slammer by now."

But Jim Irvin, deputy editor of Mojo magazine, said Gallagher was simply fulfilling his job description. "There is a tradition of the front man of a band being cocky and arrogant, and that is all he is doing."

"He is not the creative one, and when he is not actually out there performing, he is like a caged tiger. He ends up in a cycle of pent-up aggression and truculence, but one does wonder how long they can go on behaving like that and keep people interested. We must be getting close to saturation point."

The tide had certainly turned in the UK. News of the Australian tour seemed to give ammunition to those who saw the band as too arrogant, too self-indulgent and too addled by drug and alcohol abuse. The bad reviews of *Be Here Now* had also started to multiply as time had given many a chance to reflect on the material. The songs were shit and too long, many now said, with mundane lyrics and the ear-splitting volume was just an attempt to cover up how bad everything was; the band sounded dated. Noel's house had also been attacked over his comments on Princess Diana with bricks thrown through the windows. Once untouchable and revered,

Oasis were now being cut down to size – and the sight of Liam Gallagher standing trial for assaulting his own fans would be the final hack of the blade.

In his 1999 Q Magazine interview, Liam reflected on the incident. "That whole Australia incident was a nightmare. Getting arrested and banged up. Handcuffs on in court. Loads of Australians looking at me as though I was the antichrist. And it was bullshit. I was outside the hotel signing autographs and this fucking guy kept putting a flash in my face so I said to him, 'Look if you want a picture, I'll stop and do a picture with you'. But he ignored me and just carried on until I walked away."

When asked if he had hit Benjamin Jones, Liam replied: "I didn't touch him." When asked if any of his security had attacked the fan, he added: "No."

In the end, Jones decided not to proceed with the criminal prosecution in Australia but still intended to pursue the case as a civil action in the UK until the complaint was settled out of court. "I didn't want to go back to Australia to stand trial," Liam told Q when asked why he'd paid off the fan. "When we were standing in the court house I was thinking, I'm fucking stuck here. Ball and chain."

"Around the time of *Be Here Now*, people – members of the public, agency photographers and journalists…anyone trying to make some money or a name for themselves – set out to rile the band, particularly Liam, in the hope that he would kick off," recalled Johnny Hopkins. "They would then try and sell the story or sue him or the band. It was Liam in particular who was hounded by these people."

With the court case hanging over him, the final show in Brisbane was a wash-out. Distracted, Liam sang of key and eventually the show was cut short by Noel. The next day, Oasis left Australia, much to the relief of nearly everyone there: "Farewell to Oasis Oafs" wrote the Sunday Mail. "Goodbye Oasis and good riddance."

"It just turned into a travelling piss-up," Noel told the Guardian on January 29 2000 when asked about the Australia '98 tour. "Bonehead and Liam were just fucking out of control, and I was trying to keep everyone together and trying to explain that people had stopped talking about the music and were just talking about the bullshit that surrounded the band. But after about a month, I just gave up and thought, fuck it, if you can't beat 'em, join 'em."

"It was not a great time for the band's public image," he added. "Internationally, we were viewed as a bunch of lunatics who'd come roaring through town drunk, smash the place up, play a couple of gigs and fuck off again. We did some shocking gigs on that tour purely because we'd been out too much the night before. As soon as we put the instruments down, we'd go out and get absolutely shit-faced."

This rule applied as soon as Oasis touched down in New Zealand for two gigs in Auckland and Wellington.

In Wellington, Liam was clearly under immense strain and seemed hell bent on self-destruction. After drinking heavily all day and only narrowly avoiding a fight with local journalists, the heavily-bearded and sloppily-dressed Oasis singer arrived on stage that night at the TSB Bank Arena with chaos on his mind. Unbeknownst to anyone else in the band, Liam had hidden a whistle in his hand before staggering into the spotlight and proceeded to replace lyrics from the opening song with shrill blasts. Stomping around the stage in baggy shorts and an open shirt like a belligerent tramp, Liam continued to yell abuse at the sound engineers, forget words and miss out whole verses until Noel finally cracked. Throwing his guitar to the floor after the opening bars of 'Cigarettes and Alcohol', Noel stormed off stage. The rest of the band followed suit as the crowd started to boo. Backstage, Noel went forehead to forehead with his brother, bellowing obscenities in Liam's face, before striding back on to stage. After delivering a passable rendition of the aborted song, Liam then punched the microphone and stormed off stage himself only to return in an even more confrontational mood after Noel's acoustic interlude. Shouting sarcastic comments at his brother - "It's getting better, man…except it's fucking not" – the gig lurched on until Noel finally put the concert out of its misery and cut it short, leaving the venue before the last squeals of feedback had died out.

Backstage, Liam demanded a band meeting, saying that Oasis should split up. When no-one would countenance his request, he told Marcus Russell that he was finished with Oasis and that he would not be going to South America with the rest of the band the next day. Ordering a lackey to pack his bags, it looked as though Oasis had played their last ever show.

In the cold light of the next morning, the meeting that Liam had demanded was convened. While heated, the discussion ended with the band agreeing to continue and for Liam to remain. With just six concerts left on the *Be Here Now* tour, Oasis would limp on to the end before taking stock once they returned to the UK.

The opening concerts in Santiago and Buenos Aires were well-received and despite the band continuing to drown themselves in alcohol and the brothers burying themselves under an avalanche of South American cocaine, the adoration of the crowds were driving them on. Planned or not, it was a masterstroke to end the tour in one of the regions of the world where the love for Oasis was undimmed by the controversy and the chaos. This was the light at the end of what had been, at times, a very dark tunnel. When it all looked like it would come crashing down, the adoration of the South Americans would help push Oasis over the finishing line. Even Diego Armando Maradona, holding court in a Buenos Aires hotel suite full of models, took time out to meet the Gallaghers.

But in true Oasis fashion, there would still be time for some drama. Liam had spent the last day in Argentina, before and after the band's second gig at Luna Park, drinking Jack Daniels and Coke at the hotel bar. That evening, after the show, Noel had arranged to meet some local fans, who had spent hours outside the hotel waiting for the opportunity to get a glimpse of their idols. Just as Noel was preparing to meet them, Liam caught wind of the arrangement and wanted to be included. Given the state of his younger brother, Noel cautioned against it and tried to put Liam off. It didn't work. Liam insisted. Noel told him to "fuck off and get some sleep." Liam then lost the plot and smashed up the hotel lift, leaving shattered glass everywhere and the lift unable to function. Even for the volatile singer, it was a scarily unpredictable and violent outburst, one which led many within the Oasis entourage to admit concern for Liam's state of mind. With just three more gigs to go, it was hoped that the band could keep it together long enough to all get home in one piece.

The next show at Rio de Janiero's Citibank Hall may have been another triumph but the demons were lying in wait for the band after they came off stage. This time it was Bonehead's turn to become possessed. Each gig may have brought the band closer to a return home but they also brought Bonehead closer to the anniversary of his mother's death. On March 21, on the penultimate date of the tour, Bonehead's grief came to a head. After asking the hotel band at Sao Paolo's Maksoud Plaza to play 'Happy Mother's Day', a request they could not understand – let alone fulfil, the drunk and emotional Bonehead flew into a rage and began challenging all and sundry to a fight. Before the situation could escalate, one of the Oasis bodyguard's had intervened and had guided Bonehead towards the elevators. Sensing that the danger was far from over, Whitey escorted his friend back to his room and prevented a repeat of Bonehead's grief-induced hotel trashing in Australia.

The next day, Oasis flew out to Mexico for the final show of the *Be Here Now* tour. But before taking to the stage at Mexico City's Palacio de los Deportes, Noel had a pilgrimage to make. Rising early, he took a mini-bus to the ancient site at Teotihuacan, some 30 miles north-east of Mexico City, to climb the Pyramid of the Sun at dawn. But this was no tourist trip. It was the chance to connect with something "other" after months of mayhem and excess. The mysterious and ancient city provided the Oasis songwriter with a brief moment of clarity and perspective away from the madness before heading back for the last show of what had become one of the most demanding tours his band had ever undertaken.

Despite the poignancy of the visit, Noel couldn't resist making a joke as the small group prepared to leave when his guide pointed out a donkey which would drink from any bottle you put in front of it. "We should bring it on tour with us," he said. "It can keep Liam company in the bar."

That night Oasis signed off in style and as the last notes died away, Liam and Noel hugged each other at the front of the stage and jumped up and down. It was a rare public display of the brotherly love that remained buried under all the external pressures and personal differences. It was a release and a relief. They were going home.

Asked about the *Be Here Now* tour in an interview with Time Out in October 15 2008, Noel looked back with mixed feelings. "They were crazy, crazy times," he said. "That whole tour was the most enjoyable year of my whole life, because whatever you wanted, you could get two of, anywhere in the world. If you had a whim, somebody would fulfil it for you. Fucking more drugs than you could fucking possibly begin to imagine

176

your body could take, all there, all the time...Touring as the biggest band in the world, and the biggest fucking freak show in the world... It was great fun. I think it was an excuse for a lot of people to go mad...which was great because we were more than ready to facilitate that. But I feel very proud looking back on those days."

But he accepted that it may not have been that great for some of the people who came out to see Oasis play. "Everybody I meet who's been to that tour says, 'Oh fucking hell, yeah, I saw you in '97 in Hong Kong', and you're like, 'Wow, how shit was that?' and they're like, 'Yeah, it wasn't the best'. But for all our deficiencies as a group, we solved them all with volume. Because it got to the point where Paul McGuigan was not meant to be in the biggest band in the world. Neither was Bonehead. Mentally, they weren't cut out for it. Musically, they weren't cut out for it. So to hide a multitude of everybody's sins, we'd just turn it up so no-one could hear us."

On their return to the UK, Noel kept his word and shut Oasis down for a while. Inspired by his visit to the pyramids in Mexico and honouring an agreement he'd made to contribute to the soundtrack of the X-Files movie, he released his first solo material, an instrumental piece entitled 'Teotihuacan'.

Other members of the group also professed to feeling inspired creatively by returning to the comforts of home after the slog of touring. Guigsy installed a home studio and started recording dub-influenced tracks while Liam and Bonehead also dabbled with song writing behind closed doors. Even Whitey admitted to having "a symphony in my head I want to get down."

Even though he had professed a desire to do "fuck all" once he got back home, Noel kept himself busy throughout the remainder of 1998 by making a few surprise solo support appearances on Paul Weller's *Modern*

Classics tour, and recording with the Chemical Brothers and Ocean Colour Scene's Steve Craddock.

Oasis were back in the charts in October when the B-side album, *The Masterplan*, was released. It was a timely reminder of Noel Gallagher's immense talent as a songwriter and also the raw power and frenetic energy of Oasis, pre-*Be Here Now*. For all those who had forgotten what all the fuss was about, this was all the evidence needed to show that *Be Here Now* had been misstep – a bloated, chemically exaggerated folly of a misstep but a misstep all the same. The album sold over 300,000 copies in its first fortnight and reached number 2 in the UK album charts. As with most things Oasis-related, even in the increasingly downbeat and negative climate of the late 90s, *The Masterplan* raised exciting questions about what this band would do next.

It was a positive end to a year which had threatened to be the last in the band's existence. The wounded Oasis beast had survived numerous attempts to kill it off. Now it was time for it to retreat and lick its wounds. There would be more assaults in the months to come. As 1999 appeared on the horizon, it became clear that the band's fiercest battle was about to begin.

5.

gas panic!

"My family don't seem so familiar and my enemies all know my name"

Freedom at last, or at least you'd think so. After surviving the *Be Here Now* world tour, almost a year on the road playing at their physical and psychological limits, battling crushing expectations as well as each other, there would be no guaranteed respite for Oasis from the insanity and constant friction once the buses rolled home. With so little time off between playing live and recording over the previous five years, domestic life had increasingly become an extension of the madness experienced on tour and in the studio. At a time when the need for a complete break from the circus was at its most imperative, Oasis – and Noel in particular – found that there would be no escape.

"Going on the road was basically like going on an extended drinking session," Noel told Heat magazine in February 2000. "Usually before we go out on the road, nobody really wants to go but we have to because we've made a record. So everybody drowns their sorrows by getting absolutely wasted every day. I've been in some of the greatest cities in the world and have just sat in the fucking hotel room doing drugs and drinking."

This was a routine that had also become the norm back home at Supernova Heights during the breaks between previous tours and this homecoming would be no exception. Since taking up residence in Primrose Hill in 1995, the seat of Britpop power had become a magnet for London's party parasites and the cocaine and champers set. Everyone was waiting for the fun to begin again now the lord of the manor had returned. "My house in London became a nightclub and a pretty fucking good one at that," he told GQ in February 2000. "It was constantly full of people. I'd be coming back off tour, and people would go: 'Your house is lovely'. And I'd be like, 'Who the fuck are you?'"

"The bar was always open, the door was always open, there were more people coming in and out than I ever got to know," he told the Guardian in January 2000. "I must have wasted years sitting there with the curtains closed talking about bullshit - aliens, pyramids, debating 'did they really land on the moon, let's watch the footage again in slow motion' or 'crop circles - what's that all about?'" One morning, he remembers looking in the mirror at his yellow skin and popping eyes, unable to focus, with a load of strangers in the kitchen, and thinking, "Oh fuck, how did we get here?"

Even when the house wasn't full of hangers-on and comedown casualties, there was no end to the hedonism. Noel and Meg would continue bingeing in their own company with increasingly erratic results. Noel admitted in his Feb 2000 GQ interview that the couple would descend into drugs-and-booze-fuelled arguments "about fuck all," such as accusing each other of passing personal secrets to loose-lipped strangers. As the psychotic spiral intensified, cocaine-induced paranoia was beginning to pull at the threads of their relationship as well as their sanity.

Worse was to come. "During March and April 1998, the house was just fucking chaos," Noel told Uncut in March 2000. "The boys were back in town and fucking, aren't you going to know about it? It got to about June, when the World Cup started, and it was just fucking horrible. I felt like I was going to die. Not psychologically, it just got too much. I don't know what it was; it was all to do with no sleep, not eating enough or eating too much at some points. Just general lack of looking after yourself."

The years of excess were beginning to catch up with him. The man who had written the lyric 'all your dreams are made when you're chained to the mirror and the razorblade' was now in a recurring nightmare. "I would wake up at four or five in the morning having these wild, wild panic attacks," Noel told GQ in February 2000. "Anxiety attacks. Sweating. On the verge of tears. Constant racing heartbeat. Cold sweats then hot sweats. Getting the shakes. I had a spate of six months when I couldn't sleep." The man who had famously compared taking cocaine with having a cup of tea and who had reputedly sprinkled coke on his cornflakes in the morning was suddenly faced with the reality of his situation. But even though his health was clearly suffering, Noel's own denial continued to put off the inevitable. "'I'm invincible', I thought. 'I'm Noel Gallagher. I can't be packing it in'," he told GQ in Feb 2000. "'No man, I can't! I want to keep partying! I can't just go out and drink water!'"

"But my health was suffering really badly," he added in Heat the same month. "I didn't look well. I didn't feel well. You can lie to all the people around you pretending that you're fine but deep down inside you know that you're not going to last. It's just a case of accepting the facts."

"There came a point where I had a doctor out one night," he remembered in the Uncut interview. "He didn't know who he was coming to see. I was lying in bed, looking like death warmed up, and as he walked in, he's got these little half-rimmed glasses, and someone's going, 'He's upstairs, he's having a bit of a hard time'. So he walks in and says, 'Ah, good evening, Mr...' And he looks at his clipboard...'Gallagher'. And he looked up at me and this big grin comes across his face, and he shuts his book and says, 'I don't have to even diagnose what's wrong with you, sir'. He says, 'You do take drugs, I take it?' And I was like, 'Well, yeah', and he says, 'So does all this come about when you're taking drugs?' and I say, 'Yes, well, you know'. And he says, 'just stop it'. And I went, 'So you're not going to give me anything?' And he went, 'No, there's nothing to give you, sir, just stop'. And I went, 'Right'. And that was it. He just got into his car and fucked off. And I was going, 'Fucking waste of £250 that was. I could have told myself that'. And then the next day it was like, 'Do I want to go on like this for the rest of my life?"

"Do I want to be Keith Richards or do I want to be me? Do I want to do the Sid Vicious thing? Live fast, die young, fucked-up. Slashing your wrists and all that stuff. Kurt Cobain. That's mad for it gone mad," he told GQ.

"I've probably thought I would fucking kick the bucket, but only through health reasons. But I would never top myself. Fuck that. I'm too much of a coward to take my own life. So I was all like: 'right, the bar's fucking closed, I'm moving out of London, I'm stopping doing drugs'," he told Muse magazine in Jan 2000.

However, Noel's commitment to kicking cocaine would see him divert from that particular road to ruin onto a parallel street littered with similar potholes. "So I was trying to get off drugs, but I only swapped illegal drugs for prescription drugs," he told the Daily Mail in February 2012. "If you're on private health care, they're only too willing to dish them out."

"Prescription drugs are fucking worse because they come from a doctor," he added in an interview with Grantland in 2011."It's just uppers and downers that replace the cocaine and booze. It was harder coming off them than anything else."

"They give you things that make you feel calm…Valium and all that stuff," he told the London Evening Standard in June 2002. "Because of the panic attacks, I'd take them just to calm down and space out. And every

182

time I'd get an attack - which was quite regularly - I'd just take a couple of tablets and then it'd be cool."

"I was on downers reflecting on my drug past and thinking 'where did it all go wrong?' And maybe six months, a year afterwards, I started thinking 'well I'm still addicted to drugs'."

To the Supernova Heights regulars, news that Noel Gallagher had quit cocaine must have rang through the North London air like a death knell. Those who had squatted at the notorious Primrose Hill address over the past four years were on borrowed time. Some, however, weren't so willing to accept that the party was coming to an end. "When I first told Liam about it, he was going, 'You fucking what? Panic attacks? What are they? Bollocks, man. You lightweight'." At this stage, the younger Gallagher was still waking up with a pre-poured glass of bourbon on each night stand, ready for when he chose to start his day. Morning Jack, morning Daniels... The singer was in no mood to curb his own ways at this point, even when his own drinking and drug abuse threatened to destroy his marriage.

It still took a long time for many in the party crowd to get the message. "I'd made this big decision in my life to kick the drugs and there were all these people saying, 'Come on! Have a line, it's rock 'n' roll!' They wouldn't know rock 'n' roll if it bit them in the arse," Noel told Mojo in March 2000. "I thought, how did I end up in a room with all these twats? I had become the reason for all these people to justify their lifestyle. 'Wow, I'm hanging out with Oasis!' Sad, man. I wanted to get my head straight."

The establishment's hostess also took a lot of convincing to call time. Meg, who had fully embraced the rock 'n' roll lifestyle along with her circle of celebrity friends, was loath to leave her home and her mates. But after some intense soul-searching and some even more intense rows, the Gallaghers decided to leave the capital and retreat to the country in a bid to save their marriage – and Noel's life. "I just thought, 'I'm not going to end up in the Priory'. A sad, miserable fucker who is either getting high or coming down and always moaning about something. So it came to the point where I thought: 'This is it. We are going to the countryside. I'm getting off the fucking gear and that's it'. At first, Meg was a bit, 'Hang on a minute, all my friends live in London'. And I'm going, 'Get in the car'. The relationship with the missus started to deteriorate. I said, 'If you want to come, come'. She said, 'Well, I can't. All my friends are here'. I said, 'I'll get you a fucking chauffeur'."

For Noel, convincing Meg to leave her lifestyle behind was as much a struggle as getting himself straight. "Meg is hardcore, her and her fucking girlfriends are worse than any bunch of guys I've ever been out with," Noel told The Guardian on January 29, 2000. "I mean it, man. They are fucking hardcore rock 'n' roll women. They can be a bit scary when they're out, actually."

Eventually, Noel convinced Meg to sell up and the couple took off to Thailand together for a month to facilitate the break from the London scene and the start of a new life in the bucolic Buckinghamshire countryside which would begin on their return.

Despite their best efforts, it was not as easy as they had thought it would be to leave the problems associated with London life behind. The doors may have shut on the bacchanalian era at Supernova Heights once the new owner, actress Davinia Taylor, took receipt of the keys, but the Dionysian spirit which had staggered through its halls still wandered free, searching for an outlet for its energy and hunger for excess. The chaos and self-destructive elements which had brought Noel Gallagher to a state of collapse were still at large, stalking Oasis in the unrepentant form of brother Liam.

The Oasis singer had returned home after the *Be Here Now* tour but had seemingly failed to notice. Acting much like he did on the road, Liam laid waste to London nightlife in a bid to catch up on what he had missed. On one occasion, Liam and Bonehead attended the opening of the Tommy Hilfiger flagship store in the West End. The evening deteriorated quickly once the free champagne started to flow, leading to Liam abusing the designer for working with the Rolling Stones and Bonehead insulting a bouncer and a passing policeman. The rhythm guitarist was subsequently arrested and spent the night in a cell.

Devastation continued to follow in Hurricane Liam's wake and in March 1998, he found himself caught up in a raging storm of his own making. News broke soon after his return of the birth of a daughter, Molly – the result of an alleged fling with singer Lisa Moorish which apparently took place one week after his marriage to Patsy Kensit. While Justin Welch, the drummer with the Britpop band Elastica, was named as the father on Molly's birth certificate, rumours were rife that it was in fact Liam who had fathered the child after the tryst in the US. Liam denied fathering the child when Patsy confronted him but she later found out that he had been paying Moorish £2000 a month in child support. 'The week after he married me, he went to Los Angeles and slept with this girl Lisa Moorish, and got her pregnant," Patsy told Arena magazine in 2010. "What a cunt. It is his child and he was paying her to keep quiet. Everyone was lying to me about it."

This situation didn't help to quell the volatility of Liam's home life. He was still drinking heavily and taking cocaine, as was Patsy, and their collective substance abuse led to violent confrontations involving the couple with vases and other household accessories being hurled as well as insults and accusations. The police were called on occasion as neighbours complained about the blazing rows. Liam regularly disappeared on

185

drinking binges and on more than one occasion was barred from the marital home. They briefly split at the end of 1998 but reconciled when Liam promised to change his ways.

"We just had a break," Liam told Q Magazine in 1999. "We knew we weren't going to split up. I was drinking a lot and being fucking selfish. I was on the lash so she decided to have a break until I sorted my shit out."

"There are two sides to Liam," Noel told The Guardian on January 29, 2000. "When he's pissed, he's fucking horrible, and I hate him, and I really mean that. I fucking hate him. It's just psychotic alcohol bullshit and I've got no time for him. He'd think it all right to go on a bender for three days and not see his kid. He'd think that was fine. But when he's sober, he's a top geezer and you can have a rational conversation with him about anything."

"I've always wanted him to grow up and be like me, to be all nice and normal and not to be so much of a fucking headcase," Noel added, with perhaps a certain amount of tongue in his cheek. "And he always wanted me to be like him. He's going, 'You're a boring old man', and I'm like, 'You're a fucking psycho nutcase'. Whereas now it's like, 'All right, well, you do that if you want, but I'll be in a different room to you, watching telly or something'. Because I'm not into chaos. I used to be, but not anymore."

If dealing with the present wasn't hard enough, the Gallaghers then had to deal with a ghost from the past. During the twelve months between the end of the *Be Here Now* tour and the start of the first sessions for the fourth album, the Oasis name found itself cited in court proceedings brought against the band by Tony McCarroll.

The band's original drummer had been suing Oasis for some £18 million in unpaid royalties, a fifth of the band's earnings which he felt he was entitled to since being replaced by Alan White in 1995. McCarroll claimed he was "unlawfully expelled from the partnership" but there were, of course, differing accounts as to why he left. While the group questioned his musical ability after the departure, McCarroll said it had been down to a personality clash with the Gallagher brothers.

Eventually in March 1999, just before Oasis were to embark on two weeks of rehearsals at Bermondsey's Music Bank, the case was settled out of court with Oasis agreeing to pay their former drummer a one-off sum of £550,000. The High Court approved the financial settlement and a legally binding agreement severing the former drummer's connection with Oasis, and preventing any future claims on the group's earnings relating to any of the music he was involved in.

With the case settled, and Oasis preparing to start work on the sessions for the new album, Liam finally quit the booze.

"We were rehearsing and I thought, 'fuck this, I want to be there, mentally'," the singer told Q Magazine in December 1999. "I want to prove we're not a bunch of Manchester wankers who've blown it by having too much money and liking the juice too much. Because once I have a beer I get led astray and I think 'Noel will do it'. I gave it up like that, none of that fucking Priory business – lightweights, the people who go there."

"Noel used to say to the press that I didn't give a fuck about Oasis because of the drinking, so I thought, 'fuck it. I'll prove to you that I'm 190 per cent into this band and this album and if it means stopping drinking, so be it'." He suggested that pissing his brother off was also part of the motivation for quitting. "He thought I couldn't do it," Liam said. "He kept asking if I'd had a drink and I'd tell him that I hadn't touched a drop for about two months. He'd then say that I'd soon be back on it but I'm not and so he's like 'you bastard'."

"But I intend on doing this every time we work now, being sober," Liam told the BBC's O-Zone programme. "I can't remember anything of the last seven years of this band and everyone says it was pretty good."

When asked whether he thought he was an alcoholic, Liam was unsure. He admitted that he may have been heading down that road until the people around him started to make less subtle hints and he started to take their advice. "I knew all the time I could give it up, but I really loved drinking," he added." And I never had a hangover. That was the worst thing. Wake up, feel great, reach over and have another one. But then I thought, 'this is mad'."

For the coming album sessions to be a success, Noel came to the conclusion that Liam would have to stay dry. The decision was made to try and remove as much temptation from Liam's way as possible by relocating to the South of France in April 1999 to begin work on the band's fourth album.

"We were rehearsing the album a week before we went to France, and every fucking two minutes I was in the pub, and every time we'd have a break, I'd go 'fuck that', go to the pub," Liam told Uncut in April 2000. "And everyone was sitting about, listening to it back, and I'd just go to the pub. And then I'd come back, do a bit more rehearsing, and I'd be a bit pissed up, and then a little argument would fucking start so Noel goes, 'Look, if you're going to be fucking pissed in France, don't bother coming."

"Then I had a row with him on the phone and Patsy eventually calmed me down and said, 'Look, he's fucking right...and I'm glad someone's finally fucking told you because you're a knobhead when you drink'."

"So I listened to her and went, 'Right, fuck it!' So I said to Marcus, 'Ring Noel back and tell him I'll be fucking sweet. I'll be sober'. So I went there sober."

"We went to France to record because we wanted Liam to stay off the drink," Noel told Mojo in March 2000. "It makes recording a really difficult thing to do when he's pissed. So I said, no one can drink while we're there, because it won't be fair on Liam. I said I would kick it in the head for three months. We needed to give him all the support we could; everyone agreed to lay off it."

"So Liam agreed to stop while we were doing the album," Noel told NME in Feb 2000. "We agreed that we'd have the party when we got home. But by the time we got there, Bonehead had forgotten that conversation..."

Bonehead had never been a fan of narcotics but had always been a keen consumer of the grape. Removed from friends and family again – his daughter had been born just two days before the band were due to jet out to Montauroux for the beginning of the sessions – the rhythm guitarist found himself in a situation that was beginning to lose its allure. Consequently, he found it hard to cope without a drink. Ignoring the band agreement to stay off alcohol during the sessions, Bonehead took solace in wine.

"When we got there Bonehead decided that he wasn't going to stop," Noel told NME. "He would go off on the piss. I said, 'you're just rubbing it in Liam's face; if I'm not drinking then no cunt is'. So we'd all be there drinking water and Bonehead would be knocking back the red wine."

"Liam was on a drinking ban and I wasn't helping by not sticking to it," Bonehead admitted in a June 2009 interview with NME. "And, you know, Noel had his own problems at the time." The songwriter was still battling his addiction to prescription drugs while in France and continuing to have panic attacks.

After one particularly unpleasant stand-off, the situation came to a head. "I politely asked Bonehead to give it a rest and he told me to fuck off," Noel remembers. "Then there was an argument. So he said, 'That's it, I'm off!' and went back to England."

Noel elaborated on events in a May 2002 interview with Q magazine: "Bonehead was taking the piss, waving bottles of wine in Liam's face," he said. "We'd agreed to be clean and dry while we recorded and here's this cunt booting people's bedroom doors open at five in the morning, pouring wine on their faces while they were asleep. It came to a head because there was an engineer working on the album and Bonehead was doing it to him. I didn't know any of this and finally this engineer says to me, 'It's happening every night, he's getting on my tits'. So the next night I kicked Bonehead's door down in the middle of the night, dragged him out of bed and said, 'Right, how do you like it?' He got up the next day and said I was out of order. I said, 'You can do that to the band, but this engineer is working for us. He's on a wage and doesn't need a cunt like you pouring beer on his head at five in the morning'. So Bonehead decided to go."

The row over drinking had been the tipping point but Bonehead's attitude to the band had been souring for some time, ever since they had returned to the UK after the *Be Here Now* tour in March 1998. It could be argued in hindsight – given his later comments about his reasons for quitting – that he deliberately flouted the drinking ban to instigate the fight, knowing it would give him the opportunity to leave.

"When we first came out in 1994 to sign that deal we were just five lads of the street, there was a real sort of energy in that band," Bonehead told the Oasis fan blog Stopcryingyourheartout.com in June 2009. "By the time we came to record *Standing on the Shoulder of Giants* we were all living in this big rented chateau in the south of France that belonged to Christian Dior. To reach that stage, you should be having so much fun, but for me personally, that spark had gone."

190

"It was a beautiful big old rambling place with swimming pools, tennis courts, the lot...and we shipped our studio out there and set it up in the garage," Bonehead added in an interview with NME in 2013. "It should have been six weeks of pure joy and it should have been the most pleasant album to record ever – but it wasn't."

"We'd scaled such great heights in such a rapid amount of time and we hadn't had a break. I think that showed in the recording...I could feel it."

"It was the best job in the world but by the time we recorded that album, it wasn't enjoyable. No one was smiling, no one was having a laugh and it was like we'd forgotten why we started the band and why I picked up a guitar in the first place – to experience that fun, that enjoyment, that love of what you do but it wasn't there."

"I just thought, 'That's it for me, the old gang thing had gone and it does not feel right'. If I had carried on and finished that session and then gone on and done a two-year world tour to promote it, I would not have been giving 100% to the band or the fans."

"I could have kept quiet, I could have toured the album but I would have been lying to myself and I would have been lying to those guys and you can't do that. You can't lie to the other members of your band. You can't pretend you enjoy it, you've got to love it. You've got to love that band 100% to get where you want to be and that's what we did."

"I have regretted it a few times but I never thought it was a bad move or felt like I really wanted to go back," he concluded. "I was there through the good times and I look back at those days with pure joy. I have the best memories ever."

"I think he thought we'd say, 'don't leave'," Noel told NME. "But we thought...'hang on a minute!' So we said if you wanna leave you'd better make an announcement, and he did. I think he didn't want to go on tour - but I didn't wanna go on tour either, nor did Liam."

"Anyway," he added, "it's hardly Paul McCartney leaving the Beatles."

Liam initially thought that it was just one of those Oasis problems which would resolve itself. Noel had left the band a number of times over the past six years and had always returned. He didn't see Bonehead's situation being any different. "At first I was thinking, 'Right, let it be for a bit, it'll be sweet'," he told Uncut in April 2000. "You know, these things happen all the time in Oasis. Everyone gets the needle and goes home for a week and then they calm down, and then they miss it, and they go, 'Right...'"

"So we carried on with our bits, we finished the album and came home. Then we carried on trying to get in touch with him and he was still going, 'Oh, no, I've had enough of touring. I want to be with my kids.'"

When Bonehead eventually put out his announcement via Creation, it focused on the guitarist's desire to "concentrate on other things in my life, outside of the demands of being in a successful rock and roll band," suggesting that changes to his family life had been the deciding factor.

Not long after Bonehead had quit the sessions, and then the band, Guigsy was packing his bags at Château de la Colle Noire and following his old friend back across the Channel, stating that he was missing his family. It wouldn't be long before Guigs would also announce his decision to permanently leave the band. He officially left Oasis on August 25, 1999, stating in a Creation circulated fax that it was the "opportune" moment to leave with a nine-month tour planned for early 2000, something – privately – he had little desire to be involved with.

"Paul has finished his work on the recordings of the new album and feels now is an opportune time to leave before the band undertakes touring and promotional activities later on this year," the statement read. "The remaining members of Oasis have accepted Paul's decision to leave at this time. He'd like to thank the fans, as well as everyone he's worked with along the way, and wishes Oasis all the best for the future."

Noel Gallagher would later admit that he had spoken to Guigsy by phone shortly before the statement was released and that the bassist had admitted that the prospect of another tour and more time away from home had been the catalyst for quitting.

"Both Bonehead and Guigs said it was to spend more time with their families, which is a bit weird after having about a year off," Noel told Heat in Feb 2000. "I personally think it's something a bit deeper than that. Whether they didn't like the music or whether they felt they couldn't contribute anything more to the music, I don't know. Bonehead didn't like touring, neither did Guigs, so I guess they just didn't want to do it. You could recognise the signs. Both of them didn't seem into it anymore."

"I feel hurt about Bonehead because if he's got a problem with the band, which I don't think he had, then he should've been able to speak to us about it," Liam told Uncut in April 2000. "We'd been in it so long I thought we were that fucking close. When we were together, the band, we talked about things. If I had a problem with the band, I'd say it. If Noel did, and if Whitey did, they'd say it. And I just feel a bit gutted that Bonehead and Guigsy mustn't have felt like they couldn't come out and go, 'Oh, I got a problem'."

It was well reported that both Bonehead and Guigsy sought to insulate themselves from the grind of touring in their final years with the band by blocking out the monotony and the madness with drugs. Bonehead would take to alcohol and Guigsy to massive amounts of dope. While

193

Bonehead was among the chief hedonists in the early days of the band, it was only when the success and pressures took the fun out of touring that he would retreat into a bottle rather than use its contents to increase the high he got from being in Oasis.

Guigsy, always a more insular and introverted member – unless he was talking about football, had always retreated into a ganja haze as the televisions flew and the punches were thrown. It was becoming increasingly clear as the *Be Here Now* tour staggered to its conclusion that such a gentle, withdrawn figure – one which had temporarily left the band in 1995 suffering from nervous exhaustion – was finding it hard to sustain his role as a member of Oasis. At the time of his *(What's the Story) Morning Glory?*-era collapse, Guigsy said: "There was talk of it all stopping because I wasn't there, but it's bigger than that." That was then. The question on everyone's lips after his permanent departure was whether this was still the case some four years later. He may not have been a great bass player by his own admission – "When I first started I just played up and down on the top string," he told Radio 1 in 1995, "Come to think of it, that's what I still do now" – but Guigsy's worth to Oasis could be measured in more than musicianship. Guigs had a much more valuable role to play as a calming influence. Numerous accounts painted him as the man best equipped to soothe ructions between the Gallaghers and a quiet, guiding force when it came to subtly reintroducing the band to the concept of unity in times of duress. Could the remaining members of Oasis continue to hold things together without their perma-stoned peacemaker?

"There was quite a lot of disappointment at Creation about Guigsy and Bonehead quitting the band," admitted Johnny Hopkins. "They were crucial to the essence of the band and proper characters. They'd been there from the start. The fans loved them and could relate to them. They were very much part of the band's appeal. Bonehead's Barmy Army were an ever present feature of their audience at gigs, flying their banners."

"As for the brothers, I can't speak for everyone at Creation but I felt that Noel and Liam wouldn't quit," he added. "Nevertheless it was rocky."

On the same day as Guigsy officially left the band, Noel and Liam held a hastily prepared press conference at the London Water Rats venue to address this and other questions surrounding the band. It was presented as an attempted show of solidarity, which was slightly undermined by drummer Alan White's decision to stay in bed rather than attend. Despite admitting to being shocked by Guigsy's departure in particular and describing the situation as being left "holding a shit sandwich", Noel was belligerent in the face of questions on the future of Oasis. "We have to get the album out and tour... But the story and the glory will go on," he exclaimed.

"Our world tour starts in March so we need to get two guitarists quick," he added. "There might not be a stampede to join us. We have a bad reputation, you know. I suppose the big problem will be finding someone who can put up with me and our kid."

Asked whether his rumoured involvement with the band Tailgunners, former Oasis engineer Mark Coyle's new project, would lead to him leaving Oasis, Noel was quickly dismissive of such a notion: "I'm hardly going to give up this for a band that doesn't exist yet."

Liam was equally insistent that Oasis could survive the loss of its founders. "No one's bigger than the band," he said. "Unless one of us was 15 feet tall, then he would be a lot bigger..." Asked to provide some criteria that new members would have to satisfy, Liam added: "They've got to be a tad taller than me, have a nice taste in shoes, have a decent haircut - and not be a Man U fan."

Rumours had already begun to circulate that fellow Manchester City fanatic Johnny Marr had been lined up to replace Bonehead but Noel quickly shot down questions about the former Smiths guitarist's availability. "Johnny is doing his own thing at the moment," was the curt and only reply.

Bonehead later revealed that Johnny Marr had actually called him six months after the rhythm guitarist had left Oasis to assure him he wasn't joining the band. "I thanked him for letting me know and then I was like 'thank God for that'...it would have put me in a different light, wouldn't it?"

The impression that all the wheels were now slowly coming off was compounded by Alan McGee's decision to shut down Creation Records in November of 1999. With the label's promotion and distribution structure pulled out from under them, Oasis were faced with negotiating an alternative route of getting *Standing on the Shoulder of Giants* into the shops. It was another ominous development in the album's troubled birth. Not only had Noel been forced to re-record most of the album for legal reasons (as well as musical quality reasons) due to the departure of Bonehead and Guigs, the band were also contractually-bound to embark on a world tour with new members that had barely any contact with the new material. Now they were without the support of the record label which had nurtured them. The British tabloids, reduced to feeding off the band's carcass after dining on its plump flesh for the past five years, were having a field day. The Sun published a story that claimed Oasis had actually jumped ship before it became public knowledge that McGee was on his way out the door; a 'revelation' that left the band livid with its insinuation of betrayal, while the Sunday Mirror carried a foul-mouth rant from Liam in which it was claimed the singer placed all the blame on his former label boss, accusing McGee of stabbing the band in the back. In the midst of all this claim and counter-claim, Noel attempted to bring some clarity to the situation. He admitted that the record would not come out on Creation due to his belief that the label was too dispirited in the wake of McGee's announcement to do it justice, but added that – on the whole – there had been no bad feeling towards McGee over his decision to fold Creation.

"I don't know what's going on for the moment," he told NME in December 1999. "As far as I know, we're contracted to Sony Records and Sony will come up with some plan for the release of the LP. So I just don't know. People are saying that we're gonna go on our own record label. But that's just all talk at the moment. I don't really know what's happening."

"We've been going for nearly eight, nine years now and we always had the same team around us," he added. "But with Alan gone this is gonna leave a bit of a void because he was like the figurehead. So, initially, we're gonna be suspicious of people. But we just have to get on with it,"

A month later, in an interview with The Guardian, Noel expanded on the situation. "With two members leaving and then this, it looked like a big shit sandwich. But when you go to bed at night it's a crisis, and when you wake up in the morning it's just another problem to be solved."

"But if it hadn't been for Alan, I wouldn't have signed off the dole," Noel added. "It works both ways. We made him a lot of money. He gave us the chance to make him a lot of money. He left us in a pretty decent position."

"Alan was actually very concerned that we hated him," Noel told Muse in January 2000. "I was going 'if you don't want to fucking do something, then don't do it'. He started the record company eighteen years ago, set out to sell millions and millions of records, to sign the best rock and roll bands in the world. I said, 'you've done it. You've got nothing left to do, so what's the point?' He said that's exactly how he felt. It would be wrong for him to stick around if his heart's not in it."

"To be honest with you, when he phoned up and said he was leaving, I knew exactly what he meant," Noel added in an interview with Mojo in March 2000. "Creation had changed so much. When we signed, leather couches started appearing in the office, coffee tables, and everyone had to be in work on time. Our management had something to do with that...they didn't want to work with a bunch of cowboys, and Creation fell in line, and with that something went. It's quite sad that it ended up like that."

"Creation was an idea that Joe Foster and I had in 1983, and by 1996 we had achieved that idea," McGee told Vice on May 1, 2011. "But back then my ego was too big to let it go, so I continued to 1999. It got to a point where it was just drudgery – like we're all sat around off our faces, waiting for the next Oasis album so we can be number one again, waiting for the next Primal Scream album so we can be number two again, you know what I mean? It was time to get out."

"Alan and Dick (Green) had seemed pretty frustrated for a while," revealed Johnny Hopkins. "There was very much a feeling that [Creation] would be over sooner or later. The general consensus was that it would be after the Oasis and Primal Scream campaigns and I think that was originally the plan, but then things accelerated."

Liam, of course, was less pragmatic than his brother. Upon hearing the news that McGee was shutting Creation, the younger Gallagher went off the rails – and off the wagon. After a reportedly furious phone row with the Creation records boss on November 25, Liam disappeared – or didn't, depending on which reports you believed at the time. According to a number of British tabloids, Liam's wife Patsy reported the singer missing after he had not been seen or heard from for 48 hours after storming out of their £2million London town house. Fearing for his well-being, the papers reported that Patsy had phoned Peggy Gallagher, the singer's mother, with an SOS on the Saturday, prompting an emergency dash from Manchester to her daughter-in-law's side. Reports at the time also suggested that Noel had tried to track down his errant brother but to no avail.

"I was thinking, 'For fuck's sake, not again', but to some kid living in a council block in Glasgow, I bet he was going, 'You fuckin' go on, my son, you really don't give a fuck, Liam'," Noel told The Guardian on January 29 2000, two months after the incident.

However, while he had not been home and had not slept in his own bed since the row with McGee on the Friday morning, Liam was apparently at large in London and had been spotted at numerous bars throughout the capital. One confirmed sighting put him at the Metropolitan hotel where he had allegedly spent a night drinking whiskey with Fun Lovin' Criminals front man Huey Morgan and venting his frustrations. During the binge, he allegedly told a Sunday Mirror journalist who'd tracked him down that "my missus is going to kill me" and that he'd been kicked out so many times by the fiery actress that he'd lost count. He was about 24 hours away from adding another forced exit to the list...

Meanwhile, Creation was doing its best to calm the growing media frenzy over Liam's alleged disappearance and his spat with McGee, just days before Oasis were due in the US in early December to play some promotional radio shows in support of the new album. "'Despite continued reports in the media, Liam is not missing," a terse statement from the record company read. "He is currently undertaking his promotional work for the week in London as planned."

Liam's "promotional" tour ended sometime on the evening of Sunday, November 28. Returning home to his infuriated wife, the mum of his three-month-old son Lennon, and his own equally incandescent mother, the Oasis singer first took a 30-minute tongue-lashing from Peggy before his exasperated spouse ripped into him before throwing him out in much the same fashion as she did the last time, some 14 months previously. Pitching up at a London hotel, overnight bag in hand, Liam reportedly continued his diatribe against Creation and the "Judas" Alan McGee, spitting venom at anyone within earshot.

Responding to Liam's claims that he felt deserted by the man who had made an estimated £30 million off Oasis, Noel said a few days after the storm had died down: "I know for a fact he just said all that for effect, because I know he wasn't upset with Alan when he left. I don't know why he's saying he's broken-hearted because to be broken-hearted you have to have a heart, and he hasn't. He might think he does. He's got a soul, but he's not got a heart."

Two weeks after the alleged row which led to Liam spiralling out of control, Alan McGee spoke to NME about his relationship with the Oasis singer, the decision to quit Creation Records and his plans for the future. McGee told NME that he'd patched up any problems with Liam after the singer had told the Sunday Mirror that he "hated" him.

"I've spoken to him since then and that's not the situation," said McGee. "Liam's an emotional guy, that's why I love him. He was upset at first that I was going, but I spoke to him that weekend and we're 100% cool with each other. I'm sure that if you speak to him now he's totally accepted it."

Many years later, McGee attributed Liam's reaction to the fact that the Oasis singer had been under his charge from the tender age of 21 and that he'd developed an almost paternal bond with the younger Gallagher. "There was quite a gap in our ages and perhaps he found it helpful to have me around as a sort of father figure," McGee mused in an interview in the

200

Irish Post on January 3, 2014. "I hadn't meant to hurt anyone and I'm sorry if I did. But I never promised to be anyone's dad."

"Alan would have been concerned [about telling Oasis about shutting down Creation]," admitted Johnny Hopkins. "They were friends and he respected them. But he squared the situation with them. They had a strong relationship and he had always been honest with them. They trusted him. I think they were disappointed because he and Creation had been a big part of their success but they would have understood his reasons. So I think Alan is right when he says Liam's outburst was blown out of proportion by the media."

As the days turned into weeks and then months, some corners of the press started to make connections between the sales performance of *Be Here Now* and the collapse of Creation. Not content with charging the band with the murder of Britpop, the media were now accusing Oasis and their much-maligned third album of killing off the record company which signed them.

With Oasis in turmoil, some sections of the press were already championing the band's potential usurpers. Scottish band Travis, who had supported Oasis in 1997, and an up-and-coming young band called Coldplay were being set up in the media for a Blur-Oasis style Battle of the Bands as the Nineties came to a close. Oasis, the band which had defined the decade, were no longer considered worthy to be included in music press debates over who should hold the "biggest band in Britain" title. Many observers considered it only a matter of time before the events that had rocked Oasis over the previous 18 months irrevocably cracked the band's foundations and led to a final collapse.

6.

who feels love

"Found what I lost inside...my spirit has been purified"

While Noel saw his trip to Thailand with Meg as a chance to reconnect with his wife and to kick-start the process of recovering from years of cocaine abuse, the month-long break also gave him the opportunity to consider his musical future with a returning sense of clarity. The panic attacks would continue and his use of prescription drugs to manage the crippling anxiety would escalate over time but the initial decision to get back on track had been made and such a positive step infused Noel with a rare sense of purpose that he hadn't felt for what felt like years.

"You become very emotionally stunted when you're on drugs, particularly on coke," he told Heat in February 2000. "With the last bunch of albums when I would eventually come to write the lyrics, I would write any old shit that rhymed really."

"I'd come to the end," he told Grantland in 2000. "At the time, I had no reason or desire to make music. I had no drive. We'd sold all these fucking records and there just seemed to be no point. I'd lost the inspiration to work and be in a band. I'd forgotten who I was."

Wary of repeating the mistake he'd made with *Be Here Now*, that of making a record as a means to keeping the band together and paying for their lifestyles, Noel was reluctant at first to consider a new Oasis album. His initial thoughts were to go on hiatus, to let the wounds heal and to allow the public and the fans to start missing Oasis before they roared back in from the edge of oblivion. But while he was considering retreating entirely, he was given some encouragement from his younger brother.

202

"Strangely it was Liam, to his credit, who was like, 'we're going to make a record, we're going into the studio next month, and you better have some fucking songs written'," he told Grantland in 2000. "So I went ahead and did it, even though I had no inspiration and couldn't find inspiration anywhere. I just wrote songs for the sake of making an album." Noel struggled at first to make any headway on the few ideas he had for the next batch of songs and the embryonic demos that he laid down at Supernova Heights did little to stoke his creative fires.

Once in Thailand, however, the fog started to slowly clear and Noel began thinking about writing songs again. Just as the decision to quit coke and leave London had set Noel on a long journey back to himself, so this forced return to song writing was a first step to rekindling his passion for his art. The longer Noel was in Thailand, the more inspiration seemed to seek him out. "We went round all these little villages, with monks everywhere – not like the ones in Robin Hood, but proper skinhead monks in the orange gear – and we met some very spiritual people," Noel remembered. "I don't think I was really affected by that in itself, but it created a sense of well-being for me." That well-being and the calm which emanated from the Buddhist temples that he and Meg visited started to seep into the sketches of songs that Noel had brought with him on his Asian adventure. Slowly he began to gain a new perspective and the embers of creativity began smoulder once more.

"Before, I would create something to justify staying up for three days doing drugs; now it's like I create something purely because I like being creative," he told Uncut in 2000. "Whereas before we'd make records to go on the road and have a good time - so you could justify blowing 25 grand a month on drugs and lavish parties: 'It's all right because I'm a pop star! And I'll buy a stupid fucking outfit, because I'm a rock star!' Now it's like you're creating something because that's what you do...you're a creative person."

On his return to the UK, Noel continued to work on the new batch of songs, delving into his past experiences with Oasis for further inspiration. The new material was beginning to take on a very personal feel as the songwriter began exploring themes such as celebrity culture, charlatanism, loss of identity and rebirth. By channelling some of his bleakest moments of recent times, coupled with his developing addiction to Valium, the new songs started to take on a darker atmosphere than any other Oasis material that Noel had produced before.

"It's a lot more personal," Noel told GQ in February 2000. "There are certain songs that actually put into words what I was feeling at the time of writing. When you actually read the words there's something a little bit deeper which points a few things out so that people go, 'Well, I never knew that'."

Tracks which would make it onto the album, such as 'Sunday Morning Call' and 'Where Did It All Go Wrong?', dealt with the phonies and fakes who would treat Supernova Heights as a drop-in centre; the rich and famous people who would turn up in Noel's kitchen at ungodly hours of the morning to moan about their drug and booze hell as if they were on the psychiatrist's couch. "If you don't want to do it any more, then don't do it," Noel said in an interview with Uncut in 2000. "But for fuck's sake don't spend 20 grand trying to kick a habit that you can just kick by looking in the mirror and saying to yourself, 'Where did all this go wrong, man?' That's basically what those songs are about."

Others such as 'Gas Panic!' were more personal, dealing with his own drug problems and the panic attacks that had plagued him since mid-1998. "That song is about when the demons come to visit you in the middle of the night," he continued in Uncut. "If I can get pretentious for a minute,

204

'Gas Panic!' was the chosen name for the ghosts that came knocking on my window at five in the morning when my panic attacks were coming on. It was some sort of therapy. Usually I'd wake Meg up and she'd have to talk me through the night but this one time, I woke up drenched in sweat and she didn't wake up so I grabbed my guitar and just got it all out."

With the lyrics developing along almost confessional lines and the musical arrangements taking on a more experimental feel, the new Oasis material was shaping up to be quite a departure – a move that many observers felt would either make or break the band after the bombastic over-indulgence of *Be Here Now* which had alienated some fans and provided plenty of ammunition for their detractors.

"It's up to new bands to be writing all these 'life's fucking great, it's fucking mega' type of songs," Liam told Uncut in April 2000. "They don't know what's coming. When you've seen the shit we've seen...they don't know that if they get to where we were, that it can get a bit shitty. So that's for them to be writing the anthems. We're where we are now, and life's a bit shit sometimes because of what's going on, and that's coming out in the music. And all you can write is how you feel. And that's how Noel's obviously feeling."

"Most of the album is about me looking in the mirror and going, 'how the fuck did I end up in a room with a bunch of actors and supermodels? And politicians!' All that fucking bullshit," Noel told the Independent on January 22, 2000.

"I think Noel lyrically was searching for something deeper," producer Spike Stent said in the documentary which accompanied the release of *Standing on the Shoulder of Giants* in 2000. "They'd done 'Champagne Supernova', they'd proved they could do that so with this album we wanted to try new things and experimentation was encouraged throughout."

In a further break from the past, Noel had decided to drop the equipment used in the three previous albums and instead buy "loads of really weird pedals, old guitars, and small amps." Working to his own schedule with less pressure to deliver to any particular deadline, Noel spent a number of days "just messing around" with new sounds and effects in an attempt to bring something different to the material.

"I had a full year to sit in my 16-track bedroom studio with an engineer friend and make demos for this album, whereas the demo sessions for *Be Here Now* were finished in two weeks -- and they were really rough," Noel told Guitarist magazine in 2000. "This time I had basically done the album twice before it even got to the band. I had written and recorded the songs on a little Walkman, and then I demoed the tracks in my bedroom. And we ended up using a lot of stuff from the demos on the actual record because the demos were that good."

"For the other albums, I'd write a song on the guitar and before I'd record it I'd play it to people and sing it, so everyone would form their opinion on it straight away," Noel told Uncut in March 2000. "This time I didn't play anything to anyone for about six months. It was like, 'I'm not going to play it to anyone until I'm happy with it'."

"This album was written more in the spirit of the first one," he added. "The middle two are a bit of a haze - I can't remember much about them. The first one I had a lot of time to write it and a lot of time to throw stuff away, whereas the middle two were like, 'We need a record out because this thing is happening and we might as well capitalise on it'."

"*Definitely Maybe* was the young, eager, wanting to get out there and fucking blow the world away album," Noel said. "The second one was stopping in the lay-by where you catch your breath before you head off down the superstardom highway. And the third one was just fucking fat and drunk. And this one is clean, healthy, focused."

"Before 1997, I hadn't written a song without the aid of the old Colombian marching gear," Noel told SPIN in October 2008. "The whole of the first three albums were written on drugs. I remember being off my nut and going into the back room and setting the goal of writing a song in ten minutes. That was 'Supersonic'. All those albums and all the B-sides were written on drugs. That's why they're so good. And that pisses me off. I think, 'Maybe I should get back into taking drugs, and then it would be brilliant again' But that thought lasts less than a second."

"It's like being in a fucking blizzard when you're out of it all the time," Noel told The Independent on January 22, 2000. "You can't function, you can't focus, and you get lazy. You just do the first thing that comes natural to you because doing work, writing music and recording music, is a chore. It gets in the way of the party. Whereas this time, fuck, all that shit's out of the way, let's go make some music, man."

The result was surprising to all those who were allowed to hear the embryonic tracks. "When I first started playing the demos to people round at the house, they'd go, 'Are you sure you're not on drugs?' And I'm like, 'I'm telling you', and they're going, 'Because it's proper psychedelic, man'," Noel told Uncut. "Even at the early stages it was quite psychedelic. Even McGee was going, 'You wouldn't have thought you'd given up fucking powder, man'."

"What is fucking psychedelic anyway?" questioned Liam in an NME interview from February 2000. "You'd be too off your head to know you'd even hit the psychedelic period. If you're psychedelic you've got to be off your twat anyway. I certainly don't think The Beatles knew when they were being psychedelic, they probably think *Sergeant Pepper* is a punk album."

For Noel as a songwriter, to take a slightly different direction and approach to the material was also a necessary step in what had been, until then, a stunted evolution since his prolific pre-*Definitely Maybe* days. But he harboured private fears over whether the band could do justice to the new songs and provide enough quality to make the next album the success Oasis so badly needed. As the band convened for the sessions in France, Noel began to have his doubts that Bonehead and Guigsy could handle the compositions. Both had done sterling work on the band's previous three albums but had never been asked to do anything more than they were capable of doing. The material which was forming for the new album, to be called *Standing on the Shoulder of Giants*, would challenge everyone involved, even the person who conceived the songs. "Stuff like 'Gas Panic!' and 'Who Feels Love', I couldn't even get me head round those and I wrote them," Noel admitted in NME in February 2000. "There are bits of lead guitar on there that I haven't played. I haven't got a problem with passing people like Mark Coyle a guitar and saying, 'Go on then'."

"We were working with a different producer this time as well [Mark 'Spike' Stent], who was brilliant for us," Noel added in Uncut in 2000. "Owen [Morris, erstwhile producer] would never say to anyone in the studio, like to Bonehead or Guigs, 'It's not really working what you're playing, so let Noel play it'. And we'd never say that to each other because we might get the fucking needle, whereas Spike would just say, 'It's just not happening, man; it's obvious you can't do it so why don't you do it?' and I'd be like, 'Oh, right, well, I'll do it'. There was a bit of that going on."

As mentioned previously, Bonehead's refusal to adhere to the drinking ban at Château de la Colle Noire and later the confession that he and Guigs wanted to spend more time with their families were both cited as the reasons for the rhythm guitarist and the bass player leaving the band. In hindsight, Noel wondered if the discontent that finally forced their hands came from the new material; either because they didn't like it or that they felt that they were being marginalised because they weren't up to scratch.

In the end, it didn't matter. For legal – and possibly musical reasons – much of *Standing on the Shoulder of Giants* had to be re-recorded.

"To be honest, Guigs didn't play on the record but Bonehead's probably there somewhere," Noel told NME. "I played bass on six tracks. Guigs, by his own admission, wasn't the best bass guitarist in the world and he used to get away with it. It doesn't fill me with pride saying they didn't play on the album but Guigs just wasn't good enough."

The man Oasis recruited to make this new music with them was Mark 'Spike' Stent, a pioneering producer whose reputation for sonic experimentation surely helped land him the gig. Noel was also attracted by Stent's respected work ethic and sobriety, especially after the excesses of the unhinged free-for-all of *Be Here Now*.

"Spike was brilliant, because he doesn't take drugs and he rarely drinks; he doesn't join in when the party's going off, he's proper on the fucking case," Noel told Uncut in March 2000. "Whereas Owen, if we were getting pissed, would be getting pissed as well and it would end up this loud fucking din in the studio and you couldn't really make head nor tail of anything because the guitars would be double loud. Spike was brilliant because he'd just say, 'You just all go off to the pub and I'll sort this out'."

"Working with Spike was crucial, because he'd worked with Massive Attack and U2 - who I consider to be contemporary musicians," he added. "We said to him, 'Here's the fucking demos, can you make this sound contemporary because otherwise we'll turn it up and it'll be just a rock 'n' roll record?' And because the rest of the guys don't go out or go to gigs, I would go, 'You know that sound that's on that record by that band?' And Spike would pull it straight out of the fucking sky."

At a time when Oasis required something other than the Owen Morris 'brick wall' method of everything cranked up in the mix, Stent seemed tailor-made for the job of adding subtlety and colour. Morris had saved *Definitely Maybe* with his mixing of Noel and Mark Coyle's production efforts and had brought depth and power to the potentially lightweight *(What's the Story) Morning Glory?* material but he as much as anyone had been to blame for the overly-dense and undisciplined production on *Be Here Now*. The new songs would need to have space to breathe and while Spike Stent added backing singers, organs and a whole orchestra of foreign noises to *Standing on the Shoulder of Giants*, he managed to produce richness without the need to layer on track upon track of superfluous noise.

With the album finished, the next issue the remaining members of Oasis had to face was how – and if – the band would continue. After the departure of Bonehead and Guigsy, speculation about the future of Oasis started to circulate in the media with many observers convinced that the band would soon announce its demise. Despite the shock of seeing two founding members of Oasis pack their bags, Noel was less concerned than his adversaries in the press would have the public believe.

"It was a problem for that one night," Noel told MTV USA in 2000. "The next day I woke up and I'd already worked out what we were going to do. You know, other people in the band were flapping a bit. But you know these things; it was a crisis on a Monday night, and on Tuesday morning it was just a problem. It was no big thing in the end."

"I would have preferred it if Guigs and Bonehead had decided that they were going to leave before we went and recorded the album, because that would've made things a lot easier but there you go."

"We've had a hiccup and we never thought something like that would happen to us," Liam told the *Standing on the Shoulder of Giants* documentary in 2000. "We didn't think that two members of the band would leave. We thought we would be in it together forever. I'm sure they

210

thought hard about it before leaving just as we thought hard about getting two new members in and carrying on."

After Noel and Liam's press conference in London, during which they assured the press that "the story and the glory would go on," the brothers began searching for replacements for Bonehead and Guigsy.

"Johnny Marr would be good, but he's started his own band," Noel reiterated in an interview with Melody Maker on September 5 1999, when asked about his ideal recruits. "The obvious choices are Nick McCabe and Simon Jones from The Verve."

However, Noel admitted the dream team would probably not work out: "I don't think they would be right," he added. "People have to want to do it. People have to be into all the old songs and the news songs. But we've got time. We're not panicking yet."

"People were talking about Johnny Marr and fucking Aziz (Ibrahim, John Squire's replacement) out of fucking Stone Roses," Liam told Uncut in April 2000. "I don't fucking think so. You know what I mean? If you can't get it together in The Stone Roses, what fucking chance have you of getting it together in fucking Oasis? And Nick McCabe, it's the same for him. If he can't get it together in his own fucking band, he's got no chance of fucking getting it together in ours."

Hiring a new guitarist would prove the simpler of the two tasks. Noel already had Gem Archer, the guitarist and singer of Creation label mates Heavy Stereo, in mind. "In the case of replacing Bonehead, that was quite easy because I'd known Gem for a while," Noel told XFM on January 24th 2000. "I knew that he wasn't doing anything because his band had been dropped a couple of years before. So I just phoned him up. And we didn't even bother rehearsing him or doing the audition thing because we were fans of Heavy Stereo anyway, and so we knew he could play. So that was that sort of boxed off within a matter of days."

"We said 'we know what you can do, don't play what Bonehead played…do what you do and if it's a bit over the top, we'll stop you'," Liam said about recruiting Gem in the *Standing on the Shoulder of Giants* documentary. "'If you want to put your own stuff into the old songs, stuff you can hear, that's cool…if it's good we'll keep it in'."

"This is the only band that I would ever leave mine for," Gem told Guitarist magazine in 2000. "I was, and still am, a huge Oasis fan and so to join was so stupid a concept that it seemed quite rational."

"I know why he chose me," Gem added in a 1999 Q magazine interview. "Because I'm a boring studio boffin. I bring an appreciation of recording hardware which Noel likes. When I'm rattling on about some dodgy Limiter, Noel's eyes light up."

Finding a new bass player would prove to be a little more problematic. "In the case of replacing Guigs, that took about two months because we went through the audition stage with about six or seven bass players," Noel told XFM. "Some of them are currently in pretty successful bands and they sort of came down on the sly, under the cover of darkness and all that stuff, and they were saying: 'Oh if my band ever find out I'm here, I'm going to get kicked out'. So we can't say who they are. They were good players, but they either didn't look right, they wouldn't have fit in, or else they were in awe of being in the same room as us lot. But it was like being on Stars in Their Eyes for two months. 'Tonight Matthew, I'm going to be the bassist in Oasis…'"

With no bass player fitting the bill, Liam started to think outside the box. After hearing that former Ride guitarist Andy Bell had left his current group Hurricane #1 and was rumoured to be joining indie lightweights Gay Dad, Liam suggested getting in touch and offering him a shot at the vacant position in Oasis.

"I got home and we got a phone call saying Andy Bell had joined Gay Dad and I was having none of that," Liam said in his April 2000 Uncut interview. "I went, 'Fuck that'. So we got his phone number and rang him up and said, 'Look, do you fancy doing it?' And he went, 'Yeah'."

"I was amazed that Andy was up for actually playing the bass because he's such a good guitarist," Noel told XFM. "Liam said, 'Look, Andy Bell's not doing anything', but I said, 'I can't see him playing bass'. And Liam replied, 'Well we don't know until we ask him'. So we asked him, and he said yeah. I was amazed really, but he's a top bass player."

"I went out with Andy in my local in Belsize Park and said, 'just play it as you see it'," Noel told Uncut in March 2000. "The next day he came in played all the songs and he was fucking great. We were doing a version of 'My Generation', and Andy did that bass break note for note. It was brilliant."

"Noel knew Gem, and we all knew Andy, because I'd worked with his wife Idha in the past," Alan White remembered in an interview with Rhythm magazine in July 2000. "And when the five of us started jamming it all came together very quickly…in the first week, really. We're all into the same music and were instantly very comfortable with each other."

"As soon as I started to play with these guys it did feel right," Andy said in the *Standing on the Shoulder of Giants* documentary in 2000. "And they've said the same. It is hard to find people you can connect with on a musical level."

"[Creation] were in touch making suggestions in regard to the recruitment of new members," recalled Johnny Hopkins. "Andy and Gem were two of our suggestions. The band were thinking on the same lines too. People at Creation were happy for Andy and Gem as they are top blokes and top musicians. They both were fans of the band and already knew the Gallaghers fairly well. It made sense. It was all done quick. It had to be with the album being imminent."

The introduction of the two new members did more than just dispel rumours of an imminent demise, it gave Oasis a new lease of life. By his own admission, Noel's own interest in the band had begun to significantly wane after *Be Here Now*, a time during which he was sure that Oasis would split up. The idea of being in a massive stadium band, which was what Oasis was on the verge of becoming, didn't particularly appeal to him and he had mentioned in a number of interviews that he had considered leaving before undertaking the last world tour. But now, there was a new enthusiasm in the Oasis camp.

"It's like being in a new band," Noel told Heat on February 24, 2000. "It's almost like starting again. I don't play so much lead guitar anymore, because Gem is a better guitarist than I am. So it benefits my singing and backing vocals if I stick to rhythm guitar. Andy's just a mega, mega bass player. But he also has opened it up a lot for Alan. All of a sudden we've acquired this new drummer – Whitey's turned into Keith Moon! As much as I loved Guigs, he was pretty naff on the bass, and that frustrated Alan because he had to sit on the beat all the time. Now there's this whirling dervish in the corner banging everything that moves."

"The old stuff has never sounded better," he continued. "It's like a cover band doing our songs properly, but the rehearsals have been going really well, and everything sounds about 20 percent better than it ever did during our show. By the time we finish rehearsals and get to playing live, it's going to sound 50 percent better."

As well as improving things musically, the atmosphere around the band lightened with the arrival of jovial Geordie Gem and the laidback former shoegazer Bell.

"There's a better atmosphere within the band," Noel told Heat. "Everybody seems to be pulling in the same direction. Everybody who's in the band now is completely obsessed with music and just playing well really. And everybody gets on well. We still have a laugh and we still like to go out and have a drink. But the band is the band and the recreational side is something else. We seem to have put everything in its right place now at the right time."

"Oasis has completely evolved," Andy Bell added in a 1999 Q Magazine interview. "Noel's old mates have left and he's really changed his life around. He still has Liam but he needs a less extreme mate and Gem's it. Gem chills Noel out. And that makes Oasis a more stable ship."

The experience of losing Bonehead and Guigsy had also changed Noel's attitude to what Oasis had now become. From the very beginning and all through the glory days, the band had remained five friends, four of whom had grown up together on the hard-knock streets of Manchester and built a band which went on and conquered the world. Now, with Liam the last founding member still in the group, Oasis seemed less bound by the past and the bonds that had tied the original line-ups together. Noel seemed to accept that life in Oasis could now be more fluid and that, whoever featured in terms of personnel, as long as the cornerstone of Liam's voice remained, anything could happen.

"Nobody is tied to the band anymore," Noel told NME on December 18 1999. "People can come and go. Andy and Gem can go out and do other stuff if they want or they can stick around. It's totally their decision. I'd be more than happy if they stay in the band for the rest of their lives. But we'll see what happens. We won't promise anything. But, I mean, Oasis is going to be going until we physically can't do it anymore. It doesn't matter who's in the band as long as, I suppose, Liam is singing the songs."

"We're definitely together for the rest of this year and all of next year because we'll be on the road," he added, looking ahead to the new line-up's debut show in Philadelphia later that month and the world tour that would begin in Japan in February 2000. "After that we intend to go straight into the studio. I definitely want to record with this line-up. Because this album was recorded before Andy and Gem joined the band, the next album will feel like the actual rebirth of Oasis. I feel very excited about the future."

However, that future had become murkier with Alan McGee's announcement in November that he was leaving Creation Records. In the wake of its founder's departure, the label prepared to close down (it would issue its last release, Primal Scream's *XTRMNTR* album on January 31, 2000), leaving Oasis with another dilemma. With *Standing on the Shoulder of Giants* ready to go, the question facing Oasis was whether they should release their album on Creation and take the risk that the label wouldn't last long enough for the record to hit the shops or should they opt for a do-it-yourself solution?

"We didn't want to put our album out on a record label that is like a ghost town when you walk into the fucking offices," Noel said in a January 21, 2000 interview with Muse. "Was anybody there really going to give it fucking 100 per cent? Was anybody really going to be arsed?"

In the end, they set up their own label, Big Brother, under the auspices of parent company Sony, to release material in the UK and Ireland through independent distributor [PIAS] UK. The first single from the new album, 'Go Let it Out', would be the label's debut release, complete with in-joke catalogue number RKID 001, on February 7, 2000.

As the release date for *Standing on the Shoulder of Giants* approached, Noel was asked about his hopes for the record and whether he thought it would be a success.

"The album is already a success because we actually got the fucking thing finished," Noel told Heat on February 24, 2000. "It's inspired me to make more music. That's how I define success. Whether it sells as much as *(What's the Story) Morning Glory?* is debatable, it probably won't. Whether it even sells as many as *Be Here Now* is debatable. But if we make enough money on this record to go and make another one and it doesn't cost us any money, then financially it's been a success. Spiritually and professionally it's already a success."

"I don't really know what my expectations are yet of this album. I'm just glad it's finished, what with all the things that have gone on since – the two members leaving and one thing and another. At least the record's done and I'm happy about it."

"I hope that it will sell but I wouldn't bank on it," he continued. "I think it's a better record [than *Be Here Now*] but that doesn't mean that it's going to sell lots. Phil Collins sells a lot of records but he makes shit albums. The Velvet Underground didn't sell any records but they were one of the greatest bands of all time. So fucking work that one out."

Standing on the Shoulder of Giants was finally released on February 28, 2000, selling over 310,000 copies in its first week, some 40,000 less than *Be Here Now* sold on its first day of release. Compared to the 347,000 copies *(What's the Story) Morning Glory?* sold in its first week and the 696,000 copies of *Be Here Now* that were bought in the seven days after its release, sales of the fourth Oasis album confirmed that the fans and the record-buying public at large were being a bit more cautious this time out. It would go on to spend 29 weeks on the UK album chart, the fewest for any Oasis album.

Despite this, the album entered the UK charts at number one and became the 16th fastest selling album in British chart history at that time. It was also the ninth biggest selling album of 2000 in the UK.

Sales in the US would also be significantly lower that for previous Oasis albums. *Standing on the Shoulder of Giants* debuted at number 24 on the Billboard 200 on its release, selling about 55,000 units in its first week, but sales would rapidly tail off as they did in the UK, with the album dropping to number 84 in its second week.

"When we first started, we were the new Beatles," Noel told the BBC's Jayne Middlemiss. "Then we were the U2 it was okay to like. Now we're the new Rolling Stones – the records don't sell so well but you can still come and see us at Wembley."

With its title (inaccurately) pinched from the motto on the side of a £2 coin and discovered scrawled on the back of a cigarette packet the morning after the drunken night before – "I woke up to see that I'd written *'Standing on the Shoulder of Giants* ...a bum title'" – the new album already had something typically Oasis about it. Playing up to the stereotype of the semi-literate magpie that the press had pinned on him, wrongly quoting Sir Isaac Newton after a session down the pub could have suggested that little had changed in the world of Noel Gallagher – still thieving, still unashamedly unarsed with the finer point of the English language. By choosing this quote, however, Noel was also referencing another popular perception; that he had achieved his own greatness by blatantly plundering the back catalogues of his predecessors. He not only stood on the shoulders of giants but he'd ripped off their best riffs on his way up.

Despite the familiar Gallagher mischief which underpinned the story of the album's title, there was something different about its appearance and the image it conveyed. The record's cover carried a new band logo designed by Gem Archer, one which suggested a break from the past and a more contemporary future. In much the same way, the washed-out New York skyline of the main photo was a definite geographical and

218

cultural shift from the home-grown influences of the past, perhaps in an effort to shed the Brit tag that had been pinned to the previous three albums. Inside the cover, the band – which consisted at this point of Noel, Liam and Whitey – barely featured and when they did, their images were roughly chopped and blurred, rendering them barely recognisable. There seemed to be a concerted effort to leave their over-exposed faces off the record and let the music do the talking.

The music itself – at least some of it – certainly delivered a message that things were beginning to change. Oasis, against all odds and the perception of many, were beginning to evolve.

With its use of drum loops, samples, electric sitar, mellotron, synthesizers and backward guitars, *Standing on the Shoulder of Giants* divided critics with some praising the more experimental approach and the record's nod to electronica and heavy psychedelic rock, while others questioned the band's decision to attempt their comeback with the least easily digestible material of their career. As Uncut wrote, the album had "the vague air of defeat about it; as though Oasis no longer want to compete."

Rolling Stone called Oasis "Britpop's most celebrated revival band" and wrote that while the album was "sonically, easily their boldest work yet" it lamented what it saw as the band's continued plundering of the past. "Compensating for their lack of originality with overkill… *Standing on the Shoulder of Giants* doesn't really say much of anything," Rolling Stone wrote before adding "but if we must endure vague platitudes shouted from the rooftop, let them all sound as gloriously drunk with belligerence as 'Go Let it Out'."

NME called the album "a twitchy, tentative attempt at dealing with life as it really is" which seemed wrong because "Oasis in their pomp dealt in the currency of super-confidence, thumbing their collective nose at the world." Describing the album as being "recorded by the shell of a band whose musical director was confronting the massive wake-up call of abandoning the protective mask of cocaine," the NME called *Standing on the Shoulder of Giants* "half-finished" and "the transitional album Oasis had to make" and warned that "the self-doubt that colours this entire record calls into question Noel's stomach for the long-term future of Oasis."

There was no fence-sitting in the AV Club's review which called *Standing on the Shoulder of Giants* "a clear signal that the band's best days are already behind it." Criticising the melodies and lyrics as "uninspired" and "arbitrary," the US-based site complained that "*Standing on the Shoulder of Giants* picks up where the low point of *Be Here Now* left off...and is full of the sort of long, windy, forgettable songs that made that album such a chore."

Entertainment Weekly also referenced *Be Here Now* but said that the new material was "less clotted and grating" and that "the sonic openness allows Gallagher's melodies and guitar and his brother Liam's pissy bray to shine brighter." However, it added that, on this evidence, the band's destiny "increasingly involves recycling not only rock's past but Oasis' own as well."

Uncut's David Stubbs admitted he had been wondering where Oasis were going to go after *Be Here Now* and from listening to *Standing on the Shoulder of Giants*, he was of the opinion that the band had "predictably gone nowhere but a little further down, into the wet sand on which their castle has always been founded."

SPIN magazine wrote that, after dead-ending with the classic-rock sprawl of *Be Here Now*, "*Standing on the Shoulder of Giants* is bathed in electronica-inspired sonic goo, resulting in their murkiest effort yet; Oasis are a song band, and the songs are mostly missing."

Bucking the trend of those in the media who were reacting cautiously to the new album after being exposed by their overtly lavish praise for *Be Here Now*, Q Magazine gave *Standing on the Shoulder of Giants* 4 out of 5 stars and the B-side to the first single 'Go Let It Out' was featured in Q's top 500 lost tracks. The magazine said that if 'Let's All Make Believe' had been on *Standing on the Shoulder of Giants* "it probably would have carried the album to another star".

On the other end of the scale, Alex Petridis in the Guardian simply called *Standing on the Shoulder of Giants* "catastrophic."

"I wasn't expecting it to get mixed reviews at all, I was expecting it to get absolutely hammered, to be honest, because rock 'n' roll isn't fashionable anymore...Oasis aren't fashionable anymore," said Noel in the 2000 Sky One documentary *Oasis: Behind the Scenes*. "I can understand some of the criticism it got and I can understand some of the praise but most of it was just petty. But saying that, they've never really had any good words to say about any of our records, some people, so it doesn't really matter anyway. "

"People said it was shite and people said it was good, I think it's a great album," Liam told Mojo in January 2001. "People say it's amazing, it's not amazing, nothing's amazing, y'know what I mean?"

The album certainly polarized opinion and with as many hits as misses on *Standing on the Shoulder of Giants*, it was unsurprising that many reviewers couldn't provide a solid argument for or against.

The opening triptych of songs sets an uplifting and optimistic tone. Track one – 'Fuckin' in the Bushes' – with its heavy drum loops and its sampled speech from Murray Lerner's movie *Message to Love*, his documentary on the 1970 Isle of Wight festival, immediately throws the listener into a contemporary melting pot of styles before a grinding guitar line places the track firmly in Jimmy Page territory. The Led Zeppelin groove, adding a touch of *Kashmir* to proceedings, is soon joined by swirling keyboards and heavenly choirs as a crazy old woman merrily chirps about "love, life, youth" and a grumpy old major complains about "kids running around naked, fucking in the bushes". The listener immediately understands that this is something very different from the eight-minute opening opus on the previous album.

"I was working on a remix for James Lavelle's band UNKLE," Noel said of the opening track (from a run-down of the album from the Web site Oasis Recording Information). "We had a day off when we were done with the recording and we started to mess around with drum loops. I put on the bass line and some guitar and we realized that it could be quite good. We had watched a movie about the Isle of Wight Festival 1970 and we had laughed at some of the people in the movie, so we sampled them. The beginning has the promoter whining at all the hippies that broke down the fences around the concert area."

"I fucking love it, man," an effusive Liam told Uncut in April 2000 when asked about 'Fuckin' in the Bushes'. "I think that should've been the single. But it wasn't going get anywhere, it's not going get any airplay is it? It's just fucking rocking, man. You won't get a better rocker than that. For me, that's the ultimate fucking rock 'n' roll song. I know for a fact, me personally, I'll die happy being involved with such a song like that. It's just fucking mental. It's rocking, man. I love it."

The perception that this could be a completely different kettle of Oasis fish is reinforced when lead single 'Go Let it Out' swaggers in on laidback drums and acoustic guitar before Liam's vocals pre-empt a rolling bass line which is as prominent as any lead riff (something never attempted while Guigsy was on duty). It's a loose-limbed swagger of a tune complimented by obtuse lyrics about the media's obsession with celebrity. "'Go Let It Out' stands head and shoulders above anything else I was writing around that time," Noel said in the 2010 *Time Flies* documentary. "It's a right proper hipster tune though and right up there with the best stuff we've done."

'It started out like a very slow, melancholy piece, almost Lennon-like," said Noel. "But then we did the demo recordings and it went faster and became rockier. I played a Paul McCartney-like bass line and we decided to find as many instruments from the 60's as we could, old mellotrons and sitar sounds."

The album then slides into the Indian-influenced 'Who Feels Love', a spacey, psychedelic ode to self-discovery which floats along in a drug-daze dream. Liam sings the words of Noel's recovery – "Found what I'd lost inside...My spirit has been purified..." – over floating electronic keys, squelching sequencers and stoned strumming.

'Put Yer Money Where Yer Mouth Is' signals the first dip in quality on the album and hints at the lack of inspiration that Noel would later admit to suffering from on some of these songs. While it is at least five minutes shorter than comparably leaden tracks on *Be Here Now*, it is still a noisy proto-glam slog accompanied by bored whining from Liam and one which would not have been out of place on the much-derided third album.

"This song was made by a coincidence when we did the demo recordings," Noel said. "We liked the energy in it. But I would have wanted to work more with the lyrics, it's just the same words being repeated over and over."

Despite the grudging praise offered to Liam by some for his first composition on an Oasis album, the next track – his tribute to his step-son, 'Little James' - further squanders the good work achieved by the first three songs and unfortunately revives the band's reputation for lazy lyrics. "Live for your toys even though they make noise" can surely be added to the file of Gallagher rhyme crimes along with the likes of "And my dog's been itching, itching in the kitchen" from 'Some Might Say'. The song's simplicity and naivety have been used as compliments in some quarters but in this writer's opinion, these just undermine the complexity and experimentation introduced in the opening trio of tracks. The over-riding feeling is that Liam has been thrown a bone here by his older brother, who may have acquiesced for the sake of peace during an already fraught production process. Even the bolstered effects that Noel and producer Spike Stent have layered on and the Beatlesesque "la la" outro can't save what is essentially a lullaby which should have stayed in the privacy of a child's bedroom.

"One day when Liam was in one of the rooms we put a microphone on when he was singing the song for himself," Noel remembered. "We recorded it without saying anything to him. Some days later he went on holiday with Patsy and we wrote down the words, made the melody and when he came back from Tenerife the song was finished and he could go into the studio and sing."

Thankfully, the slide is then arrested by the monumental 'Gas Panic!'. Malevolently creeping onto the album on a click track which sounds like a heart arrhythmia, this is Noel's night terrors set to music: "What tongueless ghost of sin crept through my curtains…sailing on a sea of sweat on a stormy night." As Liam warns that you'd better "get on your knees and pray…panic is on the way," the waves of fear crash in on booming bass, seismic drums and wailing guitars. With doubts and paranoia swirling in the mix – "And my family don't seem so familiar and my enemies all know my name" – the song builds into a cascading, wailing nightmare. In terms of a confessional, 'Gas Panic!' is the most raw and exposed Noel Gallagher has ever been on record: "My eyes are dead and my throat's like a black hole…and if there's a God would he give another chancer, an hour to sing for his soul."

"To be honest, we could have put more break beats on that song and made it a lot more trip hop," Noel said about 'Gas Panic!' in his March 2000 interview with Uncut. "But Liam and Alan think music doesn't exist after 1969. The Chemical Brothers? Who the fuck are they? The Prodigy? Who? Oh, that geezer with the two pieces of lettuce stuck on the side of his head? Yeah, that geezer. There'd be no point in me making a record like that, if the other members of the band are just going to go, 'I don't get it'."

Derided by some as a dirge, 'Where Did It All Go Wrong' – again in this writer's opinion – is one of Noel's finest moments in the context of songs written about his darkest days of drug psychosis. Set against the times and the circumstances surrounding the band in 1999, the song sees the songwriter imagining himself back in Supernova Heights, staring in the mirror at the bloated face of a man he no longer recognizes and wondering how he got there. "You know that feeling you get…you feel you're older than time…you ain't exactly sure if you've been away a while." He then turns on the strangers and fakes that litter his home: "Do you keep the receipts, for the friends that you buy? Ain't it bittersweet, you're only just getting by…"

"This song will remind people that we are a rock band," Noel said at the time of the album's release. "The lyrics are about all the rich and famous people that used to follow me home and tell me about their problems. Many rich people are self-destructive. They think that they will be ok again if they just put themselves into private clinics every six months. But it's only themselves who can solve the problem."

'Sunday Morning Call' follows in the same lyrical vein but fails to find the vengeful energy and bitterness of the previous track – perhaps because this is the best (or worst) example of Noel's use of downers permeating the music. It's too maudlin and indifferent to effectively deliver its message to the celebrity casualty it's aimed at and lopes along on a mogadon melody which can't be bothered to break free of the monotony surrounding it.

The pace quickens with 'I Can See a Liar' but the inspiration is still lacking. Liam returns to vocals (the listener could be excused for thinking that he'd been napping on the sofa for the past few songs) and he does his best to drive this plodding rocker on with his best Lydon whine. But even his most enthusiastic nasal punk delivery can't disguise the fact that he's singing "I can see a liar, sitting by the fire", a phrase which wouldn't seem out of place in a playground disagreement.

"That's horrible isn't it?" Noel admitted in an interview with Muse on January 21, 2000 when confronted by that lyric. "I fucking hold my hands up, man. I could have come up with something better than that."

"But it's Liam's favourite song on that album and he must always get his favourites on the records," he added. "Liam is Liam and he usually always whines. He doesn't stop until he gets what he wants."

The album ends on another low-key track, one which could have been sponsored by Valium, but in this case, 'Roll It Over' sounds perfectly geared for the pace it's delivered in while the other sloggers on the album sound like they've been recorded at half speed. Noel's lyrics again target the "plastic people who live without a care" who "try and sit with me around my table but never bring a chair". It's world-weary and cynical yet soaring and anthemic; a perfect end to this mish-mash of moods.

"This is my own favourite," said Noel. "It's about people that gossip, I know lots of people that do it, especially women. It's a song that shows the direction that we like to go in the future. It's more gospel influenced, bigger and more psychedelic."

Noel initially defended the album in the face of the lukewarm reviews, and attempted to dismiss the idea that Oasis had tried to make a radical change in direction for the sake of it but had ultimately failed, falling between the two stools of their traditional rock approach and more contemporary experimentation.

"It's rock 'n' roll pop music," he told Melody Maker in September 1999. "It's not fucking drum 'n' bass. It's not a dance record. It's typical Oasis, but it's a little different. We like the way we sound. Some people reckon the album is shit, but I think it's a great album. We're not into 21st-century rock 'n' roll, but it doesn't sound like 1969 either."

"But part of me thinks I've sold out my rock 'n' roll roots, because it's not as rock, you know what I mean? I like T-Rex and The Rolling Stones and The Beatles, but some of this new album is not very rock 'n' roll. A part of me thinks, well, it is in a way, because I never got into trip hop when it was big, I'm not into fucking lo-fi punk music now and I'm not into fucking punk disco, or whatever it is. I'm into rock 'n' roll music."

"It's not a radical change from what we've been doing in the past," explained Noel in an interview with Muse in January 2000. "It's the first step on what hopefully won't be too long a journey to where we want the band to be in five years from now."

"This idea that it's some sort of reappraisal is getting right on my tits," he added in an Independent interview in the same month. "It's a tiny little step in a contemporary direction, not a fucking big side-step."

Liam also defended the album in a Radio 1 interview with Gary Crowley in 2002: "Some people reckon the album is shit, but I think it's a great album," he said "It's just a bit different."

There were some hints given by Noel in a few interviews at the time that the record could have taken on an even more radical direction. His responses suggested that a more democratic process within Oasis had begun to take hold after the remaining members had faced the possible implosion of the band in 1999.

"'I Can See A Liar' I personally wouldn't have put on the album," he told Uncut in 2000. "But Liam was, like, 'It's the fucking Sex Pistols; we've got to have some fast ones on there because it's a bit medium-paced', and it was, like, 'fair enough'."

"There's a couple of songs that got shunted off onto B-sides of singles which should have gone on the album, but it's either the singer sulking or, you know, have some semblance of fucking normality in the studio - you've got to weigh up which one's better than the other and it's better not to have a singer sulking."

Standing on the Shoulder of Giants may not have been the most triumphant of comebacks but the fact that Oasis had even returned at all was a remarkable feat. Out of all the Britpop bands who had lived fast and large throughout the mid-90s, Oasis would have been the most likely candidate for implosion before the year 2000.

As the 20th century came to a close, many of the band's contemporaries were caught up in a collective comedown; a millennium meltdown. Blur released *13* in March 1999 and it was an even darker, more introspective album than *Standing on the Shoulder of Giants*; it dealt with a number of downbeat topics such as the break-up of Damon Albarn and Justine Frischmann's relationship, heroin abuse, and mental illness. The detrimental effects of Britpop exposure and the associated fame would manifest themselves in Graham Coxon's departure from the band due to alcoholism and in-fighting before the band's follow-up, *Think Tank*, was completed.

Elsewhere, Pulp had managed to capture the desperate emptiness and frazzled psyche of the post-scene hangover with their uncomfortably twitchy 1998 album *This is Hardcore*. Shot through with self-loathing and drug psychosis, *This is Hardcore* was, as a line from the creepy album opener 'The Fear' stated, "the sound of someone losing the plot, making out that they're okay when they're not." Jarvis Cocker and Co. would make it to 2001's *We Love Life* before going on hiatus.

After finally tasting mainstream commercial success in 1997 with *Urban Hymns*, The Verve would last just two more years before splitting up for the second time in three years in a whirlwind of violence and drug abuse. Winding the band up in April 1999, singer and songwriter Richard Ashcroft would return in 2000 with his first solo effort *Alone with Everybody* but, while it attempted to put a positive spin on events, the album was a hollow affair compared to the sonic bombast of The Verve.

Perversely, Oasis started the 21st Century in much better shape than they had any right to be. Undoubtedly the recruitment of Gem Archer and Andy Bell had saved the band, not only in providing it with the personnel it needed to function but by bring new impetus and motivation to those members who had come out the other side. The disappointment and backlash that followed *Be Here Now* had also contributed. In many ways, by being written off, there was a great deal less pressure on the band. *Standing on the Shoulder of Giants* did little to reverse the negativity in the media in regard to Oasis but it did provide the band – and Noel in particular – with more breathing space. To a certain extent, the press was now off their back. There was no need any more to hide in Liam's dustbin waiting for him to pop out for a pint of milk because there were other more newsworthy people to pester. As far as the sections of the press who had set out with that particular agenda were concerned, Oasis had been knocked off their perch. Job done. It was now time to move on.

Of course, being the biggest band in Britain during one of the most important pop culture eras of modern times, Oasis would never be let completely off the hook but in the wake of *Standing on the Shoulder of*

Giants' release, the band would be afforded their first real break from the intense media scrutiny that had dogged their every move since *(What's the Story) Morning Glory?* was released some five years previously.

With their association with Creation at an end and the press off hunting for new prey, Oasis suddenly found themselves with a modicum of freedom to look to the future without the crushing pressures of the past. Noel particularly was taking the time to make plans.

"I think after about six months of this album being out, we'll find out where we truly stand',' Noel told the Boston Globe on April 14, 2000. "We've just come out of this whirlwind phenomenon that was Oasis between 1994 and 1997. The world was fascinated by British music and we were at the forefront of that. It has sort of tailed off over the last couple of years but everyone in the Oasis camp is still really positive'.'

"I would like to spend more time making records," Noel told Muse on January 21 2000. "I would like to make truly great albums, and to make truly great albums you need to be given the time and the space. With this record label thing we'll be the masters of our own destiny. We can do what we like. Hopefully what we like other people will like."

"*Standing on the Shoulder of Giants* is a small step to where we want to be with the next record and the next one will be a small step further to where we're going," he told Melody Maker on February 23, 2000. "This is album four. Five and six will take us to another level."

"I'm only a third of the way to where I want to be with the sounds and the style of the writing," he added in Uncut. "Over the next couple of albums, there's a lot to be explored. I'm not talking about experimenting, going in the studio and shaking crisp packets with six-inch nails in them for the sake of art. I don't ever see us making a radical sweep to the left, or underground music, or anything like that."

230

"I don't make art-punk records like Primal Scream, or art-pop records like Blur," he said. "I'm into making big fucking fuck off rock 'n' roll pop records. I don't think we've got to start sitting on stools and be a fucking chin stroking adult orientated rock band. I'd still like to keep the youthful exuberance and cockiness. I mean, you'll always have that with Liam standing round the microphone. Even if I'm still writing songs when I'm 43, he'll still be singing them like he's 21."

"But there's a side of it that still needs working on. The words are not amazing enough yet for me. But I'll get there. Slowly but surely my head's coming out of a blizzard of drug abuse. I'm slowly getting my shit together. All I can say is I'm really excited about making the next record."

"One day, I hope to make a masterpiece. I haven't gotten there yet, but I'm certainly going in the right direction with *Standing on the Shoulder of Giants*. It's not radical enough for my liking, but the next one, you know, the next one will be. This is the great thing about being in a band. Your last album is never your last album. There's always something else to go on with. And being in the band that we are, we're not likely to get dropped in the near future, so we've got a fair few more albums to go yet to get experimental."

"After five years I'm not too sure if I want to be doing this anymore anyway. Hopefully by then I'll have done the masterpiece album and I'll go, 'right, that's it, I'm signing off now for a bit'."

Before the future could begin, Oasis still had a world tour to undertake. Despite having managed to recruit new members in tile to fulfil the commitment – and new members, on first evidence at least, who would provide a calming influence while on the road – Noel admitted to a certain amount of trepidation. The *Be Here Now* tour had taken a heavy toll; Noel's cocaine intake had pushed him to breaking point, Liam's drinking had continued to spiral out of control and the strain of life on the road had forced both Bonehead and Guigsy to quit the band. Heading back in to that environment again would be a real test of endurance for both Gallagher brothers and the stability of the new Oasis.

"Do I really want to go on the road for nine months again?" Noel asked himself in a January 22, 2000 interview with the Independent. "I'm not looking forward to going on the road for the simple reason that the gigs we're going to play, we've played them a thousand times over, and you've been to the same cities and you've stayed in the same hotels, and there's only so many tour bus moments that you can have in your life until it becomes an absolute nightmare."

According to an interview he gave NME on January 29, 2000, Noel had reportedly asked Liam which version of himself would be coming on tour with them when Oasis took *Standing on the Shoulder of Giants* out on the road, telling him if it was the same Liam who came on tour in 1997 - "with a beard and a stupid hat, blowing a stupid trumpet into his microphone" - then it would be the last tour on which Noel would be joining him. If, however, it was the Liam that he knows and likes, then that would be fine. "I just wanted to know what weapons to pack," Noel was quoted as saying.

"The people who you have to tour with do my head in after a while," Noel admitted to this writer in 2002. "But it would be weird to put out a record and not tour it. If we didn't tour, that would mean that I'd have to give up music and I'm not going to be doing that."

He continued: "The ideal situation for me would be like when Brian Wilson had his breakdown in 1964; to just make the records and send the boys off: 'I'm not into it anymore, so have the best time you can, go and promote the record, come back and I'll have finished another one for us to work on'. But they'd be like, 'If you're not going, I'm not going'. Then, if I don't go, the band don't go, and then if the band don't go, the

232

record company are going to go, 'You can forget us trying to promote your records, you cheeky cunts'. So you end up in a vicious circle."

The *Be Here Now* experience had also soured Liam's outlook on touring. "I personally wanted to come off that last tour," he told Uncut in April 2000. "I couldn't be bothered with it because it was doing my head in. I was singing fucking rubbish towards the end and I was getting in too much fucking trouble outside the band, and that was not what it was about."

Not for the first time – and certainly not for the last – Noel wished aloud that Oasis could go back to the days when the band could pull up in their Transit van, ask to play a gig at somewhere like the Borderline, and blow a couple of hundred delirious fans away while staring into the whites of their eyes. "These days you almost feel like got the fucking people from *The X Files* following you about with a million monitor things," he sighed in Uncut in 2000. "I suppose they've got to protect the band but I'd like to break it down and start again."

There was little chance of that happening. Regardless of whether fans liked or loathed the new material – or held a grudge at being duped by the hype surrounding *Be Here Now*, there were still millions of people around the world who loved the band's collection of uplifting and inspiring songs which had helped to make them a phenomenon.

The world tour in support of *Standing on the Shoulder of Giants* would consist of 72 shows played between March and August of 2000. Oasis would take in Europe, the United States and Asia – but would pointedly avoid Australia this time. The set was essentially a greatest hits collection with only three songs from *Standing on the Shoulder of Giants* included. The *Be Here Now* material was also drastically culled with only one song – 'Stand By Me' – remaining on the list, although 'D'You Know What I Mean?' was played once on the opening night of the tour at the

Yokohama Arena only to be replaced by 'Shakermaker' for the rest of the tour. The telephone box and other relics of the previous tour were thankfully also absent, replaced by three massive video screens. It would be one of the band's best attended tours to date with the highlight being two sold out nights at London's old Wembley Stadium in front of a combined crowd of 140,000 people, the last concerts the venue would stage before being pulled down and rebuilt.

However, while the demand for Oasis live shows would continue to be huge, whatever the ticket sales said, it was clear that the fallout from *Be Here Now* would continue to undermine the band's image and status, as well as affect the sales of *Standing on the Shoulder of Giants*. As the decade came to a close, Oasis had to come to terms with the fact that the fame and success they enjoyed at their peak was unsustainable in this new paradigm. The world had changed around them as they had laboured through the *Be Here Now* world tour and the musical landscape was now very different to that which they ruled over in 1996. It was time to reassess where Oasis fitted in the grand scheme of things.

"We can have that level of acclaim again, where people thought we walked on water, but it won't be on the same scale," Liam told Uncut in 2000. "But that was when we were new. When we'd been around a bit, getting in everyone's faces and in the paper every fucking day, people got bored with that. People knew exactly what move you were making and what you were doing. So you'll never get that sense of mysteriousness about the band back again."

"Then we were about fucking getting off our tits, losing it, and all the music side of it was getting fucking missed," he added. "It was all about what we were wearing, who we were shagging, who we were rucking with."

234

"All we can do is go on and make better records and that's all I'm about now, and that's all the band is about now," he continued. "I wouldn't be doing it if I didn't think the glory can go on. I wouldn't be here today if I didn't think we can get bigger and better. But I'm not arsed about the future of British rock. All I'm bothered about is Oasis. I've done my bit for the fucking future of British rock."

Noel was of a similar opinion in the same interview: "All that madness...That's never going to happen again," he said. "That was our time for shining and we fucking did it; we put the work in and we did it and it's over. Now it's just like, 'Let's go and make some records, man'. You can't burn that brightly for that long, it's impossible."

Despite accepting that the bubble had burst to a certain extent and that Oasis were now relatively free to embark on a new chapter, there were signs that Noel was concerned about the band's legacy.

"The Nineties to me were just a phase we were going through," he told the Independent on January 22nd, 2000. "It's the next five years that will determine where we actually stand in the history of British music."

"I hope we don't just turn up on these retrospective programmes of the Nineties and we're just known as a band of the Nineties.

"Hopefully, it won't be: 'Oasis were the biggest band of the Nineties...and then they disappeared'."

With that, Oasis signed off on the decade they dominated and headed into the unknown of the new millennium.

Acknowledgements

To start with, I would like to thank all the journalists involved with compiling and documenting the career of Oasis and for releasing their work on the internet. I hope I have correctly attributed the quotes I have used from the many newspaper and magazine articles that are out there in the public domain. Similarly, I am indebted to all those authors who have gone before me and penned books about the band and the Britpop era. In particular, I would like to convey special thanks and acknowledgements to Paolo Hewitt for his work in the books *Forever the People: Six Months on the Road with Oasis* and *Getting High: The Adventures of Oasis*. Chapter three of this book would have been far less comprehensive without them as Paolo's depiction of the *Be Here Now* tour is, in my opinion, the definitive account, as very few journalists enjoyed anything close to Paolo's level of access to the band during those crazy days. Without the direct input of the members of Oasis, Ignition – the band's management company, and the majority of Creation staff contacted for help on this book, detailed accounts such as Paolo's were the only way to get an accurate overview of that specific period. I therefore thank him and hope that I have accurately credited him wherever I have quoted his work. Despite being unable to interview the band and those close to Oasis specifically for this book, I would like to extend my thanks to Marcus Russell, the band's former manager, for his respectful refusal to be involved and the subsequent good wishes he politely sent. I would also like to thank Noel Gallagher's manager Ray McCarville for his polite and measured explanation of the situation which prevents Noel and other former members of Oasis from responding to the many requests from authors who aspire to write about the band. Special thanks must go to Johnny Hopkins – former publicist for

Oasis and the Head of Press at Creation Records, the one man who did agree to speak to me on his time working with Oasis. Johnny's contribution was particularly useful in filling a number of glaring holes, specifically in chapter four. Also, respect is due to Andy Saunders, the former head of communications at Creation Records, whose offer of help led to Johnny's involvement.

On a personal level, I would like to thank my partner Benita for the encouragement – and the many kicks to my arse – she gave me throughout the writing process and the belief she had in the project from the very start. Her editorial advice also helped to hone this book into the (hopefully) coherent document you now have in your hands. Love always.

To my amazing daughter Juno: For listening intently to spoken sections of this book and laughing madly at daddy's version of 'Digsy's Dinner'.

Finally, I'd like to thank Noel Gallagher, Liam Gallagher, Paul McGuigan, Paul Arthurs, Tony McCarroll, Alan White, Gem Archer and Andy Bell for being Oasis.

Live forever.

Nick Amies
Brussels, September 2015.